PRAISE FOR *TAMING YOUR OUTER CHILD*

"This book will be an enormous help to anyone looking to let go of past disappointments and self-recrimination and get on with the essential work of healing, building boundaries, and acquiring the skills to reach your goals. I hope you will read it and do the exercises it provides."
— John Bradshaw, #1 *New York Times* bestselling author of *Homecoming*

"Are you repeating unhelpful, destructive patterns of behavior? Anderson (*The Journey from Abandonment to Healing*)...attributes this sabotaging behavior to your 'Outer Child,' a part of personality that takes over when your 'Adult' function is weak.... Anderson does not discount the role of past trauma but shows that self-defeating behavior can be changed without in-depth examination and resolution. VERDICT A helpful scenario, requiring determination and commitment, for dealing with difficult issues. This will appeal to readers seeking change." — *Library Journal*

"With more than 30 years experience working with victims of trauma, abandonment, grief, and loss, psychotherapist Anderson (*Black Swan: The Twelve Lessons of Abandonment Recovery*)...explains how to redirect 'fear and insecurity seeping out of your oldest wounds.' 'Abandoholism,' she notes, 'wins the hit parade on my website.' With a program designed to undo primal fears, she tackles such topics as lowered self-esteem, lovesick feelings, food urges, diet, chronic depression, procrastination, heartache, and a primary source of conflict with relationships, 'enormous emotional suction cups.' She also examines brain activity and factors preventing the body's production of such 'yummy neurochemicals' as oxytocin and vasopressin.... Readers under stress who are desperate for help will view this book as a valuable tool for healing." — *Publishers Weekly*

"The outer child is a bratty, angry drama queen who is responsible for unhealthful and unwanted behavior, according to the book. Anderson's three-prong outer child recovery program consists of dialoguing, guided visualization and action steps. The second half of the book addresses special applications for the program, such as dieting, procrastination, debt and depression." — *Washington Post*

Taming Your Outer Child

ALSO BY SUSAN ANDERSON

The Journey from Abandonment to Healing:
Surviving through—and Recovering from—the Five Stages
That Accompany the Loss of Love

Black Swan:
The Twelve Lessons of Abandonment Recovery

The Journey from Heartbreak to Connection:
A Workshop in Abandonment Recovery

TAMING YOUR
OUTER CHILD

Overcoming Self-Sabotage and
Healing from Abandonment

Susan Anderson

New World Library
Novato, California

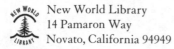 New World Library
14 Pamaron Way
Novato, California 94949

Text design by Casey Hampton

Library of Congress Cataloging-in Publication Data
Anderson, Susan (Psychotherapist)
Taming your outer child : overcoming self-sabotage and healing from abandonment / Susan Anderson.
    pages   cm
Originally published: New York : Ballantine Books, c2011.
Includes bibliographical references and index.
ISBN 978-1-60868-314-7 (paperback) — ISBN 978-1-60868-315-4 (ebook)
1. Self-defeating behavior. 2. Habit breaking. 3. Change (Psychology)
4. Self-management (Psychology) I. Title.
BF637.S37A53 2015
155.9'3—dc23   2014034691

First paperback printing, February 2015
ISBN 978-1-60868-314-7
Originally published in hardcover by Ballantine Books, New York, January 2011
(ISBN 978-0-345-51448-6)
Printed in Canada on 100% postconsumer-waste recycled paper

 New World Library is proud to be a Gold Certified Environmentally Responsible Publisher. Publisher certification awarded by Green Press Initiative. www.greenpressinitiative.org

10   9   8   7   6   5   4   3   2   1

PAUL ASA COHEN
May 13, 1952–March 20, 2003

Contents

PART THREE: SPECIAL APPLICATIONS

Author's Note

In presenting information about the impact of Outer Child behaviors on human life, I drew from research data I collected for over a decade as well as my own personal experience. In the case studies cited here, the names are fictitious and other identifying details have been scrambled or changed to protect the privacy of the individuals involved. The anecdotal data I collected are confidential, whether taken from interviews, submissions to my website, clinical cases, workshop discussions, call-ins, or the experiences of others I know. Therefore, the examples you see in this book are composites of those individual stories and do not reflect any one person's experience. This is the case with the quoted material as well. Any similarity to myself or the people in my life—friends, family, workshop members, clients, colleagues—is purely coincidental.

Part One

GETTING TO KNOW YOUR
OUTER CHILD

ONE

Welcome to Your Outer Child

What makes you break your diet, or run up your credit card, or be attracted to all the wrong people? You know these aren't healthy things to do, you know you're sabotaging your own best interest, but sometimes you just *can't help it*. Sometimes you want what you want and there's no reasoning with the devil on your shoulder!

Each of us has self-sabotaging tendencies, the origins of which elude us. Be confused no longer! I'm here to tell you that these behaviors are attributable to a part of your personality that perhaps you didn't even know you had: your Outer Child.

You may already be familiar with the concept of an Inner Child, a psychological construct developed by John Bradshaw, Charles Whitfield, and others. Your Inner Child is your emotional core, the innocent, vulnerable, often needy part of your personality. Many of its feelings emerged at a tender young age and still reside in your psyche; others arise anew from fresh experience. Whatever the origins of its feelings, your Inner Child needs tending to, it needs to be heard, it should be honored.

No less important, your Outer Child is a psychological concept that I have identified to describe the part of your personality that *acts out* your

Inner Child's feelings in self-defeating ways, without giving you, the Adult in charge, a chance to intervene. Simply put, your Outer Child is responsible for your *misbehavior*. Think of your Outer Child as the impulsive and willful adolescent in you: the person who has trouble regulating behavior and resisting primal urges. Your Outer Child says yes to a third glass of wine when you, the Adult, had already decided on a two-drink limit. Your Outer Child decides to watch the game when you'd resolved to clean out the garage. Your Outer Child wants what it wants and pulls out all the stops to get its own way.

As with an Inner Child, we all have an Outer Child; it is not a flaw. It is, however, the obstinate, selfish, self-centered part of us we all *share*—a part that until now we have failed to recognize as universal. Outer Child is universal because we all have primal feelings we are barely aware of but that drive our most deeply entrenched defense mechanisms and knee-jerk reactions—if we let them.

Your Outer Child manifests *out*wardly what your Inner Child feels inside. For instance, if your Inner Child's core fear is *abandonment,* it is your Outer Child that manifests this fear with all sorts of inappropriate behaviors. When you feel insecure in a romantic relationship, Outer acts out your vulnerable feelings in ways that can only be interpreted as desperate. You might freak out, freeze up, or blow up when your date keeps you waiting more than a few minutes for a call back. In fact, Outer Child usually has a hair trigger when it comes to abandonment fear—the nerve that jangles so easily when any of us feel slighted, dismissed, or rejected. Hence waiting those few minutes for the phone to ring triggers an overriding fear that you will wind up all alone, bereft of love *forever*.

Lest you think that I'm giving a name to this part of your personality in order to let us all off the hook for bad behavior, think again! Being able to identify and recognize your Outer Child is an important step toward taming it. I have found with my work in private practice with clients and with countless workshop attendees that being able to separate the personality in this way is the first important step toward controlling your actions and your own emotional destiny.

I initially coined the term *Outer Child* for my book *Journey from Abandonment to Healing* (2000). I didn't introduce the concept and a list of Outer Child traits until nearly the end of the book, but Outer Child somehow managed to take center stage. Almost immediately after publication I began hearing from readers wanting more information about how to tame

INNER CHILD	OUTER CHILD
Feels	Acts out feelings inappropriately

their wayward Outer Children. I have spent the past decade applying this tool to a broader range of issues and clinically testing exercises I've adapted to overcome Outer Child's most entrenched behaviors, a program you'll read about in the following pages and chapters.

YOU DON'T HAVE TO BE *THAT* PERSON

Think of the things you yearn for—to have a happier love life, to break free of debt, to achieve greater recognition in your field—and consider all the impulsive little things you do that actually hinder your progress toward those goals. Your Outer Child represents that hindrance; it's all the counter-productive habits and tendencies that keep you forever wanting to achieve, but always falling short.

Let's say your Inner Child feels a little anxious in a social situation and urgently wants you to make a good impression. Your Outer Child acts out your nervousness, insisting on making its own impression. It might share information that's way too personal for cocktail party banter, or express an opinion with the kind of vehemence best reserved for competitive debate. So much for that good impression.

One of Outer's favorite ploys is procrastination. It creates as much sabotage by what it *doesn't* do as by what it *does,* gumming up the works with indecision and passivity. For instance, it ignores you when you tell it what to do, like *"Go to the gym."* Instead Outer just goes right on eating potato chips and lounging in front of the TV. Outer Child is the guy who talks constantly about how he's going to move to a cattle ranch out west, but never gets around to it. You don't have to be that person. You *can do something* to tip the balance in favor of your Adult Self when those internal power struggles arise.

The concept of the Outer Child is a revolutionary self-awareness tool that lets you look at your own behavior from a powerful new perspective. It reveals the third dimension of your personality: the self-rebellious dimension. In exploring this new dimension, you gain access to a part of yourself that was operating undercover, until now.

Those of you familiar with the terms *Id, Ego,* and *Superego* may wonder how the concept of an Outer Child fits in. They're closely related, though Outer Child is a newly identified component of the psyche, one that expands Freud's theory of the Id by taking it into the behavioral realm. We'll explore this relationship in more detail in the next chapter.

For now, I want to reassure you that you can redress and redirect your Outer Child's subterfuge; it doesn't have to hold you back any longer. Whether Outer Child has been preventing you from sticking to a diet, curbing your spending, overcoming performance anxiety, ending procrastination, improving a relationship, becoming a better parent, or reaching your potential, you can finally create the change you've always dreamed of.

In the interest of full disclosure, it's important to know that your Outer Child isn't going to give up its power over you without a fight. Which is why the program I created offers powerful tools for overcoming its resistance. Outer Child doggedly fights change—especially change directed at its favorite bad habits. It balks at doing the right thing and hankers after precisely those things that are bad for your health, reputation, marriage, career, figure, or bank account.

That's because Outer is a glutton for immediate gratification and adept at foiling your best laid self-improvement plans by cleverly substituting self-indulgence for self-nurturance. The difference between the two is vast, but Outer, a master of rationalization, does its best to confuse them. Self-nurturing is taking action to truly benefit your life. Outer prefers self-indulging, in other words, momentary feel-good things like buying an extravagance on credit, or taking another nap—things that are easy to rationalize in the short run, but sabotage your goals and dreams in the long run. You will learn exercises throughout this book to help you delay gratification, remain goal-directed, and guide your behavior in the direction of your highest potential.

OUTER CHILD AS LOVE ADDICT

So who, exactly, can benefit from this program? For starters, many of the people who read my first book on abandonment. I mentioned above that a lot of your self-sabotaging behaviors hearken back to unresolved abandonment issues. Depending on your earlier losses, heartbreaks, and disappointments, Outer Child can wreak havoc in romantic situations by acting too needy. When you become unsure of your partner's love, you grow these enormous emotional suction cups that are irresistibly drawn to your lover. You frantically try to hide them lest they scare her away, but to no avail; new emotional suction cups keep surfacing, making it increasingly difficult to appear self-contained. The Outer Child program shows you how to redirect that neediness at yourself—so that you, and not an unwitting partner, become ultimately responsible for fulfilling your deepest emotional needs.

Outer Child has lots of other relationship issues. One of its patterns is so prevalent that in one of my books I coined a special term for it: *abandoholism*—addiction to the emotional drama and love chemicals of abandonment. Abandoholics are exclusively attracted to people who are unavailable. Their Outer Children only feel passion when in "pursuit mode"—when they are trying to win over someone's love. This puts many an otherwise secure marriage (in which partners sometimes take each other for granted) in the doldrums and has many a single person chasing after hard-if-not-impossible-to-get lovers. There are those who are well aware of the fact that they're love addicts and would readily admit they *"get a high on abandohol"* and complain that *"otherwise life feels too humdrum."*

Abandoholic Outer Children are addicted to the biochemistry of abandonment, which is why they suddenly feel no chemistry when a previously unavailable romantic interest actually does become available. Learning to tame your Outer Child helps you uncross your brain wires so that you can feel love and passion without having to chase an emotional challenge.

WHEN OUTER CHILD TAKES CONTROL

Outer Child specializes in power and control. Its primary adversary is your Adult Self. When you try to achieve a goal, Outer Child can act like an oppositionally defiant 10-year-old. Outer is bent on wearing you down, on getting you to fall back into one of your old habits, addictions, or compulsions. That's why awareness alone isn't enough to stop it. You'll need my program's specialized tools to learn how to take the reins securely into your own hands.

Outer Child has been known to grab control of the celebrity spotlight. We've all witnessed some of our most honored officials, athletes, and movie stars whose Outer Children got caught in the act of philandering, using steroids or other drugs, perpetrating financial scandals, or shouting "politically incorrect" epithets in public—all examples of their Outer Children breaking through their public personas and gaining control.

Speaking of control...

Beware: Outer can catch you off guard and take control when you least expect it, especially when you are angry. Outer overreacts to anger. Sometimes it overreacts by *under*reacting. This is because many people are too insecure to risk expressing direct anger toward someone (like their boss or lover); they fear losing that person's acceptance. Outer can *act out* your fear and lack of assertiveness by getting you to take your anger out on yourself. One of my workshop attendees described just such an episode:

> The other day when I failed to speak up for myself for the millionth time, I started slamming things around the kitchen. I accidentally broke a dish I really liked. That was my good old Outer Child acting-out in its usual self-destructive way.

In other cases, Outer takes your anger out on innocent bystanders and makes you look like a monster. As one workshop attendee put it, "When my Outer Child is cranky, it tries to bite someone's head off."

Outer's control issues really kick up in relationships: When Outer Child gets into power struggles with other people's Outer Children, watch out. Outer Children tend to battle one another for control and wrangle over "who's right." They also take one another as emotional hostages, demanding reparations for hurts and betrayals inflicted by old relationships, dating all the way back to childhood. (If only you could send your respective Outer Children out to play—or to Outer Childcare!—so that the Adults could work things out rationally and fairly.) The Outer Child program I will offer in this book shows you how to nip these Outer Child shenanigans in the bud and untangle the interference. My program provides a powerful new model for couples counseling as well.

Your Outer Child doesn't just try to bully your partner or other people; it bullies you: When your *Adult Self* is too weak and your *Outer Child* is too strong (as it is for many of us), Outer can become so powerful that it completely controls the *person*.

Some people, like this former client, are almost *all* Outer Child:

> I ate what I wanted, even though I got fat and lost my looks. I drank want I wanted, even after I got arrested a few times for drunk driving. I spent what I wanted, even though I eventually defaulted on my mortgage.

Think of your Outer Child as a horse—an untamed horse—and your Adult Self as a trainer trying to mount it. Sometimes the horse is more determined, more powerful than the trainer and you're thrown from the horse. Then Outer Child goes galloping off in his own direction. The Outer Child program in this book educates you about the creature you're trying to control, offers tools for the job and lots and lots of opportunities to practice using these tools so that eventually you'll be the one in control.

OUTER CHILD UNDERCOVER

Outer's maneuvers can be subtle. It wears many disguises. It slyly masquerades as free will, while leaving you, the Adult, in shackles. It poses as your ally, but is really distracting you from attending to your true needs.

Since Outer Child is an outward manifestation of your emotional self, some of its characteristics are on prominent public display, *out* in the open for others to see. We don't mind owning up to some of these behaviors, but there are others we don't like to acknowledge. It's far easier to identify those in *other* people. Take self-centeredness for example: Outer loves to project this less-than-stellar trait onto others, usually behind their backs. (*"I can't stand the way she grabs center stage; it's always all about her. I never get a chance to say anything."*) Gaining Outer Child awareness allows us to own up to our *own* self-centeredness and transform it into a positive force.

Think of it this way: Outer is you on autopilot. Its mission—to hijack your Adult Self's best interests—keeps you forever stuck in old patterns. Outer is always waiting in the wings to spring one of its knee-jerk, defensive strategies, especially when you're trying to change.

In addressing self-sabotage, many experts focus primarily on symptom relief. But teaching people how to save money or lose weight doesn't address the powerful component of our personalities that acts out in spite of our best intentions. The advice from personal finance and nutritional experts is valuable; it's just hard for a lot of us to put their counsel to good use while our Outer Child is in control of driving. That's why we relapse or substitute one problem so readily for another. For example, we pay off one credit card only to run up another; we give up smoking only to gain 30 pounds.

To extend the metaphor, by learning about your Outer Child, you take yourself off of Outer Child autopilot and switch to manual transmission for a while. In doing so, in taking charge of the wheel, you expose your Outer

Child's true identity. What had been unconscious now becomes conscious. Outer Child's cover has been blown and you take control of your life's mission. In the course of reading this book you'll learn how to lovingly and effectively deal with the emotional *source* of Outer Child's power—your primal needs and neglected feelings buried underneath maladaptive defense mechanisms. You will heal from the inside out. Deconstructing your Outer Child defenses allows you, the self-nurturing Adult, to finally take command and rechannel your emotional energy constructively.

AWARENESS IS THE FIRST STEP

This book will take you through a life-changing program of self-discovery. In the process you will own up to behavioral traits most people prefer to deny—traits that have formed an invisible infrastructure of self-sabotage deep within your personality. This distortion-free view of your psyche also gives you an edge. You'll gain a foothold on your impulses, attitudes, and habits, which elevates you above most others, who remain in a haze of their own denial and self-manipulation.

Awareness is only the first step. The Outer Child program will take you beyond insight to action, into taking behavioral steps to overhaul your old patterns and at last move your life forward.

The *Outer Child* program is a three-pronged one. In Part One, I explain the Outer Child framework and help you take a personal inventory of your own Outer Child tendencies. This is the start of a life-changing process of self-discovery and self-mastery—a process that will deepen and unfold as you make your way through the book.

In Part Two, I introduce the exercise program that helps to resolve the underlying source of your self-sabotage—feelings and needs that have been long neglected within you.

In Part Three, I show you how to apply the exercises to each of the pressing issues in your life. You discover that Outer Child is not just an awareness tool, it is an action plan; with it you can achieve your goals.

Taken together, these steps have catapulted the forward growth of my clients, workshop participants, and myself—and they will do the same for you. Let's get started!

TWO

Three Parts of the Personality

The concept of the Outer Child isn't something that emerged wholly formed out of nowhere for me. In fact, it owes a lot to Sigmund Freud, whose groundbreaking three-part model of human consciousness provides a structure for psychotherapy. In Freud's theory, the Id represents our innate biological drives—such as the drives for pleasure and survival. It's the mammal within us—the ape or squirrel within us that's driven to procreate, nurture our young, fight threats, and avoid pain. At the other end of the spectrum is the rule-driven Superego, the part of us that upholds morals, social conventions, and laws essential to co-existing with other human beings. Between them is the mediating Ego, which (hopefully) keeps the Id's urges in check—unless it's safe or appropriate to express them.

Freud formulated his revolutionary Id/Ego/Superego triumvirate to explain the dynamics of neurosis—a malady caused by the self-blaming, self-shaming, and repressing we do when we are burdened with guilt over the Id's urges and desires. Clinicians who practice Freudian therapy believe that gaining deeper emotional insight into internal struggles is a catalyst for change. In other words that by airing conflicts between the Id and Super-ego, by bringing them out of the subconscious and experiencing emotional catharsis, change will come. The trouble is (as we've seen over the century since Freud first invited a patient to recline on a Viennese couch), you can remain in psychoanalysis for many years, growing ever more self-aware, without any discernable change in behavior.

In Freud's time, science was not advanced enough to know about the inner workings of the emotional brain structures, but it is today. Recent evidence from neuroscience makes it possible, I think, to extend Freud's theory by identifying a new component of the psyche.

Our mammalian urges, as I see it, aren't the problem; they are biological givens with which we all must contend by learning to accommodate and modulate their expression. It is when we *act out* these urges in impulsive, annoying ways that the problem arises. Freud did not create a separate construct for this acting-out component, but I now believe that it's essential to do so in order to effectively change self-sabotaging behaviors. And that's how the concept of Outer Child was born.

The reason I believe we've had so little success changing our unconsciously driven behaviors in the past is that we didn't know enough about the mechanism that generates their persistence within our personalities—within our brain structures—a mechanism involved in habit formation and learned behaviors. These behaviors are *automatic,* mediated by our *auto*nomic nervous system rather than under cerebral control. That's why emotional catharsis alone isn't sufficient to stop them—and neither can conscious will. Fortunately you won't need iron willpower or searing insight into your childhood (most of us have gaping holes in our childhood memories anyway) to overcome your self-defeating patterns. More on that in Part Two.

This chapter starts you on a journey of growth and discovery by exploring a new three-part concept of personality, the Outer Child framework. Through the course of the book you'll learn to get all three moving parts of your psyche working together—Inner Child, Outer Child, and Adult Self. It's important to understand that these are psychological components we all have. This isn't about being wounded; they just *are*. Early wounds, however—and we all have some of these—cause these three selves to act out of turn or to co-exist uncomfortably. That discomfort, this walking out of step, is what causes us all to sabotage our own best interests and to fail ourselves.

LITTLE YOU

The Inner Child goes by many names in therapeutic circles—Child Within, Emotional Core, Child Self, Innermost Self, Little You, to name a few. Your Inner Child represents your pure emotional essence, not your behavior. Inner Child consists solely of *feelings and needs*. When you are sad, it is the defenseless, innocent Inner Child tucked within you who is sad. When you are mad, it is your Child Within who is upset about something. When you are joyful, it is your Child Self feeling happy and excited. When you are tired, hungry, cranky, or bored, it is Little You feeling these things. When you are emotionally eating, it is your Emotional Core that is craving to be soothed or fulfilled. The obtrusive *Outer,* not the innocent *Inner,* is the one busily stuffing the feelings with substitute pleasures, like food. When you are eagerly looking forward to something—a holiday, perhaps—it is Little You whose childlike awe and wonder are at play. And when you can hardly wait, it is your Inner Child feeling expectant.

You may already be well acquainted with your Inner Child. There are many self-help books, workshops, and therapy practices that focus almost exclusively on this concept. Some of you have been doing "Inner Child work"—a technique involving written or spoken dialogues of love and acceptance with your Inner Child.

The Inner Child concept was created to help nurture and love yourself—to become your own loving parent. But like Freudian therapy, it's hard to demonstrate that this concept alone can effectively help us change unwanted behaviors. While the Inner Child concept helps us connect with the source of deep-seated feelings, there is another step we need to take to overcome the acting-out behaviors triggered by those feelings—and that is where the Outer Child exercises come in.

THE MISSING LINK

Both your Inner Child and your Outer Child developed during childhood —first Inner Child when you were a just a wee thing, experiencing life purely through your needs, instincts, and feelings. Outer Child emerged later, as you developed language, motor, and other skills that enabled you to act (however primitively) on those needs.

Outer Child began its rise to power during the terrible twos—when you were a little tyrant, seeking pleasure and avoiding pain at all costs. As you

REVISING THE THREE-COMPONENT PERSONALITY

Psychology and self-help books have addressed "self-sabotage" in the past, but their authors tended to make these behaviors a function of the Inner Child. Following Freud's example, they didn't make a point to distinguish between "inner" and "outer" processes. In not creating a model that delineated reactive behavior as an *out*ward manifestation of an *in*ward emotional process, they unwittingly allowed feelings and behavior to remain merged.

In Freud's Id, feelings and reactive behaviors are merged. The Id represents emotional drives along with their behavioral discharges. Rather than divide these stimulus-response processes in two, Freud divided the Adult in two—Ego and Superego—thus completing his personality triangle. His superego represented an internalized parent figure (sometimes overpunitive) whose role was to manage and limit the primitive emotional drives of the Id. Freud's Ego represented the executive in charge who mediated between the overzealous, guilt-inflicting Superego and the legitimate needs of the self.

Many people are familiar with the Parent/Child/Adult framework from Eric Berne's Transactional Analysis. This framework follows Freud's same three personality divisions. Berne's Parent, like Freud's Superego, manages (and overmanages) the Child's needs and impulses. Berne's Child, like Freud's Id, needs to be compassionately managed and nurtured. And Berne's Adult, like Freud's Ego, guides the individual rather than impugns or chastises the Child self.

From Freud onward, conceptual models have differentiated two adult components while leaving feelings and behavior merged. The Outer Child framework is also a triangle, but instead of dividing the Ego in two, it divides the Id (or Child) in two. Inner Child represents the Id's emotional drives and Outer Child represents its *motoric discharges* (behaviors in reaction to those emotions).

Like the other models, the Outer Child framework posits the Adult at the top of a triangle. The only difference is that our Adult Self integrates Freud's Ego with constructive elements of the Superego, combining the roles of mediator and nurturer. The Adult Self is the executive in charge of the personality, ever striving to get stronger to better guide your life's mission. A stronger Adult Self, en route to becoming your higher self, no longer blames your self-defeating behavior on your feelings, no longer shames and blames your Inner Child (that would be a punitive Superego), but tames your Outer Child's behaviors, nurtures your Inner Child's needs, and chooses positive goal-promoting behaviors.

grew, so did your Outer Child, eventually developing into a kind of crusader and defender. The Outer Child is a hedonist (that pleasure-seeking part doesn't change!) as well as protector of your Inner Child, attempting to shield you from fear and hurt. Indeed, Outer is the embodiment of all your defense mechanisms—including those that can later sabotage your efforts to live a better life.

> When my parents tried to get me to do things like my home-work or clean my room, I resisted—I guess you'd say passive-aggressively—by doing the absolute minimum. My Outer Child still relies on this strategy; I still perform at a minimum.

> Outer Child is the "yes but" of my personality.

The Inner Child within you remains a helpless, innocent child of about five—an embodiment of your most vulnerable feelings, completely dependent on the other parts of your personality. In contrast, Outer continued gaining strength over a longer period of time and got stuck somewhere between the rambunctious age of 10 and the restless, hormone-driven age of 13. In terms of the way your Outer Child acts out, it is a lot like you were at that age—old enough to have a willful mind of your own but not yet old enough to understand the consequences, let alone the rights and feelings of others. That is why self-centeredness is age-appropriate for Outer Child. Outer isn't cognitively developed enough to make well-considered decisions, so it *acts out* instead.

When responding to your Inner Child's need for pleasure, for instance, Outer might choose to binge on candy in spite of the fact that you, the Adult, are steadfastly sticking to a diet (or so you thought). Intellectually you know for certain that your desire for pleasure is better served by keeping trim—better for both your health and your self-esteem. But Outer Child, a glutton for *immediate* gratification, wants to satisfy these urges *now* and grabs for the candy.

WHO'S IN CHARGE HERE?

Your mental capacities continued developing beyond pre-adolescence of course. Somewhere in your teens an Adult Self slowly emerged. You used your expanding cognitive abilities to limit your Outer Child's self-rebellious behavior, trying to free yourself from the bonds of crippling defense mechanisms you didn't even know you had. But try as you might, even as a full-fledged adult, Outer Child can still get the better of you. Outer was there first, and there's a powerful psychological inertia supporting its behaviors. And it can act out when you least expect it.

IS IT MY INNER OR MY OUTER CHILD?

In trying to control Outer's maneuvers, it's sometimes hard to tell Inner's voice from Outer's. When your Inner Child starts pining for something specific—a second helping of ice cream, a car you can't afford, or a particular lover you know to be "commitment phobic"—be suspicious. This is not your Inner Child, but your Outer Child disguising itself in your Inner Child's voice. Your Inner Child is not attached to specific things like a particular food, car, or lover. Its needs are more basic and substantial—to feel special, loved, and fulfilled—and doesn't want to become fat, broke, or heartbroken getting there. Your specific cravings are nothing more than Outer Child trying to take over your life.

Imagine that you are feeling slighted by your colleagues—lately they've been dismissing all of your ideas. You've started to think about other ways to pitch them when your Outer Child suddenly swoops in and takes over, going on a hotheaded rant, telling everyone in a crowded conference room that *this* time they're going to give your idea due consideration (your Inner Child was feeling hurt and angry, no doubt). You got their attention, all right, but probably not the way you intended. Did I mention that one of Outer's favorite mottos is: Negative Attention Is Better Than No Attention at All? In fact, it's only made things worse—you feel more isolated and misunderstood than before.

"My Outer Child has OPD—obnoxious personality disorder."

Your Inner Child still has wants and needs, but is desperate to break away from Outer's clumsy, destructive way of handling things. That pesky devil child has been butting into your Inner Child's life, behaving like the typical overprotective older brother who's "only trying to help." Meanwhile Inner's been waiting—most likely for decades—to be rescued. It's time for your Adult Self to step up to the plate.

The Adult Self we're talking about here is, of course, *you,* the person

INNER CHILD	OUTER CHILD	ADULT SELF
Feels, needs, and wants	Exhibits reactive behavior patterns	Acts as executive in charge of nurturing Inner, parenting Outer, and achieving your goals

reading this book, and the executive in charge of fulfilling your life's mission. I salute you for taking this opportunity to become a stronger, more capable person. I wrote this book to offer practical tools for integrating feelings and behavior—Inner and Outer Children—to help us become our higher selves.

UNDERSTANDING YOUR FEELINGS IS NOT ENOUGH

The concept of the Inner Child has made a potent psychological contribution, helping millions of people get in touch with and nurture their most difficult to reach feelings. Many who apply the concept, though, get stuck when it comes to changing their behavior. They gain awareness, but still seek clear-cut ways to *use* it.

Let's look at just one example. The concept of the Inner Child has helped us understand that when we overeat, we're often *"emotionally* eating." We've come to recognize that overfeeding ourselves is a misguided attempt to fill the empty, needy Child Within. But when hunger overtakes us again, we wonder, Now what? How do we translate this valuable awareness into action? Lacking concrete answers, we remain a nation of overeaters.

The Outer Child framework offers access to the mechanism perpetrating these self-destructive behaviors as well as effective exercises to overcome them.

The unrecognized voice of the Outer Child has been interfering in the internal dialogue we all have between our Adult Self and our Inner Child. Identifying and isolating Outer Child's voice quells its commotion and allows our heart to finally communicate with our head, and vice versa. The Outer Child concept transforms what had been a two-dimensional dialogue into the integrated, three-dimensional, dynamic approach we have needed all along in order to get unstuck.

Gaining Outer Child awareness allows us to finally love ourselves unconditionally. Until now, we've tended to blame our behaviors on our *feelings*—especially intrusive feelings like anxiety.

My anxiety holds me back. It makes me tongue-tied and brain dead when I'm around the higher-ups in my company.

I hate my insecurity; it makes me act too needy with my girlfriend.

It's my anger that makes me say the wrong thing.

When you blame the way you acted on your anxiety or any other feeling, you are, in effect, blaming your Inner Child. There's no question that your Inner Child's feelings are what triggered that moment of mental or verbal paralysis or what prompted you to become too attention-seeking in a social situation. So, if you ask yourself, *"How do I feel about my anxiety?"* you'd probably answer, *"I hate it."* But wait. How is it possible to simultaneously love your Inner Child unconditionally and hate its feelings for holding you back? That's been the hidden problem.

Attributing the behavior pattern to Outer Child resolves that internal conflict. It's natural to feel as if you've let yourself down in the wake of a self-defeating outburst. Most of us judge ourselves mercilessly for these self-sabotaging behaviors. But when you blame them on your feelings, you compound the self-abuse. You allow self-anger and self-hatred to silently leach into your internal dialogue, contaminating your relationship with your innermost self. Identifying the third dimension of the personality— Outer Child—removes the contamination.

Many therapists recommend positive affirmations as a way to cleanse and heal your relationship with yourself. Maybe you've tried it and wondered what all the fuss was about because it didn't seem to change anything. Why? Because when you stood before your mirror and said things to yourself like, *"I love you just the way you are,"* you unwittingly made that "you" the object of your frustration and fix-it energy. You're saying the words *"I love you just the way you are,"* but you're hearing this: *"I love you even though you're a basket case and ruin my life with your damned anxiety!"* or *"I'm trying to love you, if only you weren't so needy and reactive around people."* Your well-intended affirmations became contaminated with subliminal negative messages.

Before you can truly benefit from self-affirmations, you must first attribute the self-sabotaging behavior to something *out*side of the Self—namely, the *Outer* Child. When you feel frustrated with yourself, you can direct your fix-it energy toward your *Outer* Child. This spares your innermost self—your tenderhearted Inner Child—from the toxic subtext.

THE BLAME GAME

Letting Outer take the flack liberates your Inner Child from blame. It allows you to get beneath the unconscious contamination to zero in on your Inner Child's true needs and feelings for the first time. This is self-love at its purest and most healing.

A former client, Sarah, illustrates what a difference this makes: When she first came to see me, she was 32 and single.

My beauty is buried under the 50 pounds I've gained over the last 10 years. I'm always on a diet, but I keep getting bigger. I guess that's what happens when you just keep eating. I used to be a model in college. Now I'm stuck in hell.

Sarah understood that her overeating emerged from unresolved emotional needs. She'd already connected the dots between traumatic events in her childhood and the struggle to lose weight. She'd met with a therapist weekly to work on her self-image and strengthen her resolve—and that therapist had been a good analyst and supportive coach. Sarah had also done Inner Child work, writing letters of love and acceptance to herself through a series of "Healing the Child Within" workshops over the years. But she continued to struggle with emotional eating; although when she grabbed for the second helping of pasta, she did so with greater self-awareness.

What stood between Sarah and the physical appearance she desired was (you guessed it) an unrecognized Outer Child. For the past 10 years, Sarah's Outer Child had been busily misappropriating her drive for pleasure and tension-reduction by gratifying all of her yearnings with food. When Sarah got wise to her Outer Child, everything changed:

When I saw my Outer Child for the cunning, obstinate, gluttonous, don't-take-my-candy-away-from-me addict that it was, I was ready to face it down. But I knew Big Me needed to be stronger and I knew I had to love Little Me more.

Doing the Outer Child exercises is what did it. In isolating Outer's interfering voice, I was finally able to hear my Inner Child begging me to make her beautiful. I no longer resented her or blamed her. I actually grew to feel real compassion for her, even love, for the first time. It got me to care enough about myself to put an end to the self-sabotage.

Sarah used Outer Child tools to feed her long-standing need for love and connection in a direct, new way. She *behaviorally* addressed her oldest, most hidden emotional issues without food-feeding them. Instead she healed them. (You too will learn how to accomplish this, when we explore Outer Child and your Diet in Part Three.)

Giving Outer Child its own separate identity provides the conceptual backdrop for Inner Child to finally emerge as the pure and innocent little child its authors—Bradshaw, Whitfield, Peabody, and others—always meant it to be. It was never their intention to blame the victim—to have Inner Child take the heat for the self-sabotaging, impulsive, habituated behaviors. The problem was, we simply didn't have a framework that clearly separated our self-sabotaging behaviors from our blameless emotional inner selves.

We all have a relationship with ourselves—whether or not we've ever written a letter to our Inner Child—a relationship sustained by an *unconscious, internal* dialogue. The quality of that dialogue, be it adoring or self-loathing, has been asserting itself beneath the surface of your life, all along silently affecting your ability to love yourself.

Outer Child is a conceptual tool that functionally separates behavior from feelings. Outer personifies *out*put while Inner personifies *in*put, thus creating simple language for articulating the dynamic interplay between *IN*COMING emotional sensation and *OUT*GOING behavioral reaction. In case there's any doubt: Emotions are not right or wrong, they just *are*. Behavior, not emotion, is what is judged culpable. Once you tease the two apart, you can effectively short-circuit the unwanted behaviors that have been holding you back.

BEING A BETTER PARENT

The ability to separate feelings from behavior is a critical skill not only for people attempting to parent themselves, but also for those looking to better parent their children. I led parent education workshops for over 15 years and meted out this advice, coined by my colleague Nancy Steinbach, over and over again:

Validate and nurture your children's feelings, but never accept those feelings as an excuse for unacceptable behavior.

(*"I know you are angry at your brother, but hitting him is unacceptable."*)

Once parents learn this principle—that feelings and behavior need to be dealt with differently—they're able to comfort their scared child (or calm their angry child) and show her how to express that fear (or anger) without taking it out on a sibling or herself, or anyone else. As an added bonus, they are learning to better parent their own Outer Children.

NOW IT'S YOUR TURN

Once you can separate feelings from behavior, your Adult Self can finally deal with Outer Child, and not just the isolated embarrassing incident, but the overarching personality dynamic that embodies your storehouse of defense mechanisms, repetition compulsions, personality tendencies, impulsive behaviors, habits, quirks, and knee-jerk reactions. You'll deal with these behaviors as part of an interrelated phenomenon that acts in response to, but *is separate from,* your internal needs, urges, drives, and feelings. The latter you can finally validate, cherish, and love. In fact, you'll find that developing a strong emotional connection to your Inner Child is what prevents Outer from galloping away with your life's mission.

Reading this chapter may already have given you a few ideas about your own Outer Child's more prominent traits. In the next chapter I'll introduce you to tools for taking an inventory of them—including some of the more difficult to observe behaviors and the emotional triggers that set them in motion. You will find that in taking your Outer Child inventory, what would normally take hours of morose soul-searching is an easy empowering task that propels you forward.

THREE

Exposing Your Outer Child

Years ago, when I was writing my first book on abandonment I arranged meetings with my colleague and friend Peter Yelton to engage his fertile mind. I'd been searching for ways to help people overcome the deeply entrenched patterns that arise from unresolved abandonment and other experiences. Peter and I were groping for a word, a phrase, a concept to target those repetitive behaviors that interfere in people's lives—not the emotional wounds, but the *out*ward manifestations of those wounds, the behavioral warts and scars and habits that show on the *out*side. "Not the *Inner Child*," we said aloud to each other, "but the . . . *Outer Child*!"

Naming the concept led to a fireworks display of new insights. As sparks of self-illumination came raining down on us, we were inspired to offer up our own worst traits to each other. Our revelations were alternately funny and shocking, and soon we were trying to outdo each other with the outrageousness of our Outer Child tendencies. Along the way we saw that the concept encapsulated a new level of insight about how our defense mechanisms and unconscious motivations function as a kind of embodied presence within the self, dividing us against ourselves. Peter and

I could both see that here was an awareness tool with enough oomph to dismantle the whole infrastructure of self-sabotage.

I brought the Outer Child concept to one of my workshops as a test and saw it elicit the same explosions of insights for others, breaking through denial and opening the door for change.

I wish I could magically transport you to one of my workshops. Doing Outer Child work in a group is always such raucous, good fun. It's everyone's favorite activity—including mine. As soon as I begin explaining the concept, the group lights up. I post a list of Outer Child characteristics to help people get a sense of the scope and diversity of Outer's machinations—how multifaceted, devious, and subtle its behaviors can be. After reviewing the list, people are quick to join in, topping one another with the outlandishness of their own Outer Child traits. The atmosphere in workshops is lighthearted, yet the depth of self-disclosure is unprecedented. People admit things to one another (even in larger groups) they have never before admitted to themselves or anyone else.

Let's create a reader's workshop right here. You already have some idea about what your own Outer Child is up to, at least its more prominent behaviors. Below I'll present a list of some of Outer's common tendencies and later look at what might be going on emotionally (within your Inner Child) to trigger them.

The idea is to take a sideways glance at your own Outer Child's behaviors. By the way, you'll want to situate your Adult Self squarely in the driver's seat, because Outer Children hate this kind of assessment—they're by nature extremely defensive—so we'd rather not have any at this party.

REMIND YOU OF ANYONE?

Remember that no one's keeping score here; we're just taking a broad look at the remarkable and sometimes ridiculous things we do to get in our own way. You're most likely to see your Outer Child acting out when your Inner Child is tired, cranky, or stressed. Any number of triggers can arouse Outer's antics, including having an argument with a friend, losing your keys, or feeling overworked. People with extremely stressful, traumatic childhoods tend to have easily stressed-out Inner Children and their Outer Children use this as license to act out.

Ready? Have a quick read through the list below and see if you don't find a few of these traits familiar. Outer Child...

Is excessive

Outer is the addict, the alcoholic, the one who runs at the mouth and does everything to extreme.

Outer has a hole in its pocket when it comes to either anger or money. Outer must spend.

Outer loves chocolate and convinces you that bingeing on it is good for your heart. Likewise with wine.

Outer is the hidden "Chuckie" of the personality. Even the nicest people we know overreact like a 10-year-old with a full-blown conduct disorder (perhaps not in public) when they feel even slightly rejected, dismissed, abandoned.

Is a drama queen

Outer thrives on crisis and chaos.

Outer enjoys playing the victim; that is, when not playing the martyr.

Outer underreacts when a friend steps on your toes, pretending to be gracious—*"Oh, that's all right"*—but holds on to resentment for decades.

Outer uses crying as a manipulation. But this ploy is so automatic, primitive, and unconscious, if you call Outer on it, it cries louder.

Outer provokes anger in its subtle ways and then accuses the other person of being abusive.

Outer loves to play the injured party.

Outer acts submissive so it can seethe at being dominated.

Loves distraction

Outer makes huge messes that take forever to clean up. Outer distracts you from things you're trying to get done.

Outer uses projection as a defense. Outer projects your shortcomings onto other people to keep the heat off of itself.

Outer is like Cleopatra: Queen of da Nile. In fact, denial is Outer's favorite defense mechanism. If all else fails, just deny it.

Is uncompromising (for no good reason)

Outer is a fairness-junkie. It fights valiantly for what it considers fair. Outer has been known to commit injustices (or declare war) in the name of fairness.

Outer can be a perfectionist. Perfectionism, for Outer, is a form of bargaining: Outer is saying, *"If I do this perfectly, I merit a reward."* Outer's perfectionism contains a built-in vise grip; if you don't get rewarded, Outer's iron fist may protrude through its velvet glove.

Outer can be self-spiteful—make you miserable in order to punish someone else. For instance, Outer can keep you heartbroken for*ever* just to prove the injustice of the breakup. As illogical, primitive, and totally self-defeating as you know this to be, Outer continues its spiteful siege against you.

Is completely devoted—to itself

Outer is devoted to its own self-interests. Outer is the self-centered part we all share; it's just that some of us hide this selfish part better than others.

Outer is reactive rather than active or reflective. It is defensive rather than open to feedback, self-justifying rather than self-aware.

Loves the blame game

Outer specializes in blame. When Outer loses something, it blames it on one of your children.

Outer revels in taking other people's inventory. It has a *negative* attraction to their faults. Outer happens to be especially obsessed with and intolerant of other people's Outer Children. If you have an uncomfortable feeling, Outer needs to find somebody else at fault.

Outer enjoys making the other person wrong. Sometimes Outer makes the other person *pay* (even though he may be entirely innocent).

Outer talks about your friends behind their backs. Outer hates it when your friends talk behind *your* back.

Is a master of disguises

Outer acts pure and innocent to show other people up.

Outer will use almost any diversionary tactic, no matter how convoluted or unattractive, to keep your vulnerability out of sight. For instance, Outer hates asking for either help or directions. It would rather get you frustrated or lost.

Because your Inner Child so fears abandonment, your Outer Child developed a pleasing persona—but the only reason to please anyone as far as Outer's concerned is to prevent them from rejecting you. Outer finds someone who is easy to take for granted and then treats her badly since it no longer has to worry about being abandoned. When this fear is dormant, your true personality can emerge; you no longer have to charm and seduce the other person.

When Outer does something mean or selfish, it hides behind altruism, moral superiority, righteous indignation, and benevolence.

Outer can express your anger by becoming inconveniently passive.

Outer has a favorite disguise: compliance. Outer uses compliance to confuse others into thinking it doesn't want control. But don't be fooled—Outer Child is a control freak.

Outer has a split personality—it splits its personality between home and office: nice at office, a tyrant at home . . . or vise versa.

Outer is an award-winning actor that believes its own act. This makes it challenging to recognize the true face of your Outer Child or anyone else's. Since other people's Outer Children are so well disguised, you may have thought you were the only one with an Outer Child.

Outer tries, but the truth is, you can't hide your Outer Child from your spouse or children. They get to see the real you—bad habits, tirades, and all. In fact, we could redefine intimacy as the mutual exposure of our Outer Children.

Is demanding

Outer is a people pleaser with ulterior motives. It will give others the shirt off your back. But what does it expect in return? Everything.

Outer seeks emotional salve from others.

Outer can't stand waiting, especially waiting for that special someone to call. It loves to test new lovers to the limit. One of its favorite games is hard-to-get. Rather than endear you to your lovers, though, Outer's games leave your partners confused, agitated, and fed up.

Outer is always looking for love insurance and refuses to believe there is no such thing. For instance, Outer might chase after someone who is very hard up and become his "caretaker" in hopes of becoming so valuable that the poor slob will never want to leave you. But this strategy backfires like all of the others; you wind up abandoned again.

Wants it, and wants it now

Outer is highly principled, but the only principle it obeys is the pleasure principle.

Borrowing from author Elizabeth Gilbert in her memoir *Eat, Pray, Love,* when heartbroken, the best way to get over someone is to get under someone else.

When it comes to self-improvement programs, Outer wants to skip the work and get straight to the benefits. Outer prefers to learn in pill form rather than have to *do* something constructive, like go through the steps of a linear process (like this program). Outer lies back, holding out for the next magic pill.

Loves the getting, not the having

As one workshop attendee so cleverly put it, Outer is an environmentalist when it comes to pursuing women (or men)—it just likes to tag them and then throw them back in.

Outer can be very cunning and put its best foot forward when pursuing a new lover. It seems the picture of altruism, decency, kindness, and tolerance. It becomes seductive, funny, charming, full of life, deeply interested in the other person's life. But once it catches its prey, it suddenly clams up, becomes cold, critical, intolerant, irritable, and sexually withholding. Outer makes us pity the person willing to love us.

Outer can't resist the emotional candy of pursuing an emotionally challenging lover. Outer thinks unavailable people are sexy. This goes against what's good for your Inner Child, who needs someone capable of giving love, nurturance, and commitment. But then, since when does Outer Child care about what's good for Inner Child?

Is all about surface

Outer can't commit because it's always "looking to trade up." It is plagued with bigger-is-better syndrome.

Outer is attracted to people's form rather than substance. Outer finds status and external beauty more attractive than integrity or kindness.

Outer tries to get self-esteem by proxy—it tries to attract someone higher than you in the pecking order.

Outer identifies with Groucho Marx: It would never join any club that would have you as a member.

Thinks it's my way or no way

Outer doesn't obey the golden rule. Outer obeys its own Outer Child rule: Get others to treat you as you want to be treated, and treat others as you feel like treating them.

Outer is never wrong and must never be told so, or it will break something.

Outer keeps up an endless protest against any reality it doesn't want to accept. It can stay in protest mode no matter how hard you try to let go. It sustains a tenacious protest against loss, homework, annual checkups, taxes, rejection, global warming, and death.

Outer believes laws and ethics are for everybody else. It obeys rules only to avoid getting caught.

Outer doesn't hesitate to sacrifice intimacy in search of satisfying its own desires. In fact, it does its best to defeat the two major tasks of intimacy: Task one is to get *your* Inner Child to become friends with *your mate's* Inner Child. Task two is to make sure you don't take each other's Outer Children too personally. But Outer prefers to beat up on your mate's Inner Child and goes head-to-head with her Outer Child.

To borrow from Elizabeth Gilbert again, Outer believes what it wants to believe. It has a wishbone where it should have a backbone.

These and many other Outer Child issues will be explored in depth in the chapters to come. But let's highlight a few of them now to look at some of the triggers that set them in motion.

OUTER WANTS EVERYTHING THE EASY WAY— IN PILL FORM, IF POSSIBLE

Your Inner Child could be feeling hopeful about the possibility of having a better life (as a result of reading this book) but also impatient, helpless, worried that it might never happen—all normal Inner Child feelings. In the Adult Self's hands, these feelings become motivation to create positive change. But your Outer Child prefers to act out these feelings by seeking

INNER CHILD	OUTER CHILD	ADULT SELF
Feels, needs, and wants	Grabs for quick fixes	Nurtures Inner, parents Outer, and achieves your goals
	Self-sabotages	

quick fixes. Outer balks at having to go step by step through any process that takes time. It tries to convince you that awareness is enough—that insight alone is magic, that it's not necessary to have to actually *do* anything differently. You just have to sit and read and think and *feel* about yourself and you will have a breakthrough and your behavior patterns will spontaneously change for the better and your life will turn into a bowl of cherries.

Your developing Adult Self realizes that you resolve long-standing issues not by thinking or talking your way out of them, but by *doing* your way out. In fact, learning to tame your Outer Child is a lot like learning to swim, do yoga, or play tennis. You can read all you want about the technique but the only thing that improves your game is actually doing it. Practicing. And lo and behold, you get better at it! When your Adult Self overrules Outer's insistence that insight gets your behavior to change spontaneously, then you're ready to take action.

THE VIRTUE OF SELFISHNESS

Your Inner Child is afraid people won't like you if they can see your selfishness. Yet Inner can't help but stay focused on its own feelings and needs; it just doesn't want to be criticized for it. Maybe one of your parents called you selfish during your childhood and it hurt and confused you. You tried to hide your self-interests and felt guilty for having them.

Now as an adult, you see other people get away with selfish behavior—and perhaps your Inner Child is resentful and envious that it doesn't have the guts to do the same. Your Outer Child takes these perfectly normal feelings and uses the emotional energy to point the finger at others.

The truth is that self-centeredness is not something to be ashamed of—in fact, it's universal to the human condition. Everybody has this self-serving part, so why not you or me? After all, if you're not looking out for your most basic emotional needs, who will? By identifying and recognizing these needs for what they are, you become enlightened.

Self-interest hails from a primal, primitive place built into the mammalian brain (the stomping grounds of your Outer Child). The function of this primitive part of the brain is to promote the biological and emotional needs of the self. Your Adult Self's role is to identify the self-driven part without causing shame. No one's indicting you, the whole person, for having these perfectly normal needs. But by identifying this part of yourself, you will no longer be unconsciously motivated by it. You can now make *conscious* choices based on self-acknowledgment rather than self-denial. Owning up to the primitive Outer Child trait of selfishness rather than denying it, masking it, rationalizing it, or projecting it onto others offers a real boon to your personal growth.

As Joe, a former workshop attendee, puts it this way:

> Outer Child was like a jolt of self-awareness. I'd always prided myself on NOT being selfish. But learning that we all have a self-centered part and that we all have an Outer Child was freeing. Now instead of accusing everyone else of selfish motives, I am more prone to catch myself in the act. It allows me to take a step back, maybe laugh about it, make amends if it's appropriate, grow a little more self-aware, and move on. It's helping me evolve to a higher place. I'm a work in progress.

COMING CLEAN

What might your Inner Child be feeling when your Outer Child makes a mess of things? How about nervous about how you're going to make ends meet now that you've left your job and your Outer Child has stalled about finding a new one? Or how your boss will respond to the proposal that is now a month overdue?

Or maybe you're just craving pleasure; your day wasn't rewarding enough. So right in the middle of a project, Outer Child goes off to rest, eat, or call a friend instead of letting you finish what you're doing. Or it might go deeper. Your Inner Child may have an undercurrent of anxiety or depression stemming from old wounds. Your Outer Child is reacting by forestalling real work with self-soothing quick fixes.

Your developing Adult Self learns how to recognize Inner Child's feelings and conduct an internal dialogue that soothes and assuages your underlying needs so that you can delay gratification to get your work done. Having postponed your Inner Child's needs, your Adult Self must eventually follow through and gratify them in a healthy way, like eating a nutritious snack or reading the next chapter of a good book. We all need to take breaks from hard work; you'll read more about how to do that kind of self-nurturing in Part Two.

PEOPLE PLEASING

In your childhood, your parents may have been emotionally unavailable due to any number of reasons—alcoholism, grief, workaholism—and you groveled for their attention and love. You felt worthless and inadequate when you were not able to get them to parent you. Outer Child runs with these long-standing feelings of worthlessness and re-creates that same dynamic in your adult relationships. In other words, you chase after people who don't, can't, or won't give you what you need. When Inner Child feels needy, Outer springs into action to practice what it knows best—its excellent groveling skills. Practicing scratches the itch of the old pain, but that only aggravates the rash. There are better ways to connect with other people, as you'll read about in chapters on relationships in Part Three.

DRIVEN TO EXCESS

Your Inner Child desires pleasurable things like love, connection, and fun. Outer Child finds that satisfying its sweet tooth is the most immediate way to get pleasure—it's instantaneous! Outer, the hedonist, is a champion of pleasure and will valiantly smuggle cookies to your bedroom, especially when you're dieting.

Your developing Adult Self learns to gratify its need for pleasure in more substantial ways, such as developing a new relationship or building a new career, rather than relying on quick fixes that are not good for your health, reputation, or waistline.

ALL THE WORLD'S YOUR STAGE

What's with all the Outer Child drama? In acting out Inner Child's feelings, you would think your Outer Child was preparing for a career on the stage! Inner Child may have a whole backlog of feelings stemming, perhaps, from having been raised by dysfunctional, neglectful parents, and Outer takes these feelings and uses adult circumstances as a stage on which to reenact the same dynamics. This is Outer's way of *externalizing* your internal feelings. So, for example, your boyfriend has a habit of cheating on you, but instead of moving on, you catch him over and over again, each time enacting your long-standing angst of unrequited love with a live person. He's a substitute for the parent who abandoned your needs in childhood. Or you drive a malfunctioning jalopy instead of a more reliable car, and—surprise, surprise—it breaks down a lot. Your "incompetent" mechanic then becomes the perfect target for your feelings of helplessness and frustration.

People, places, and things become props on Outer's melodramatic stage.

Your developing Adult Self knows what is going on inside and becomes self-constructive—no need to create dramas involving other people, as you'll read in the chapter on Trauma in Part Two.

SHE'S SO...

Sometimes Outer Child behavior is anything but deep-seated. Inner Child might simply be cranky from a long day's toil, so Outer goes looking for someone to use as a scratching post.

Or it might go deeper. You might be feeling frustrated with yourself for not landing that new client, or for carrying around those extra twenty pounds for the last decade. When that sort of self-criticism simmers inside, your Outer Child may eventually displace feelings onto other people. *"Why can't he get it together and find a steady job?"* *"She's so inconsiderate; there she is, late again."* Your Adult Self recognizes your fault-finding as a warning sign. It reminds you to focus on improving your own life conditions in order to meet your Inner Child's needs in more substantial ways.

PERFECTION IS A TRAP

When Outer Child insists that nothing but perfection will do, your Inner Child might be feeling empty, disconnected, or worthless. Maybe as a child you felt left out, perhaps resentful of one of your siblings for being the "special" one or grabbing more attention. So your Outer Child takes these longstanding feelings of jealousy and inadequacy and acts them out by trying to be perfect. There's still a chance to steal the spotlight from your older brother (the smarter, taller, more popular one), isn't there? Of course, you're no longer in competition with anyone but yourself!

Situation: You're planning to go to a party, but you haven't been shopping in months. There's *nothing* spectacular enough in your closet to wear. Clothes you liked yesterday are suddenly hideously passé. If you can't find the perfect outfit, you're not going. You'd rather stay home and feel miserable.

Your Adult Self finds a middle ground by accepting the fact that we all have imperfections, shortcomings. We are all bent twigs. The knuckles, knots, and bends in your twig are what give your personality its special contour and distinctiveness. If perfectionism is one of your traits, rather than be ruled by it, accept it as a part of your Outer Child portfolio, and balance this trait with wisdom coming from your more reasonable, self-accepting higher self.

TEMPER, TEMPER

Anger is Outer's favorite emotion, because anger is so energizing. And self-justifying! When your Inner Child feels angry, your Outer is charged to *do* something about it. Anger is Outer's excuse to strike out. It becomes bloodthirsty; its rampage is fueled by adrenaline and other brain chemicals that increase your impulsivity and decrease your reasoning capacity.

Anger is not a primary, but a secondary emotion. First comes pain. When you stub your toe, it hurts: pain. Then you scream in anger because the pain makes you angry. Pain first, anger second. When something in your life creates chronic emotional pain (failed attempts to start a new career, a partner who withholds emotionally), you might direct your anger at the person triggering it or any inanimate object that gets in your way.

Being rejected by a loved one can create abandonment rage, which can trigger Outer Child's most destructive, dangerous, and self-justifying behaviors. In the extreme, abandonment rage has been responsible for some of the most infamous headline-grabbing murder-suicides. You might remember the case of the man who, in a jealous rage, set fire to the Happy Land Social Club in the Bronx, killing 87 people.

Your developing Adult Self knows that anger is head-bending. So when you become angry, Adult takes precautions, learns how to assume complete responsibility for your behavior, learns to avoid alcohol and other substances that reduce one's control, learns how to nurture and calm this most volatile of emotions.

BENEATH IT ALL

Why, when we're faced with a new challenge, does our Outer Child pitch a hissy fit? Since when did the failure to assemble a futon frame spell the end of the world? Your Inner Child might be feeling frustrated or inadequate and beset with primal abandonment fear, the fear of being deemed unworthy of love and left behind. This primitive fear is residual of our Clan-of-the-Cave-Bear days, when banishment or abandonment meant death.

Your developing Adult Self realizes that your helplessness is learned helplessness and knows that you must calm down so that you can use your cognitive resources to override this learned response and accomplish the task—whether it's hanging those shelves or learning to apply the tools of the Outer Child program. Adult also knows it can ask for help.

And help is on its way. Next, in Part Two, as we continue exploring your Outer Child behavior and what motivates it, I'll guide you through a program for overcoming all your self-sabotaging behaviors.

In the meantime, keep tabs on your Outer Child. To this day, I still keep a daily inventory of my own Outer Child characteristics. It helps me stay honest, in tune with myself, and motivated to keep my higher self in the lead. One of my most productive Outer Child insights involved locating evidence of egotism that was hiding out in my seemingly humble demeanor. I thought I had already gotten rid of most of my egotism, but as I peeled away the layers, I saw it. The clarity proved to be both humbling and empowering. For instance, I noticed, because now I wanted to notice, that sometimes I assumed I understood something when in fact I had not understood it.

Owning up to this trait didn't make me want to beat myself up because I figured if I had it, my colleagues had it, Freud probably had it, and just about everybody had it, at least to some extent. I was just grateful for being able to detect it in myself. Thank you, Outer Child! This new awareness helped me look *beyond* my own egotism to *see* my egotism.

I started to have multiple sightings of this Outer Child trait. For instance, I'd catch myself nodding my head in a knowing way as if to say *"I understand,"* when in fact I hadn't. I noticed this happening when doctors used medical terminology in giving me test results or when someone expressed a complex worldview. I realized that I'd walked away perplexed instead of asking for clarity. I saw how this behavior caused so much going on around me to remain unquestioned and poorly understood. In correcting this, I began learning new things by leaps and bounds, but it meant first acknowledging my ignorance to myself and then, of course, to others.

I don't know exactly at what point in my life this *presuming to know* set in—probably becoming a psychotherapist gave it a good boost—but I do know that this Outer Child trait had been hiding out in my Adult persona, protecting my insecure feelings and serving my egotism quite nicely. I also know that when I can't tell the difference between understanding something and *thinking* I understand it, it blocks me from knowing more. Catching myself in the act of *presuming to understand* got me to delve further into many truisms I had taken for granted. What a gift. Discovering my Outer Child helped me penetrate the surface reality of things and take a giant step forward as a theoretician and person.

Here's an example relevant to doing the research for this book. It got me to continually question the assumptions I was making about exactly how Outer functioned within the personality. Thanks to my new awareness, I'd peel away another layer of assumption, take a second look, and realize there was something about Outer's underpinnings that still eluded me. For instance, I discovered I wasn't exactly sure where Outer's outbound energy derived from. So I removed yet another layer of preconceived assumption and asked myself more probing questions. I dug further into the newly unfolding neurobiological research, seeking help from research mentors, and consulted again with co-creator of the Outer Child concept, Peter Yelton. In this digging, questioning manner, I was able to penetrate many uncertainties I had about Outer Child (the hardest part was realizing I had uncertainties) and to admit to the ones I still had.

It was in this tentative, searching manner that I was able to resolve the conundrum about how it's possible to have emotional insight but not know how to use it. I slowly honed specialized power tools that allow you to actually *use* your insight. The solution involved trial and error, and realizing error when I saw it.

Presuming to know was just one facet of my Outer Child persona. I have identified hundreds of others (none terribly flattering). If you add up all of my Outer's features, they'd tell the backstory about the many ways I manage to get in my own way. Many of these discoveries are included in The Outer Child Inventory posted on my website www.outerchild.net.

As you discover the unique maneuvers of your own Outer Child, please send them to me. Contributions from around the world help me continue building the Outer Child Inventory. It's clear the concept has an enormous impact on people's lives.

Remember, you don't want to bind and gag your Outer Child. It will only fight harder to act out. It's when you acknowledge your Outer Child and learn constructive ways to use its energy that your life begins to change.

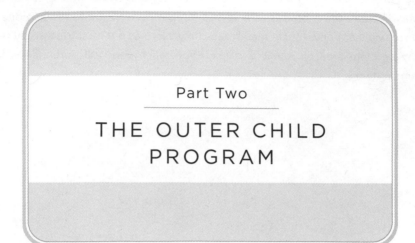

Part Two

THE OUTER CHILD PROGRAM

Now that you understand the Outer Child concept, it's time to get started on putting that good knowledge to use. Part II introduces you to the three prongs of the Outer Child program: separation therapy, guided visualization, and action steps. I have been developing these techniques for over 30 years as a psychotherapist and workshop leader. Gurus with whom I have studied and colleagues have shared their techniques, which I have integrated, and some are my own, practices molded by trial and error as I have worked with clients. I've included some of these exercises in previous books, but since introducing the Outer Child concept, I've adapted these exercises to the special task of overcoming our most entrenched self-defeating patterns, taking into account new advances in brain science and other related research along the way.

The Outer Child program involves working directly with all three components of the personality—Outer Child, Inner Child, and Adult Self—to resolve internal conflicts so they no longer interfere from within. You learn to calm your Inner Child, tame your Outer Child, and strengthen your Adult Self. The goal is to get those three parts of the psyche working together on your behalf, toward your dreams.

Your insight into these inner workings of the personality will increase chapter by chapter to a level beyond where you've been before—to the point where you're taking action to eradicate old patterns and create healthy new ones. We will explore important areas affecting your life, including abandonment, self-esteem, unresolved childhood issues, and stress, and we will apply the exercises to help you effectively work through each one. Once you learn how to use these tools, they serve as a template to apply to any problem area of your life, helping you reach your full potential as a human being.

FOUR

Outer Child and
Your Abandonment Issues

Abandonment casts a wide net, snaring anyone who has ever felt a loss or disconnection. Those old abandonment wounds form the basis for Outer Child's most intrusive defense mechanisms. Still, it rankles some people to hear "grown men and women" talk about their abandonment issues. Their knee-jerk reaction is: *"Stop all that whining!"*

We're not whining. In fact, the purpose of the Outer Child program is to focus you on very specific goals. It helps you heal your deepest issues *without* dwelling on them.

Abandonment is the crux of the human condition. Exploring this issue takes you on a journey to the center of the self, where deep healing can begin. The tools I'll describe in this and the next four chapters will help you redirect the residual fear and insecurity seeping out of your oldest wounds. By the time we're done you'll be redirecting energy you once used to beat yourself up to propel your life to a better place.

WHAT IS ABANDONMENT?

Abandonment is the feeling of being left behind and it's a primal fear, a fear of losing life-sustaining support. Its pain can be acute, a burning feeling of rejection and betrayal. Or it can be chronic, an under-the-skin anxiety you can't trace back to a specific event but which has left you feeling hypersensitive to rejection and loss.

Abandonment can be an intermittent feeling; you might occasionally feel aftershocks of old losses when a friend drops out of your life, when your partner just doesn't seem to understand, or when you worry about ever finding someone to love. These anxieties rise up from your core, unwelcome reminders of your vulnerability.

Abandonment can also run like a current beneath your conscious awareness. Left unresolved, the primal wound of abandonment festers below the surface, silently eroding your self-esteem, infecting your relationships, and triggering your most self-defeating Outer Child patterns.

Depending on your earlier losses, your abandonment wound can be tender, a raw nerve highly sensitive to anything that makes you feel...

excluded
misunderstood
overlooked
unappreciated
taken for granted
ignored
belittled.

My aim here is not to explore the whole abandonment spectrum but to zero in on one aspect that's particularly relevant to our work: self-abandonment, the emotional root of self-sabotage.

LEAVING YOURSELF BEHIND

The important message here is that while adults can *feel* abandoned, they can't actually *be* abandoned by another person. Unlike children, who depend on caretakers for their very survival, able-bodied adults can take care of their own basic needs. Only children can truly be abandoned.

However, adults *can* abandon themselves.

My colleague Peter Yelton once created a metaphor that he called "the invisible drain of self-esteem." As Peter explains it, abandonment trauma is powerful enough to create a drain deep within the self that leaks self-esteem. No matter what you do to bolster your self-image, the invisible drain is always working to funnel away feelings of self-worth.

The invisible drain of self-esteem is driven by self-abandonment. Why do we flush our self-worth away? It's something we do to ourselves unconsciously. Fortunately it's something we can *undo* through the Outer Child program. By administering to our long-neglected primal needs and feelings, we reprogram the trigger points for our automatic behaviors and heal our emotional core at the same time.

WHY WOULD I DO THAT?

Self-abandonment started early, when you were too little to know what to do with your own or other people's strong emotions. When children feel disconnected, hurt, or criticized they tend to take it to heart and blame themselves (e.g., *"Dad's mad all the time, I guess it's my fault." "Mommy never likes to do things with me, I guess I'm just not special enough to make her happy."*) When children feel culpable and disappointed in themselves, they move further away from a core belief in their value and lovability. To a child, rejecting this worthless screwup (who just happens to be themselves) makes perfect sense. And so it begins.

As an adult, a variety of situations can lead to self-abandonment, especially if you happen to be:

- going through a painful breakup
- alone (again) and having trouble finding a relationship
- feeling a loss of love in your current relationship
- dealing with the loss of a friend, a job, or a dream
- experiencing echoes of past hurts whenever you feel a hint of rejection

A major event—someone you love chooses to leave you—can trigger a full-blown abandonment crisis, one that throws your whole sense of reality into an emotional time warp. Old familiar feelings of dependency and panic rush to the surface. As if a small child again, you suddenly feel you can't live without that person—that you'll die without him. We've all heard stories about people, aging but apparently healthy, who die just a few months after a beloved partner. Like them, it feels like you too will succumb to terminal heartbreak. You're panicked and weakened and ashamed about losing someone you love and for falling apart over it. You hate yourself and your emotional excessiveness. This self-recrimination is self-abandonment in its most virulent form. In fact, it is responsible for the severe depression and plummeting self-esteem that accompany a heartbreak.

As painful as feeling abandoned is, it's the things you do to yourself in the wake of "being dumped" that cause the most damage. It's the *self-abandonment*—the self-criticizing, blaming, and shaming—that fractures your sense of self and keeps you mired in a swamp of self-doubt. This attack on yourself heightens your fear of future abandonments. In fact, Outer Child develops its most entrenched patterns in a misguided effort to defend you against these fears.

We are barely conscious of it when we commit self-abandonment. It's a silent process, one that creates a fertile breeding ground for an Outer Child to secretly gain power within the psyche and create self-defeating defense mechanisms.

IT'S CONDITIONING

The Outer Child is a function of brain activity. It represents the behavioral manifestation of our most deep-seated human fears that reside in the *amygdala,* an almond-shaped structure located within the brain. This tiny organ has everything to do with who you are emotionally and how you react to those emotions. Thanks to what goes on in your amygdala, you're conditioned (think Pavlov's dogs) to respond to certain situations with learned knee-jerk behaviors.

Think of this tiny brain structure as the seat of primal fears (Inner Child) and the trigger-point for your reactive patterns (Outer Child) to those fears. Just as feet and noses vary from person to person, so do our amygdalae. Some of us have more prominent, easily activated amygdalae than others.

My amygdala must be huge. I'm a train wreck if I even think about attempting a new relationship.

I have a hyperactive amygdala. My Outer Child is off to the races if my partner disagrees with me. It takes over before my Adult Self has a chance.

Your higher thinking brain can send messages to your amygdala, but that's a dial-up connection compared to the information superhighway that links the amygdala with the part of your brain that carries out your behavioral impulses. The amygdala's job is to prepare you to act first, think later. It creates a state of action-readiness to prime you for an instant emergency response. You fight, flee, or freeze if your amygdala perceives any potential threat to your well-being. And this all happens under the radar of your conscious awareness.

Long ago the time it took to react to a threat could be the difference between life and death. You ran or were eaten for lunch by a tiger! Today's threats to safety and well-being take different forms. And they're individualized. Your amygdala's stimulus-response system has been conditioned by your own personal history of emotional experiences, stemming all the way back to when you were born—experiences you've mostly forgotten. The way you respond, which emergency defenses you use, that's uniquely yours too.

The amygdala is always on the lookout for a threat and it picks up subliminal triggers. This causes you to react automatically before your higher thinking brain has a chance to consider a more prudent course of action. In other words, you flinch before you think. Yes, flinching can save your life if you're jerking away from a rock hurtling in your direction, but when there is no physical threat, flinching can make you appear jumpy and extremely nervous.

When you perceive a threat—you fear your partner may be falling out of love with you—your amygdala sends an urgent warning down through the brain (to areas like the brain stem) to activate a behavioral response. These behaviors stem from a two-part process: first a buildup of emotional arousal in your amygdala; then a behavioral discharge of activity. In this sense, emotion and behavior—stimulus and response—function like symbiotic twins: One feels; the other reacts. Inner feels; Outer acts it *out*.

I screamed at my boyfriend over this little thing, knowing my outburst would be the last straw, but I couldn't stop myself.

Your primal fears and your learned automatic defenses are coupled, and this coupling is what my program is designed to undo. Until the advent of the Outer Child concept, we lacked a tool for untangling feelings from behavior. But now we can separate them, empowering our Adult Self to use

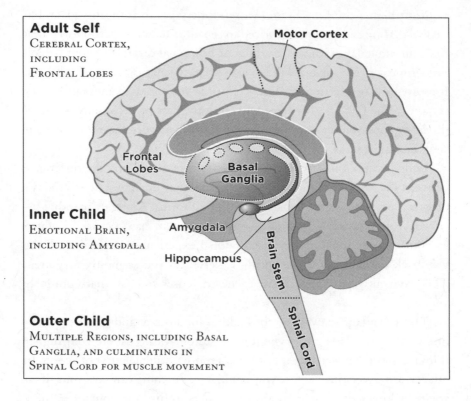

Adult Self
CEREBRAL CORTEX,
INCLUDING
FRONTAL LOBES

Motor Cortex

Frontal
Lobes

Basal
Ganglia

Inner Child
EMOTIONAL BRAIN,
INCLUDING AMYGDALA

Amygdala

Hippocampus

Brain Stem

Outer Child
MULTIPLE REGIONS, INCLUDING BASAL
GANGLIA, AND CULMINATING IN
SPINAL CORD FOR MUSCLE MOVEMENT

Spinal Cord

our higher brain to intervene, even in moments of passion (which are, of course, amygdaloid in nature).

YOUR ADULT SELF

Outer Child, Inner Child, and Adult Self all stem from functions in higher, middle, and lower regions of the brain. The Adult essentially comes from the *higher,* cerebral brain centered around the frontal and parietal lobes. The Inner Child's fears and other emotions come from the *mid-range* area, containing your limbic structures, centered around the amygdala. And your Outer Child's repetitive behaviors, while triggered in the amygdala, are behaviorally discharged primarily through brain operations connecting from the motor cortex and basal ganglia, to the *lower* region of the spinal cord, which controls movement.

Learning about the amygdala and how it connects to higher and lower brain areas helps us understand why we might lash out at someone or freeze up instead of having the mature conversation we had planned. That lashing out can catch you by surprise because abandonment fear and other primal emotions can be triggered by seemingly ordinary life experiences (e.g., an offhand comment). Your emotional triggers may be subliminal, but they are often powerful enough to induce reactive behaviors (from the lower brain) that go against your better judgment (in the higher brain).

> I went to the movies with my boyfriend, and all of a sudden, I got to worrying that he might not love me anymore. He didn't know what hit me and neither did I. It ruined our whole evening.

THE MONSTER UNDER THE BED IS GROWING

Joseph LeDoux, leading research expert on the amygdala, has produced another piece of information so vital to the work we are doing that I can't say it often or loud enough:

> Fear tends to incubate rather than dissipate over time.

In other words, fear develops and grows fuller over time rather than fading away. When I first learned that fear incubates, I finally understood the dilemma for abandonment survivors. Their fear tends to burrow beneath their conscious awareness, where it intensifies and rebounds with greater force when they attempt to start a new relationship.

Did it ever occur to you that certain fears might intensify? That the monster under the bed was growing larger and more threatening? If you're like most people, probably not. So when you attempt a new challenge, the intensity of your abandonment fear can come as quite a shock. Abandonment survivors tend to experience more than their share of these unexpected bouts of intrusive insecurity and anxiety.

Let's say you've been through a painful breakup and decide there's no need to rush back out there to replace your ex. You're not ready. You're prudently taking time to heal, to find your balance, to reduce your emotional neediness. No rebound relationship for you (you're way too smart for that). But when you finally think you're ready to meet someone, one of two things can happen:

1. No one turns you on (even though they look great on paper) *or*
2. Someone *does* turn you on and you're suddenly so vulnerable you can barely stand being in your own body.

What's going on here? In the first instance, no one turned you on because your overefficient amygdala was short-circuiting the attraction, triggering the release of numbing opiates and other anti-passion neurohormones (similar to the ones creating numbness during early bereavement) designed to blunt your emotional responses. Uninvited, it was doing (overdoing) its job to protect (overprotect) you from getting attached and potentially hurt again.

In the second instance, your amygdala declared a mini state of emergency *precisely because* you were attracted to someone. In fact, it pulled out all the stops, sounding the alarm to warn you about a full-blown abandonment crisis in the making. Your amygdala had learned (through fear conditioning) to perceive losing someone as a life-threatening situation. After all, to children, losing a caretaker could mean life or death and this fear incubates and remains into adulthood.

All this neural activity takes place beyond your conscious control. Powerful stress hormones, triggered by your primal abandonment fears, went coursing through your body and sent you into an involuntary state of fight, freeze, or flee. This put you at your most defensive just when you thought you were ready to get back on that horse.

I really liked this woman, but my heart raced and my mouth went dry when I tried to ask her out on a date. So much for trying to act casual.

Therapists and self-help books might tell you that if you are emotionally overreactive to a new person it means you're not ready, but often, that's simply not true. You could have waited another decade to become "ready" and still freak out when you find yourself genuinely connecting with someone new. Why? Because the fear instilled by your last breakup didn't dissipate; it had grown.

The same is true when you avoid taking any other positive risk in your life, such as making a career change, moving to a new area, or asserting yourself to your boss. The longer you procrastinate, the more your anxiety and inhibition can escalate. Avoidance and its cousins procrastination, isolation, and inertia are probably the most common ways we abandon ourselves. While you're isolating, your ever-industrious Outer Child builds new walls and spins ever-thicker cocoons of defenses in response to your incubating fear. Ultimately they're roadblocks to moving forward into a new venue or relationship.

I've become increasingly awkward around attractive people. It's become easier to avoid those situations.

I've created a romantic fantasy life that no real relationship can compare with.

I've been alone so long my love map has changed. It no longer matches other people's.

What to do? The good news is, you don't have to avoid relationships and other risks just because you have performance anxiety or feel awkward. The heightened vulnerability you feel is involuntary. And it has nothing to do with how intelligent, strong, and independent you happen to be. It has to do with fear conditioning (reinforced by your past breakup) that took place in your amygdala (beyond your conscious control). It's an automatic reaction, part of being a human being who has experienced a painful loss, disappointment, or hurt.

IS IT TOO SOON?

I don't mean to suggest that you should seek a new relationship while you are still in the throes of abandonment's initial stages. In my previous books, I outlined the five stages of abandonment—Shattering, Withdrawal, Internalizing, Rage, and Lifting (S.W.I.R.L.)—and explained what to expect during each phase, as well as how to deal with each one. During the final stage, Lifting, you are learning to manage the painful feelings of the breakup, find your balance, and establish a new normal. Depending on the length of time you were in the relationship, it could take a year or more of going through the S.W.I.R.L. process before you are emotionally ready to make a new connection. Even then, you may still feel vulnerable and yearn for your lost love, which is normal. But vulnerable or not, during Lifting it is usually better to practice making connections with new people than to avoid relationships altogether.

When you do stick your toe into the unknown waters of a new relationship and your amygdala declares a state of emergency, don't fault yourself or deem yourself incapable; likewise, don't assume you are biting off more than you could chew with a new job or big project. Just accept the feelings as feelings and push through the fear. Get on with your life. Have a little faith and summon some courage. Don't let Outer Child use your breakup to gain new ground. Rising to this challenge will do more to promote your emotional growth than avoiding it will.

Please note that I'm not suggesting you use someone new—exploit her without consideration for her needs and feelings. The highest degree of personal responsibility is in order here. What I am saying is that avoidance is one of Outer Child's favorite forms of self-sabotage, one that does more harm than good in the end. Why? Because while you are avoiding, your fears are secretly gaining strength (not melting away).

When you attempt a new relationship, Outer Child may be chomping at the bit to act out your incubating fears in all sorts of obnoxious ways, like imposing excessive emotional demands on your new significant other; or playing childish games of hard-to-get; or haranguing her for "making" you feel insecure; or ending things rather than trying to work them out. Outer has a whole bag of inconvenient-to-romance tricks. But no matter what your Outer Child is up to, it's time to stop avoiding, worrying, and self-blaming—and get your Adult Self to take command. We'll be learning about a whole battery of tools in this section of the book, designed to put your Outer Child in its place, and we'll pick up the first one now.

UP FOR ADOPTION

When the diagnosis is self-abandonment, the first course of treatment is to adopt your Inner Child. We'll be using a guided visualization (a directed use of your imagination) to put your Adult Self in the role of caretaker of this most vulnerable part of yourself. You won't need pen or paper here, just a quiet few minutes alone. Ready?

> *Imagine a child, one who's been abandoned and is living on the streets in a distant foreign city. (Imagine this child is of the same gender you are.) This child is cold, hungry, wounded, and scared. Her fondest wish is for someone to care for her and protect her from harm.*
>
> *Picture yourself coming upon this poor abandoned child as you are on a trip, walking the streets of the city where she lives. You sense something familiar about this child. You don't know why, but you feel compelled to approach her and offer her your jacket and something to eat. At first the child shrinks from you in terror, but you patiently and gently convince the child you mean no harm, that in fact you want to help.*

After she's eaten, you go together to the authorities and through them learn that she has no living relatives who can take her in. Worse yet, there is no social service system that can care for her in the way she needs.

Now you make a critical decision: You decide to care for this child yourself. You're going to do whatever it takes to assuage her fears and meet her long-neglected needs. And not temporarily either. You promise to never abandon this child. You've decided to adopt her.

The child becomes an important and meaningful commitment and focus in your life. Adopting her is a gift of love and connection unlike any you've ever given.

This child is you, your own Inner Child—and she's counting on you.

Now that you've committed yourself to your Inner Child, you're ready to start nurturing a stronger, healthier relationship with yourself.

IMPROVING YOUR BRAIN HEALTH THROUGH SELF-LOVE TECHNIQUES

Neuroscientist Richard Davidson, using fMRI brain scans, shows that when people are directed to visualize compassion toward themselves or others, the practice stimulates neural activity in the left frontal cortex, a site that mediates positive emotions. When we feel happy, energetic, or enthusiastic, the left frontal cortex lights up, whereas our negative emotions make the right side light up. Victims of a stroke or injury to the left frontal cortex can succumb to "catastrophic worrying," while those with damage to the right side "appear unduly jovial and seemingly unconcerned about their condition." Researchers can induce positive emotions by applying transcranial magnetic stimulation (TMS) to the left frontal cortex. Most significant is that yogis who have been practicing mindfulness meditation for many years show greater development in this area, suggesting permanent beneficial changes in their brain.

The upshot is that by developing compassionate, nurturing feelings toward your imagined Inner Child—including them in a daily practice of mindfulness and positive intention toward self and others—you are improving your emotional set point and increasing your brain health. I'll be showing you hands-on tools to help you give loving kindness to your newly adopted emotional center both imaginatively and behaviorally—all to become a more self-loving, mindful, self-responsible Adult Self.

FIVE

Outer Child and Your Self-Esteem

The relationship you have with yourself is the most important relationship in your life. It is the template upon which all your other relationships are built, the source of your self-esteem, and the driving force behind your choices and behaviors. It's the very foundation of your psychological functioning. Whether or not we realize it, we've been trying to improve the relationship we have with ourselves all our lives—often not very effectively. This chapter presents you with tools for changing all that.

The way you feel about yourself affects the way you relate to other people. This in turn affects the way they view you.

> I have a desire to show off my talents, but I'm so inhibited, nobody knows what I've got inside.

No two people feel the same way about themselves. You developed the way you feel through many experiences, especially interactions with other people—your parents, peers, teachers, and significant others. You strove to live up to what they expected of you and unwittingly absorbed the way they responded to you—their affection, disapproval, esteem, acceptance, rejection, criticism, and indifference. You measured your worth against certain standards you came to believe in and compared yourself—sometimes favorably, sometimes not—to others. Through this haphazard trial-and-error manner, you calculated your rank in the pecking order, a process that was neither deliberate nor conscious. The net quotient of this automatic process constitutes your self-esteem (the way you feel about yourself) and your self-image (the way you think other people see you).

We all know people who seem to have come out of this process feeling terrific about themselves. They have a healthy and appropriate sense of entitlement. They're confident, self-possessed, and hold themselves with great personal dignity and pride. Many of us wish we could be like that and fault ourselves because we can't get there. It doesn't have to be that way.

Consider the quality of your current relationship with yourself. Do you hold yourself in high esteem? Would you like to? Can you identify any areas that could use improvement? I've never met anyone who didn't wish they had more self-esteem!

I'm oversensitive to rejection. Any hint of criticism makes me defensive and impossible to be around.

My Outer Child is self-spiteful. I punish myself when someone treats me poorly instead of standing up for myself.

I put more pressure on myself than anyone else ever could. I drive myself to overachieve. I'm a type A for sure.

A member of one of my workshops, Steve, presents this testimonial about how the program helped him develop a nurturing, loving relationship with himself:

My self-image was a disaster. My father had brutalized me as a kid. People could SMELL the shame on me somehow. But then I figured...if I don't hold myself in high regard, why should they? I had no confidence in me, so why should anyone else? So I tried to cover up my shame and self-doubt by putting on this big act. I acted like I thought I was a pretty together dude (the way my father acted). I was faking it, not just with them, but with myself. I was trying to make the feelings go away.

Steve's as-if persona meant he was not being genuine with himself or others. His sometimes jokey, sometimes overearnest manner came across as hollow.

I couldn't be real because I was ashamed of being ashamed. It was a vicious cycle. I'd been ACTING for so long, I sometimes forgot how low my self-esteem was. But then something might happen, like me getting laid off at work, and I'd hit bottom and come face-to-face with my self-loathing once again, petrified that I would die a loser.

Steve's Inner Child had feelings of anxiety, self-doubt, and inadequacy, but as uncomfortable as these feelings were, they were not the problem. The problem was the way he *reacted* to these feelings—the Outer Child defenses he had erected to avoid having to deal with them. Steve's attempt to *cover them up* (remember, Outer Child loves to put on an act) interfered with his ability to be himself.

It didn't take Steve long to grasp the root of the problem and his next question was a universal conundrum: So now I know why I do it, but how do I change it? People gain insight but don't know how to *use* it. A program I call "separation therapy" provides a hands-on solution—a way to use your insight. I borrowed the term from the late Richard Robertiello, MD, a psychoanalyst, my mentor, and the co-author of *Big You, Little You: Separation Therapy.*

SEPARATION THERAPY:
PHYSICAL THERAPY FOR THE BRAIN

The Outer Child framework accomplishes something revolutionary. In separating the parts of the personality, it gives you access to an internal dynamic that dictates how you relate to yourself (and others) and what you accomplish in life.

The separation therapy we'll begin in this chapter gives voice to the three dynamic parts—Inner Child, Outer Child, and Adult Self. Through

simple dialogues you get these parts to talk to one another and work together productively.

Think of separation therapy as physical therapy for your brain. It effectively builds your self-esteem—just as physical exercise builds cardiovascular health and muscle mass—and improves your confidence. The idea is to zero in on your deepest emotional recesses so that you can heal and resolve any underlying sources of self-doubt or inhibition.

You've already begun preparing for separation therapy by increasing your awareness about your Outer Child and adopting your Inner Child. The next step is separating your Outer Child from your Inner Child, freeing that Inner Child to receive your unconditional love. At last! Separation therapy provides a hands-on way to give love and esteem directly to yourself. What used to be an easier-said-than-done aphorism—love thyself—now becomes a goal within reach.

If all this talk about separating constructs from one another sounds theoretical, that's because it *is* based on a theory, but fortunately one that's easy to put into practice. In this chapter the practice will be writing simple letters and dialogues.

No one's asking you to become a fluent writer if you are not so inclined. I'm talking about jotting down a few notes, not writing volumes. To the Outer Children out there looking for a magic bullet—kindly take a backseat. We know how good you are at avoidance. As we practice using this and the other tools, we're going to override Outer's passive-avoidant tendencies and engage the more action-oriented areas of your brain—in this case by putting pen to paper. The patterns of self-sabotage we are deconstructing here are so deeply entrenched that they call for hands-on measures to undo them.

If you've already decided to excuse yourself from actually writing anything down, stop and read that last paragraph again and ask yourself who's in charge here. *You won't get the same benefits just reading about the exercise.*

If you want to tackle your most important goals, you simply must go beyond digesting the Outer Child framework intellectually. You need to take action. Committing your thoughts and feelings to the written word engages a wider range of brain functions than just reading about them does—it changes the brain, strengthening existing neuronal pathways and triggering structural changes.

Separation therapy is more like physical therapy than it looks at first glance. When you put pen to paper, you activate neurons connecting to tendons and muscles in your arm, hand, fingers, etc. You are using a graphomotor task to bring diverse brain activities to the table at once, engaging mental functions involved in reasoning, emotional memory, imagining, practicing, and those that integrate multiple brain systems. In fact, strengthening the brain's integrative functions—the neural networks coordinating emotion, cognition, and intentional behavior—may prove to be the most valuable aspect of all this incremental brain exercising you are doing.

As with any other type of physical therapy, you won't instantly see improvements. It may take a few sessions before you feel something, but then one day, there it is—you feel less inhibited and more confident. With multiple sessions, over time you begin to feel and act like a new person. The more regularly you exercise your brain, the greater the positive change.

Let's get started so you can *feel* the difference between understanding the concept and truly experiencing it.

NOTE TO SELF

First, dedicate a special notebook to taming your Outer Child. Now write today's date along with your intention to improve your relationship with yourself—remember, that's the point of all this.

Get specific about what you want and need in your life to feel better about yourself. Think of a goal you have been trying to reach but have not yet achieved. Zeroing in on this goal is central to our work here. All of your goals are to be honored. Each one becomes a friend who accompanies you throughout this book to help you build your relationship with yourself. When you focus on your goal, you center your energy and improve your aim toward the target.

Some examples from my workshops:

My goal is to become solvent. I'm three months behind in my mortgage and it makes me feel irresponsible and ashamed.

My goal is to get in shape; I've let myself go. If I fixed this, I'd feel more comfortable in my own skin.

My Outer Child blocks me from getting recognition, though I'm not sure how. I know my performance at work is excellent but I haven't been able to get it across. My goal is to learn how to get the recognition I deserve.

Now it's your turn. Zero in on a specific goal and write it down.

WHAT'S STOPPING YOU?

Next, list the little things you do that interfere with you achieving your goal. These counterproductive tendencies are, of course, prime examples of Outer Child's underhandedness. Let me use another example from one of my workshop attendees, Bob:

> My goal is to make more money. Being broke all the time makes me feel like a loser. If I had a better job, I'd like myself more. I don't make enough money because I don't feel good about myself. And I don't feel good about myself because I don't make enough money. But when I thought honestly about what I could be doing to reach my goal and what I had done, I could start to identify behaviors. Here's what I wrote:
>
> *My goal is to make more money. My Outer Child interferes by:*
>   1. *Procrastinating*
>   2. *Coming home and vegging out instead of networking*
>   3. *Forgetting to buy the paper to check out the help-wanted pages*
>   4. *Falling asleep in front of the TV instead of researching jobs online*
>   5. *Being self-indulgent instead of taking initiative*
>   6. *Avoiding making phone calls to promote myself*
>   7. *Succumbing to distractions.*

Okay, in what ways does *your* Outer Child interfere with your identified goal? Write them down! Like this:

My goal is _____ and my Outer Child interferes by:
_____, _____, _____, _____, etc.

WE CAN DO BETTER

Your next task is to list behaviors you *would like* to perform, productive behaviors that would help you reach this goal. Here's what Bob wrote, as unrealistic as they seemed to him at the time:

> *These things would help me reach my goals:*
> 1. *Every day, find out more about how other people make money—what jobs, businesses, or other ventures are more financially rewarding than what I've done.*
> 2. *Take positive risks.*
> 3. *Change my daily regimen; take a small step every day toward finding a better job or venture.*
> 4. *Avoid distractions.*
> 5. *Stay determined until I reach it.*
> 6. *Pursue training or a degree if that's what I need to do.*

Now it's your turn: Write down a list of things you could do that would take you a step closer to your goal. Writing them puts these *would-be* behaviors on your radar screen. It helps you lay the groundwork for a new way of thinking. Just fill in the blanks:

My goal is _____ and here's what I would like to do to reach it:_____, _____, _____, etc.

FROM NOW ON

Great! Now it's time to put your Outer Child on notice. Explain what your goal is and let Outer know about the changes you *plan* to make to achieve it. Make sure that when you address your Outer Child, you do so affirmatively. For instance, rather than say what you *would like* to change, speak as if you're actually *going to do it* (even if you've never considered making these changes). Like the exercise we did in the previous chapter (adopting your Inner Child), visualization is involved in this exercise. It helps you picture yourself making changes, which in turn stimulates brain cells that neuroscientists have recently dubbed mirror neurons. These newly discovered cells are the focus of numerous ongoing research studies that demonstrate a remarkable brain function: When you visualize taking an action, you activate the same areas of the brain that would light up if you were actually *taking* the action. Thanks to your mirror neurons, visualizing something allows your brain to take a trial run, strengthening the neural connections that would be involved in the action you plan to take, increasing your skill set. This neurological practice increases your capacity for and likelihood of reaching the goal you are aiming for.

Writing this note has another benefit. It performs the work of separation therapy I've been telling you about: It identifies your automatic, habit-prone Outer Child as apart from your Inner Child or your Adult Self. Once separated, these voices can interact in constructive new ways, with Adult Self in the lead, gaining strength along the way.

Bob shared his note with the group:

Dear Outer,

My goal is to make more money. I want you to cooperate. I want you to stop doing these things: [here he listed his Outer Child's self-defeating behaviors]. Now I, the Adult, will be taking responsibility for the situation.

I know you were only trying to help...and that I've been letting you run around loose out there on your own. But now *I'M* going to be calling the shots. Here is how I'm going to do things differently: [here Bob listed steps he would like to take].

Sincerely,
Bob's Adult Self

Now write a note like this to your own Outer Child.

Don't expect this simple exercise to make you feel better on the first try. In fact, it probably will feel more awkward or hokey than anything else. Remember, this is physical therapy for the brain. And just like physical therapy for the body, it involves a series of small steps. Raising your right arm five times or writing this exercise may seem pointless, but that's only because it is too early to expect results. When you put your Outer Child on notice, you are beginning a new internal dialogue with yourself whose benefits reach fruition through practice.

The note focuses your mental energy on how you would like (*plan*) to resolve the issue. You're picturing yourself as free from self-sabotage and taking goal-directed actions. Picturing yourself in this way actually increases the possibility that you will ultimately act out those behaviors.

Writing focuses your mental energy on the solution rather than letting it stagnate on the problem. It gets you out of a rut and creates a new mental space where productive behaviors begin to germinate.

If you slip back the next day into one of your self-defeating behaviors, don't beat yourself up. Remember, Outer has a penchant for immediate gratification and has only been trying to help in its own misguided way. Outer has remained unsupervised for so long that its habits are entrenched. You can always write Outer another quick note to firmly call him on the behavior, saying *"Thanks but no thanks"* and restate your adult action plan.

CREATING A RECIPROCAL DIALOGUE

Writing to your Outer Child is the first stage of separation therapy. To stretch your mental muscles further, we go to the next level and create a dialogue between your Adult Self and your Inner Child. This second-level dialogue builds on the legacy of Bradshaw, Robertiello, and others, getting you to exchange communications with your Inner Child. The reciprocal dialogue gets underneath the problem to deal with the *cause*. Working with the primal source taps into your motivational core, approaching your Outer Child at an oblique angle. You discover that what had been the source of your interference and pain now becomes a wellspring of motivation and forward-moving energy.

THE CAST

Before you open a dialogue, first take a minute to clarify who's in your psyche, and cleanse the concept from any debris that may have inadvertently collected on it.

Remember, Inner Child represents your feelings, not the behaviors those feelings may trigger. To get in touch with your feelings, consider how much you'd like to be rid of those self-sabotaging behaviors and how frustrated and trapped you feel right now. These feelings—desirous, frustrated, impatient—all belong to your Inner Child.

Like any small child, Inner Child is full of hopes and dreams; it wants to be loved, heard, indulged, cherished, and freed. Your Inner Child is that child on the street corner: small and helpless and incapable of providing for itself. It's up to your newly emerging Adult Self to meet the child's needs. When you care for yourself, it is called "self-love." When you value yourself, it is called "self-esteem." As I've said, your most important adult responsibility (the one we are all most likely to shirk) is to perform the tasks of *self*-love, *self*-esteem, *self*-acceptance, and *self*-nurturing on your Inner Child's behalf.

For the purpose of this dialogue, let's borrow terminology from Kirsten and Robertiello's book, *Big You, Little You*. Think of your Adult Self as "Big You" and your Inner Child as "Little You." This dialogue works to resolve the relationship between these two voices. The universal dilemma for most people is that Big You has been too weak, Outer too strong, and Little You neglected and growing ever needier. As a result of this exercise, Big You gets stronger and is able to finally validate, nurture, calm, and love Little You. When this happens Outer no longer has the opportunity to act out your Inner Child's stray feelings.

So consult your notebook and revisit your goals. Write them down again and add today's date. As you write your goals, remember to honor each one no matter how big or small, no matter how outlandish someone other than you might think it is. Your goals give your life aim, trajectory, and vision.

Now zero in on one particular goal and think about how you feel about not (yet) achieving it—and attribute the feelings to your Inner Child. Bob explained how he got started:

> My goal was to increase my income but I was afraid to go out there. I was afraid I'd fail. So I wrote a dialogue and gave this feeling to my Inner Child—my Inner Child was afraid. I also wanted to feel better about myself. If I made more money, I wouldn't feel so inadequate. I gave that feeling to my Inner Child too. I imagined that he was feeling a whole combination of things: hopeful, afraid, impatient, angry, frustrated, and sad.

Now get in touch with your own feelings. Might Little You feel impatient about fulfilling its dreams? Frustrated? Hopeless? Excited? On edge? Desirous? Desperate? Any feelings that come up belong to your Inner Child. Capture those feelings in your notebook, like this:

> My goal is _____ and I haven't reached it yet. My Inner Child feels the following ways about it: _____, _____, _____.

As you get these two parts of your psyche talking to each other, remember Little You is your *inner* self. The individual who will write the dialogue is your higher Adult Self, who creates your Inner Child's voice, giving it a vocabulary befitting a five-year-old (or younger) child. Your higher self also creates the voice of the stronger Adult Self you are becoming. In creating a persona for Big You, you are once again using the regenerative powers of the imagination, this time to create an image of a loving parent-self fully capable of administering to your deepest emotional needs. For inspiration, you can look to people you've admired for qualities to emulate. Your goal is to create the kindest, most empathic, nurturing, wise Adult Self you can give voice to.

Here's Bob's experience:

> I had a beloved aunt. She genuinely cared for all of us: children, pets, my parents. I trusted her to always be there. She was warm, kind, intelligent, and understanding. When I created an image for my Adult Self, I based a lot of it on my aunt. As I wrote the dialogue between Big Me and Little Me, I channeled my aunt and started to *BECOME* her.

Creating the image of a higher-functioning Adult Self—and staying in character for the duration of the dialogue—stimulates your mirror neurons and provides high-level physical therapy for the brain. By first creating and then writing from this character's perspective, you give your mind a powerful picture of you to digest. Doing this exercise is part of the process of becoming the adult you always wanted to be!

YOUR TURN

Here are a couple of examples to help inspire you to get started. A member of a workshop offered the excerpt below of one of his first dialogues. His goal was to get in shape. Getting started was awkward, he admitted, but he found a way.

> BIG FRANZ: How do you feel about getting fit, Little?
> LITTLE FRANZ: Scared.
> BIG: Why?
> LITTLE: Because you won't do it.
> BIG: Why do you think so, Little?

LITTLE: Because you don't do anything to help me. I feel so bad about myself. And you don't care.

BIG: But I'm changing that, Little. I want you to feel better.

LITTLE: I don't feel good like other people. They go to the gym, but you don't take me. You just let me look like a blob and feel worthless and bad.

BIG: I've let you down in the past, Little, but I'm going to change that. I want you to feel good about yourself.

LITTLE: Yeah, but you won't bother. You'll just do the same stupid stuff all over again.

BIG: Little, I'm going to care more. I'm going to make things better.

LITTLE: I'm just not important enough for you to take me to the gym. Other people are important enough to take care of themselves, but I'm not. You just stay home and watch TV instead of doing anything to make me healthy and strong.

BIG: I will from now on, Little, because I'm finally listening to you and I won't let you down again.

LITTLE: I don't trust you. I'll feel even more mad and upset because you won't bother to do what you say.

BIG: Yes I will...

Franz told us he didn't expect to be confronted by his Inner Child, didn't know he had such a resentful, hurt little kid inside. It both moved and motivated him. He reported later that he had to hear about his Inner Child's feelings more than once before he started to change his habits, because he felt a strong pull to go back to his old ways, but dialoguing set him on the road to developing new, more constructive habits.

One more example and then it's your turn. A woman from the same workshop offered a sample of her first dialogue, which focuses on her career development. Like a lot of people in my workshops, she began by asking her Inner Child how she was feeling.

BIG CARLA: How do you feel about the job, Little? I was thinking about moving on, maybe starting my own business.

LITTLE CARLA: I want to be somebody. I feel like a nobody.

BIG CARLA: I'm glad you're telling me, Little. You *are* somebody. I want you to feel better about yourself.

LITTLE CARLA: But you act like there's something wrong with me.
You think I'm not capable of doing anything right. You think
I'm not good enough for you to try harder. I don't count.

Carla's Inner Child remained impatient with her Adult Self throughout
the three-day workshop and that was quite an eye-opener. When Carla got
home, she kept the conversation going to get closer to those feelings and soon
understood where those feelings came from. Her parents had both been alcoholics. No matter what she did as a child, it was never enough to get them to
stop drinking or to parent her. That, she realized, was why she'd been wast-
ing her life at a dead-end job, being loyal to a boss who took her for granted
and underpaid her. But hearing Little Carla's voice lit a fire under her—she
realized she had an Inner Child who needed her. It gave her a mission.

Time to get started on your own dialogue.

Big You will speak caringly and consolingly to Little You. You, the
individual writing the dialogue, often have to reach up pretty high into the
top of your human potential to find the words to coax Little You out of its
secret hiding place. Remember, this stretch is good for your changing brain.
Some Inner Children don't want to leave their protective shells, but don't
be surprised if once you get it started, it won't shut up. Whatever the initial
response—whether it's complete silence, verbal diarrhea, or angry tirade—
just let it flow from pen to paper.

Go for it... Write your dialogue. Big You begins the dialogue by asking
Little You to open up and explain (in its own five-year-old words) how it
feels having had to wait so long to reach its dreams.

BIG ME: How are you feeling, Little, about... (restate your goal and
the fact that it has not yet been achieved) _____?
LITTLE ME: I feel _____, _____, _____, etc.
BIG ME: I want to help you by telling you _____, etc.

How did it go? Was the hardest part finding words to comfort and reassure Little You? Join the club. Some Littles remain inconsolable for the first
several dialogues. They force Big You to try harder and harder to soothe
them. The idea is to comfort with solemn promises that things are going
to change. As you make those commitments, you will give your brain a
good physical stretch. (Remember, later you have to follow through: Never
break a promise to a child. In Chapter Eight, you'll learn an exercise for

increasing your follow-through efforts.) Your first attempt might feel clumsy, but no matter, you're just practicing. Every bit of practice you do helps your Adult Self (and your brain) grow.

Writing about your feelings and behaviors involves integrative brain functioning. It gets you to tune in to your primal emotions, which activates the primitive mammalian center in the brain (the amygdala). As you weave freshly aroused feelings into your dialogue, you engage neural pathways that link this emotional brain and your higher cognitive regions. Having personified the three components of your personality—Inner, Outer, and Adult—and getting these distinct voices to talk to one another, you have been engaging brain regions involved in visualization, simulation, practicing, creativity, symbolization, as-if reasoning, working memory, problem solving, prioritizing, decision making, and language processing—phew! It's a real workout for your changing brain. It also enervates regions of the brain involved in inhibiting acting-out. When this area functions properly, you can have a vivid mental picture of throwing a punch without having to carry out the action.

On a conscious level, by addressing your innermost self, you're learning the fine art of self-nurture. Your relationship with yourself will improve to a level you never thought possible, but it will do so incrementally. Soon you will learn this physical therapy for the brain like the back of your hand. You'll integrate it into your relationship with yourself. It will become effortless, automatic, a new habit.

All it takes is practice and I'm here to inspire, guide, and support you along the way. My former clients and workshop members continue to offer their help throughout. Earlier you met Steve, whose low self-esteem made it difficult for him to "act real." Steve used the Outer Child program to reverse the impact of years of self-abandonment. He became both more self-assured and self-possessed—attractive qualities people gravitated to—because he'd taken on the role of commander-in-chief of his Outer Child.

> The dialogue helped me connect to my most vulnerable feelings in a way that got me to heal from the inside. I didn't need to look to other people to make me feel okay, because I was able to give acceptance to myself.

> My Outer Child is now under house arrest. I don't punish him—I actually like the guy, especially now that he answers directly to me

instead of running around loose out there. I keep Outer busy doing healthy, fun things. But anytime I fall back into my old patterns, it reminds me to get closer to Little Me. That starts the self-love-fest all over again and the self-consciousness around other people slips away.

With a stronger Adult Self, Steve felt good enough about himself to present "the real Steve" to other people. His false self dissipated. He no longer seeks validation from the outside world, but instead gives validation and love directly to himself, dissolving the root system of his problems in a bath of healthy nourishment.

As dialogue-writer-in-chief, it is up to you to decide which issue to address in your dialogues. You can stop the writing anytime if you feel it is unproductive or if you get inundated with a lot of uncomfortable feelings all coming to the surface at once. It is up to you to set the pace for the process. No need to rush it. You can pick up on it again anytime. The important thing is that you remain in complete control of the dialogue at all times, even when you find yourself surprised by the things Little You says or the depth of the emotional needs it reveals.

The dialogue performs the work of separation therapy in that it provides a practical, hands-on way to effectively separate feelings from behavior—Inner from Outer—while also strengthening Adult Self.

Separating feelings from behavior—stimulus from response—will become progressively easier and, as you'll discover, nothing short of life-changing. With this shift in the paradigm, and the tools we'll discuss in the coming chapters, your stronger Adult Self can turn your life around.

SIX

Outer Child and Your Future

Building a better relationship with yourself includes developing a more confident sense of future. Everyone has a sense of future. Though they're not always conscious of this sense, it looms in the background, working for or against them. For most people, it's a vague assortment of assumptions ranging from positive to negative about where life seems to be taking them. Take a moment to reflect on the quality of your own sense of future. Does it stretch before you like a yawning vacuum? Is it tinged with a subliminal sense of dread? Is it punctuated with events you are looking forward to, like a trip you've planned or a move to a new home?

In conjuring up your "future," you can't help but use your imagination because the future doesn't exist yet. You have to *imagine* it. When you engage your imagination in this automatic manner, you can unintentionally project worry, anxiety, or pessimism into the scenario—or you might infuse it with an unhealthy dose of wishful thinking—maybe you're unrealistically expecting a risky business venture to land you on easy street, so you let more solid prospects fall by the wayside.

The good news is that once you start using your imagination in a more deliberate, conscious way, you can get it working for you, rather than against you. The exercise in this chapter exemplifies the second component of the Outer Child program: guided visualization. In the last two chapters, we worked on separation therapy, personifying the Inner Child, Outer Child, and Adult Self parts of the personality. This chapter uses your imagination to create a Future Vision—a powerful image that helps to nourish the mind and restore your dreams. As you continue to build a better relationship with yourself, you'll become more open and alert to new opportunities. Your self-esteem will manifest itself in more forward-looking, goal-directed behaviors.

You can think of the mind as divided into two camps. One camp strives forward, while the other, plagued with self-doubt, tries to sabotage it. Intention, when it is not fully crystallized, can be defeated by self-doubt. Visualization exercises use the powerful resource of your imagination to develop and crystallize your intention. There will always be self-doubt, but when your intention becomes stronger and moves to the forefront of your mind, the opposing camp has a much harder time sabotaging it.

The rigors of everyday life have a tendency to weaken intention. In fact, when most people think about the future, they muse about things they *would like* to achieve, but never get beyond fantasizing about it. Without realizing it, they live in an if-only world:

> If only I'd meet the woman of my dreams.
> If only I could make more money.
> If only I could lose the weight.

People become tacitly resigned to never reaching their dreams. *"I wish I could feel better about myself"* is more pessimistic lament than aspirational goal. Our aim is to move beyond fantasy about a would-be future. We're going to take forward steps toward a future of richer possibilities.

To reach your dreams you need a crystal-clear picture of what constitutes that dream come to life. Originally, the Eiffel Tower was nothing more than an idea, a picture in Monsieur Eiffel's mind. The building stands today because he stayed focused on that image, coupling it with the steadfast intention of seeing his dream realized. He also took action; in other words, he did the design and drafting work that conveyed his vision to those who could build it. Bottom line: The Eiffel Tower would never have been built without the vision, intention, and follow-through of the man who conceived it.

No doubt many brilliant ideas have formed in other brilliant minds and never reached fruition, most likely because the people who conceived them lacked the necessary intention and initiative. Perhaps all they needed were better tools to help them direct their energy at the intended target. The exercise I'm going to show you provides those tools. It uses your sense of future to improve your aim and increase your trajectory toward your goals. I call this powerful but simple exercise "Back to the Future." It's especially effective when used in tandem with the Outer Child dialogues.

BACK TO THE FUTURE

Like the separation therapy exercises we've been working on, this exercise creates a distinct mental boundary, in this case between the *future* and the *past*. It separates your future *potential* from your past *failures*, the higher Adult Self you are *becoming* from your *former* Adult Self, who was mired in self-defeating patterns. In marking a bold line between past and future, it places you directly in the now, where all of your power resides.

This exercise serves a practical purpose. In focusing your cognitive mind on your imagined future, it takes your imagination to acrobatic heights. Stretching your mental resources this way stimulates significant areas of your higher brain functions.

The idea is to create an image of yourself at some time in the future— say, two years from now—an image of yourself feeling happy and at peace because you've left all the problems of today behind you.

Pretend you are in the future. And that the future is now. Your needs are fulfilled, your goals achieved. Imagine that you are enjoying the benefits and how good you (would) feel to have left all your self-sabotaging Outer Child patterns behind.

Working backward from the future, see yourself overcoming obstacles and taking steps to move your life forward. Imagine how confident you (would) feel now that you have achieved these gains, and that you, not anyone else, made it happen. Here's how Sarah, a woman we met in Chapter Two, applied this tool:

> My dilemma was that I was 50 pounds overweight. So I imagined it was two years from now and that I'd already lost the weight. I imagined how thrilled I felt to get my sexual power back. It felt great.

By picturing yourself in this already-there state, you are stimulating your mind's problem-solving and as-if reasoning functions, giving your changing brain a good workout. It is important to picture your stronger Adult Self as the one who resolved your problems. Don't make the achievement of your goal dependent on someone else's actions—it's you who made it happen! This exercise borrows strength from an essential truth: The only control we have is over our own behavior. We have no control over how someone else might act or react, so the solutions to our problems must be centered on our own actions and no one else's. Another client illustrates:

> When I learned to use this exercise, my younger daughter was a single parent and always looking for handouts. My older daughter had drug problems. I felt completely overwhelmed. I didn't know what to do, how to get around these problems. But I tried this exercise, pretending it was two years from now. In this future timespace, I imagined having peace of mind, and that the contentment didn't depend on what my children were doing. I'd made something better within me.
>
> I know that I have no control over what other people might do or not do to change. So I imagined that two years from now, I was feeling loving toward my children, enjoying them, able to focus on the positive things about them and their lives. I also imagined I had set up new boundaries. I imagined I was no longer buying into the guilt-trips they tried to lay on me to excuse their own behavior. I imagined how rewarding it was to see them trying to manage their responsibilities and how good it felt to have made these important changes within myself.

There are five easy steps to the Back to the Future exercise:

1. Create an image of how good you would feel two years from now if your current problems were behind you. Remember you've *already* achieved your goals.
2. Identify the goals you achieved.
3. Then identify what obstacles you had to first overcome to achieve them.
4. Working backward from the future, imagine the steps you must

have taken—*behaviorally*—to overcome those obstacles. See yourself taking those steps.

5. Now imagine how wonderful and blessed you feel about this
change—grateful to your higher self and the powers that be.

Paul offers an example. His highly critical mother had devoted a lot of
energy to putting him down in childhood, much to the detriment of his
confidence and self-esteem.

I didn't feel good about myself. The ways Outer was handling these
feelings—avoiding competition, people-pleasing, keeping a low
profile—were the biggest obstacles I had to getting anywhere in
my life.

I had to practice being more vocal instead of trying to avoid any
chance of criticism. I pictured a more confident version of myself.
The image felt like pure fiction at the time, but it was a nice idea
all the same.

It was hard to imagine myself overcoming these obstacles—they
were so ingrained. But I pictured myself taking a step—going to a
Toastmasters club because it seemed like it would be a step in the
right direction. I pictured being surrounded by new people, supportive people from the club. And I pictured practicing some of
my newfound confidence at work.

Do you see what Paul's doing? Rather than focus his psychological
energy at the level of the problem—the unfairness of his mother's criticism,
the fear of confrontation and ridicule—Paul placed his energy at the level
of the solution, at where he wanted to be. This strengthened his intention
and helped illuminate steps for him to take in his real life.

YOU, TWO YEARS FROM NOW

You won't reap the benefits of this mental exercise until you try it yourself,
so let's get started. Get your notebook and record the date—two years into
the future. Then:

1. Conjure up a mental image of how you would feel with all of your
current problems behind you: *"It's October 4, 20__ and I feel*

_____, _____, _____, *because I have achieved all of my goals."*

2. Now identify the goals you achieved between now and this future vision time: *"In this future year of 20__, I have already achieved the following goals: _____, _____, _____."* Circle one of these goals for target practice. (You may stick with the goal you selected in previous exercises or select another one.) You can repeat this exercise for each one of your goals.

3. List the obstacles you had to overcome to achieve this targeted goal. Some of them involve Outer Child patterns that have been interfering, whereas others involve impediments imposed by external circumstances. *"My goal was to _____ and to reach it I first had to overcome the following obstacles: _____, _____, _____."*

4. Use your imagination to create a picture of yourself in the act of overcoming these obstacles. Get as specific as possible about the action steps you would have to take. *"I took the following action steps to overcome my obstacles: _____, _____, _____."*

5. Finally, envision how fulfilled, happy, and grateful you feel to have taken these steps and achieved your goal(s). Write these positive feelings in your notebook. *"Here's how grateful I feel now that I have achieved my goal(s) in 20__: _____, _____, _____."*

As you picture yourself taking constructive action you are creating space for new activities in your mindscape. This mental exercise stimulates mirror neurons, which allow your brain to mentally rehearse positive new behaviors. By conjuring up gratitude for this future achievement, you're implanting your intended outcome more deeply in your brain and increasing its sense of as-if reality. These activities strengthen your ability to take these steps.

Where, you may be asking yourself, will you get the energy to actually accomplish all this? Believe it or not, the energy will come from Outer Child. As you learn to manage Outer, you will be able to direct its energy toward your intended goals.

DEAR ME

Some people have an easier time writing this exercise in the form of a letter. Try it; write a letter from your future self to your present self. I call it a "Future Letter."

Get your notebook and start by writing a future date (anywhere from two weeks to two years from now). Then imagine yourself in that future, acting as a guide to your present self, guiding the way to a life free of self-sabotage. Like this:

Dear Present Self,

I'm writing from the future to tell you that thanks to your efforts, you are in a wonderful place in life. Outer's patterns are resolved. Here is how positive you feel: _____, _____, _____. Here are the goals you achieved: _____, _____, _____. Here are the obstacles you overcame between now and _____ (your future-time space): _____, _____, _____. Here are the new actions you took to overcome them: _____, _____, _____. Here is how wonderful you feel about our accomplishments and how grateful and blessed you feel to the powers that be: _____, _____, _____.

Looking forward to meeting you.

Sincerely,
Your Future Self

Paul illustrates how it works by the power of example:

Something happened at work: I was convinced I was going to get a promotion, but was overlooked—again. It was unfair, no question about it. My old Outer Child patterns of avoidance and sucking it up were poised and ready to kick in.

I had to deal with it soon or lose my opportunity, so I used Back to the Future and placed the future time-space about two weeks ahead. Then I wrote myself a letter to reinforce a picture of myself resolving this problem through my own actions. I didn't start with clearly articulated ideas of what I could do; the ideas developed as I was writing. This was different from my usual daydreaming. It was realistic problem solving. I was working backwards from the future to chart a realistic course of action.

In my letter, my future self explained how I'd first written a few Outer Child dialogues until I'd calmed some of my fears and felt more self-possessed. When I felt strong enough, I spoke to my boss in a calm, confident voice, stating my case simply.

The amazing thing was that I was able to accomplish what I'd previously thought impossible. About a week later, having clearly pictured myself several times calmly communicating with my boss, I went in and carried out the plan. I felt even better about *THAT* than the promotion I garnered from it.

You can incorporate writing a Future Letter into your journal writing whenever old patterns seem to be holding you back from achieving a goal. Go back to the future to find your way forward. Just use your imagination and picture yourself feeling happy, as if you had already overcome the obstacles and resolved the problems. Like Paul, give some thought to how long you might realistically need to get to that future. In his case, two weeks made sense—waiting years to have a conversation with his boss about his career aspirations would have been giving free rein to his Outer Child's avoidance behavior.

Like all of the Outer Child tools you're learning in this book, this one works by strengthening your Adult Self to take command over your automatic behavior patterns. And in this case the process is not a purely intellectual one. Creating a Future Vision overrides the limitations of the intellect by increasing the trajectory and aim of your mindscape. *Thinking* your way out of deeply ingrained habits rarely eliminates them. Witness the smokers who are fully conscious of the health hazards of smoking but are unable to use this information to stop smoking. This exercise increases your intention to get past your usual sticking points of compulsivity or complacency. Your imagination helps you use your increasing awareness and sense of future to reach your potential.

As you continue through the book, I will guide you through additional visualizations designed to exercise your mind. These exercises engage the laws of attraction, the idea that by mentally focusing on future outcomes, you increase the possibility of those outcomes. If you've ever skied through a glade (translation: lots of trees to avoid) you've experienced a situation where mental focus is essential to avoiding a nasty collision. Ski instructors will say over and over again, "Don't look at the trees!" because when you look at one you'll find yourself skiing right at it! Of course, you can focus on positive outcomes instead, which is our whole purpose here.

As you're working your way through the logjams of life, it helps to make frequent visits to this future time-space where your problems have been solved. It's pleasurable enough, and only takes a minute. Let the picture of your future be a kind of visual mantra, something to return to again and again as you go through the day. It gives your brain a pleasurable, healthy stretch each time, engaging the laws of attraction.

DREAM HOUSE

Let's try another visualization, one I call "Dream House." Like the previous exercise, it's designed to bypass the internal gatekeeper, otherwise known as your Outer Child, the hidden barrier to achieving success. Outer's defenses have created a veritable obstacle course to reaching your potential. One obstacle is having a low sense of entitlement. When you have an appropriate sense of entitlement, it means you feel deserving of an equal share of the rewards and benefits of life. When you feel less than entitled, Outer Child acts out your feelings of self-dismissal and unworthiness through passivity, avoidance, and underachieving. Outer acts out similarly with your feelings of despair and helplessness. When you feel "I can't" or "I don't know how," Outer seeks substitute fulfillments, like food, alcohol, spending, or resting. Visualization uses your sense of future to break through these internal stumbling blocks. Dream House nourishes your mind with a fully crystallized, positive image. Gazing upon this imaginary view provides an opportunity to engage your mind's solution-creating capacities and strengthens your motivation to *behaviorally* follow through to reach your goals.

Some of you might be relieved to hear this exercise doesn't involve writing. But like all of the exercises in this program, you still have to do it. In this case, the doing is creating a mental image of a house and frequently referring to this image throughout the day. Once you create the Dream House image, it only takes a few seconds to conjure it up. You can focus on it at any time, any place—driving your car, running on the treadmill at the gym—whenever you have a few minutes to hone your thoughts.

I know Dream House works because I've used it myself with remarkable results, and I've seen it transform the lives of my clients, workshop attendees, friends, and colleagues. It is an active, strenuous form of physical therapy for the brain that works by stimulating growth in areas that promote focus, trajectory, aim, forward motion, and goal-achievement. Einstein formed pictorial images in his mind to engage in a process referred to as "synesthesia"—the merging of sensory images with mental content—to solve complex problems of the universe. When his brain was examined during an autopsy, one part was particularly large—the parietal lobe. That's the brain's imagination factory, the part that creates pictures in the mind's eye. For now, though, we can forget about the mental mechanics of how this exercise works. The important thing is that it gets results.

First I want to remove any pressure you might be feeling to *believe* what you're about to imagine. You don't have to believe you will one day live in your Dream House. You are just creating a crystallized image to nourish your mind.

EXTREME MAKEOVER, HOME EDITION

Begin by imagining that in the near future you come into unlimited financial resources—a distant, improbably wealthy relative has bequeathed you a fortune, or maybe you win the lottery, who knows. Imagine that your ethical, spiritual, and financial advisors all urge you to acquire some land and on it construct a home that expresses your personal dreams. It can be a vacation home, permanent residence, or way station on another continent from which to explore the world. In fact, they advise, the more you invest in this property the better. You'll be boosting local economies and offsetting some of your personal tax burden as well.

You're in the enviable position of being able to put all your financial worries aside. Your trustworthy advisors have helped you safely invest more than enough of these finances to fund ongoing philanthropic projects closest to your heart, as well as to bankroll your family's security for generations to come (you are using your imagination, remember). So you're free to indulge in your dream property.

Many of you will likely want to build your home with green principles in mind, perhaps using your Dream House to create a showcase for new sustainable, environmentally friendly materials and building practices. Your Dream House can set an example, serve as a model to instruct and inspire others.

Think about where you would like to build your Dream House: What

BACK TO THE LAND

Some people, rather than construct a Dream House, prefer to mentally construct a Dream-Scape—a place in nature they leave mostly undisturbed. Perhaps they help the economy and the planet through intensive conservation projects over a great expanse. Dream-Scape is often the preferred option of those grieving the loss of a loved one (since it is difficult to visualize the benefits of a luxurious house when someone you love has died). Others who might prefer the Dream-Scape include those who have just built a new home (their real-life dream home, perhaps), as well as those dealing with a serious chronic illness who might prefer a natural, peaceful setting. If Dream-Scape is your preference, just read along, conjuring details of your ideal natural landscape rather than an enclosed one.

climate suits you? Is it warm? Tropical? Dry? Breezy? Are there changing seasons? Does it snow in winter?

Think about the larger community in which you'll want to live, about places where you'll find productive outlets for your Outer Child's energy. Is it tucked in a dense forest? In a farming community? Is it on a cliff overlooking an ocean? Is it neighborly, with friendly people all about? Is it private and remote, surrounded by lots of property? Is it an apartment whose windows look down on a bustling street? Is it a houseboat? A communal living co-op? Create a mental picture of yourself wherever that is, scouting out the location.

Now start thinking about the house itself. Is it spacious or cozy? Create an internal space not only for your Adult Self, but for your Inner and Outer Children as well. Within this space your behavior will be channeled constructively and you'll enjoy security, peacefulness, and joy.

Remember that money is no object. In creating the Dream House, the more money that flows into the pockets of tradesmen, artisans, sustainable environment consultants, suppliers, and construction workers the better. Imagine yourself distributing this money to all of the many people who help you build your Dream House.

Don't worry if you don't believe you'll ever come close to living in a place like the one you're imagining. You'll reap the benefits of this exercise simply by visualizing the Dream House—you don't have to believe it's going to be built. You just need to pretend. You can remain a Doubting Thomas (like I am) as much as you like, as long as you *do* the exercise.

Now think about which room you'll enjoy the most, the room where you'll entertain your (current or potential) friends and loved ones. This room is the emotional center of the house (regardless of its actual location within the floor plan). What is this room like? Is it open with lots of space, lots of light? Or is it a cozy nook tucked in an upper loft?

Now think of your favorite chair in that room—a chair enticingly welcome and familiar. It's the place you're most likely to plop yourself down in after a long day of satisfying work or exercise—the place you like to read your mail, write in your journal, return phone calls, or just collect your thoughts. Imagine yourself in this chair, happy to be resting in it, even when you are in the Dream House alone.

Picture a captivating view from this favorite spot in this emotional center of your house. This view gives you endless pleasure. Can you see it? Can you hear it? Is there a sound of rushing water or ocean waves? Is there birdsong or wind rustling through the trees? Can you smell salt air, chlorine from the pool, or loam from the dense surrounding forest? These sensations bring you awe and wonder, capture your full attention, bring you out of your thoughts and into the moment. What a gift life is, you think, gazing upon this view, taking it all in.

What about the rest of the house? Is there an observatory? Library? Porch? Gym? Deck? Kitchen nook? Meditation room? Home theater? Are there balconies? Sleeping lofts?

Are there outbuildings on the property? Guest houses? Garages? Communal living spaces? Stables? Barns? A chapel? Art studio? Concert hall? Wine cave? Lodge? Let your imagination run wild.

One important enjoinder: In creating your Dream House, you can't rewrite the laws of nature. You can't, for instance, bring people back from the dead, make houses fly to other planets, or control other people's behavior (to make them love you or behave properly). Staying within the laws of reality allows you to integrate your imagination with the practical, problem-solving regions of your mind.

Let's return to your favorite room, the center spot of the house. Imagine that it's two years from now and you are alone in the house, sitting in your special seat. Why two years? Because two years is a reasonable time in which to solve almost any problem, overcome Outer Child patterns, and transform your life. Two years is also a reasonable time in which to overcome any technical obstacles that you might encounter in building. Don't think of your Dream House as perfect in every detail after these two years— instead think of it as a work in progress. There are still craftspeople, artists, and consultants at work on particular details, though you (and yours) can now stay in it very comfortably anytime you want.

Maybe you are sitting on a comfy stool in your kitchen, elbows on the counter, gazing at your beautiful view. Maybe you are on an amazingly comfortable sofa in the den or living room. Maybe you are sitting near a huge stone fireplace or enjoying the breeze on your porch swing. Imagine yourself contented and at peace in this space.

Think about what other things are in the room with you. These are things that bring you enormous pleasure just to look at. Indulge your fanciful imagination. Maybe your floors have precious seashells or even jewels embedded in them, or are made of 100-year-old reclaimed oak. Maybe you have an exquisite set of dishes, an old potbellied stove, a beautiful rug, a beloved piano, a bouquet of fresh flowers, or photographs of loved ones. Add all of the comforts and materials that might delight you and your loved ones (both current and potential).

Glance around the room in your Dream House for a moment. Take it all in. Imagine how grateful you feel to the powers that be for being alive in this space, so satisfied within yourself, so confident about your achievements. If you can picture yourself this way, you can become this. In creating a Dream House you've created a crucible in which to forge your higher Adult Self. Every time you conjure up your Dream House—even if it's only for seconds at a time—you place your energy in this crucible that holds the possibility of your growth and nourishes your brain with healthy new messages.

Conjure up the whole house—its climate, landscape, architecture, favorite room, and space for loved ones—gathering up as many details as you can in a single image. This house, as you might have guessed, is *you*. And it's the you you're becoming. Its overall shape, location, and embellishments represent your emotional needs, your potential to overcome obstacles, your most deeply held dreams, and your future. By visualizing it, you are projecting all that you are, all that you need, all that you will be into a single, vivid image. In your real life, this image guides your future in the direction this house symbolizes.

Conjuring up your Dream House is designed to be pleasurable. It provides its own built-in reward. When your brain receives rewards for performing a behavior, long-lasting changes occur in the neurons of the basal ganglia, the region involved in learning new patterns. The basal ganglia are rich in receptors for dopamine, a neurochemical that mediates reward, and which we will explore in Part Three. There is another area in your brain rich in dopamine that is also sensitive to reward (and punishment)—the orbitofrontal cortex (OFC), part of a neural circuit that mediates between impulsive behaviors and the higher thinking brain. Dream House spritzes these significant brain areas with healthy doses of dopamine to reward your problem-solving efforts each time you mentally rehearse new skills. Conjuring up an image of your Dream House nurtures, satisfies, and pleasures the brain, effectively reinforcing the positive new behaviors you are learning throughout the course of this book.

It isn't necessary to rebuild the house every time you visualize it; you've already created it. You just need to take a few seconds three or more times a day to conjure up the image of it. Repetition and consistency are what make the difference. If you do this consistently for up to three months, you will surely see your life change.

LIKE LEARNING TO WALK

In creating a Dream House, you've become engineer of your own life, master designer of an environment suited to your greatest needs, goals, and desires. The process has transformed you into a virtual architect engaged in a problem-solving activity whose intention is to promote goal-achievement in your real life.

When you bring the image to mind, you might want to take that moment to tweak or change some of the details. As you make virtual decisions, like how to enlarge a closet or where to put the stereo speakers, hold in mind your goals. Holding those aims in mind stimulates integrative regions of your brain that allow you to simultaneously design, mastermind, and plan for a projected future outcome. This integrative mental activity is akin to what happened when, as an infant, you learned to walk. Your new-found mobility inspired your developing mind to explore the world around you as you hadn't been able to before, helping you grow by leaps and bounds. Similarly, in creating your Future Vision, you are strengthening an ability that will free your Adult Self from the constraints of Outer Child and bring you closer to your dreams.

So add this Outer Child exercise to your toolbox along with your Outer

Child dialogues. Use the exercises frequently. Soon you'll notice you're incrementally developing greater self-entitlement, increasing your confidence, fine-tuning your goals, and moving your life ahead on many levels and in many areas.

As you change—achieve goals and then set new ones—you can change your Dream House accordingly. Renovate it to reflect your evolving self. You may decide to move it to another country. Or make it smaller. Or larger. You may decide to add a room or delete one. You may change your favorite spot from one room to another, perhaps to enjoy a different view.

If you'd like, you can sketch your evolving Dream House and map out its floor plan. Many of my clients carry a diagram of the house with them. You can also cut ideas from magazines for your Dream House and keep them in your Outer Child notebook or make a collage of them. The important thing is to keep this Dream House prominent in your mind.

In focusing your mental energy on your Future Vision, you add mortar to the foundation of your new relationship with yourself, something we'll continue to build incrementally, tool by tool, chapter by chapter.

SEVEN

Outer Child and Your Past

Have you ever wondered if forgetting long stretches of your childhood means you are not of sound mind?

What some people "remember" aren't their own firsthand experiences, but what family members have told them—for instance, you may have been hospitalized or separated from a parent for long stretches of time but have no conscious memories of the experience.

Does that mean you need psychoanalysis to uncover your past? If you don't get it, will you suffer psychological problems indefinitely? Do you need to remember your childhood traumas in order to set yourself free?

The answer to all these questions is no. The reason has to do with the *hippocampus*, a seahorse-shaped structure set deep in the brain. The hippocampus is the site of our factual or context memory. It is responsible for storing the who, when, what, and where of the event. The hippocampus provides us with this information so that our emotions can be appropriate to context. For instance, it's normal to feel sadness when someone dies, but depressed people feel sad in contexts that don't seem related to their low mood, suggesting a glitch in hippocampal functioning.

The hippocampus functions in a radically different way from the amygdala, the brain structure that stores emotional memories—how an experience is *felt*. Understanding the difference between these two memory systems, *emotional* memory (amygdaloid) and *informational* memory (hippocampal), throws the very concept of repression into question. More importantly it lets you off the hook for any gaping holes in your childhood memory.

Here's why: Whereas your emotional memories are nearly indelible, the memories stored in your hippocampus are prone to distortions and deletions of all kinds. Hence, you might experience echoes of an emotional memory—feelings that stem from a childhood of being scared, lost, or excited—but have no historic context for those feelings. Lose a friend or a job and suddenly an old unwelcome feeling resurfaces. You know you've had the feeling before because it has a strong and all-too-familiar aspect to it. But you don't know where it came from because the circumstances surrounding the feeling may never have been stored in the hippocampus in the first place. That's a far cry from repression as Freud conceived it. You can't repress a memory you don't have!

FEELINGS CAME FIRST

All this raises another fascinating question: How do events we can't even remember affect the way we react to things happening now?

Whereas your amygdala was fully operative before you were born, your hippocampus didn't develop fully until a few years later. This means that feelings dating back to the womb have been retained in your amygdala (but not in your hippocampus). Incredible as it may seem, even feelings that old can intrude into your current life. That you have no memory of the details of the originating event matters not at all.

When your hippocampus did develop enough to start storing circumstantial details, the process was subject to interference from stress hormones. Stressful events trigger the production of cortisol and other stress hormones known to hinder your hippocampal memory while having just the opposite effect on your amygdala. In other words, stress hormones can weaken informational memory and simultaneously strengthen emotional memory. So it's possible to pick up emotional baggage (amygdaloid) from childhood without the context information (hippocampal) to help you make sense of it.

MEMORY: FEAST OR FAMINE

People try all kinds of things in an effort to recover lost memories, including dream interpretation, hypnosis, trauma reduction therapy, and even truth serum, but the past often remains elusive. And now we know why. Thanks to an underdeveloped hippocampus or the impact of stress hormones on its neurons, you're having hippocampal memory malfunctions. The events were either never recorded in the first place or some of the data got recorded but later stressful events caused the memory connecters in the hippocampus to corrode, preventing the memory cells from making the necessary connections. So people remember only fragmented, distorted parts of the original event, if they remember it at all. They experience emotional reactions to triggers installed by traumas they've mostly forgotten.

Some stress hormones can also cause the exact opposite phenomenon to occur: *flashbulb* memories. Depending on the severity of the stress, another hormone involved in the stress response—*adrenaline*—can actually *heighten* context memory. A former client recalls one such event:

I have a clear image of Lonny saying he didn't love me anymore, even though it happened over 15 years ago. It's a vivid scene: every word we spoke, how he was looking at me, the feeling in the room, the expression on his face when he turned away. It creeps into my mind whether I want to think about it or not.

Most of us can remember exactly where we were on September 11, 2001, when we learned about the planes striking the Pentagon and World Trade Center. The shock gave us flashbulb memories, a symptom of posttraumatic stress disorder shared, in this instance, by the whole nation. We can remember not just the feelings but the *details* of where we were and who we were with.

I was sitting in a coffee shop, calmly reading the paper. The radio was playing in the background and the announcement came on and everyone started to listen. Then the door swings open and this guy comes up and asks for a coffee like nothing happened. We knew but he didn't. I'll never forget the guy breaking the silence.

Thanks to the variety of stress hormones released during an intensely stressful experience, it is possible to have a flashbulb memory of one part of an event and a black hole where the rest of the details should be.*

A CALL TO ARMS

Stress hormones play a big part of Outer Child's automatic reactions. The stress hormones most people are familiar with are cortisol and adrenaline, but there is a whole variety of them. When something triggers an old abandonment fear, your amygdala calls for a release of cascading stress hormones that you are barely aware of on the surface but that greatly impact your behavior. Surging stress hormones signal your emergency defense system (fight, freeze, flee) to go into full swing.

Stress hormones would come in handy if you were preparing to fight a mortal enemy because they keep you on edge, hypervigilant—ready to sprint out of harm's way or to mobilize muscular strength to fight off an attacker. When there is no mortal enemy present, the hypervigilance, hyperactivity, and agitation (caused by surging adrenaline and other chemicals) are extremely unpleasant and feel out of proportion to the actual event.

In adult life, things happen that barely register on the Richter scale of cognition but nevertheless can trigger the release of stress hormones. This subliminal readiness for the fight-or-flight response impinges on your sense of composure. Some of these stress hormones stay in the blood for hours or even days to keep you hypervigilant and on-edge—ready to defend over the long haul. They create a background tone of emergency-readiness, which means it takes less provocation to prompt an automatic response. On the surface you experience this as being more reactive than usual, more prone to anger, perhaps wakeful at night.

Some of these longer-acting stress hormones (such as cortisol) increase your appetite, an interesting and important fact we will discuss in the diet chapter in Part Three. They can also keep you *emotionally hungry*. For abandonment survivors, the chronic arousal of abandonment fear and the release of cortisol and other stress hormones can cause you to continually

---

* For an addendum about the impact of stress hormones on cognitive brain functioning, please click on "topics" at outerchild.net to download information on this subject.

seek reassurance from other people, which explains your incessant need for approval and your sensitivity to any hint of rejection.

REMEMBERING WON'T SET YOU FREE

Freud theorized about the inner workings of the psyche without the benefit of 21st century neurological and biochemical research. Yet he understood the importance of airing your unconscious emotions. Separation therapy—communicating with the vulnerable and impulsive part of your psyche—helps your unconscious emotional conflicts bubble to the surface. You tune in to your innermost self through the emerging voice of Little You, who opens up and reveals your most neglected, long-standing emotional needs (which have been stored in your amygdala).

Many people (including a lot of therapists) believe that remembering the events that led to your current emotional vulnerabilities helps release you from their hold. Conversely, the thinking goes, if you have memory blocks, you might be mired in an unresolved conflict from the past. Though pervasive, I simply can't find good support for this belief. Memory gaps are understandably confusing; it's frustrating to have an undercurrent of fears from a past you can't remember; and they may be a point of inquiry for your therapist. But rest assured, your emotional memory of earlier events remains intact, and that's all you need to connect with your emotional core and reap the benefits of separation therapy.

When your hippocampal memory does provide some information about stressful events from the past, a new question arises: How reliable is it? One of my clients helps to illustrate:

> My family had this big violent episode when we were kids. I can remember who was there, exactly where I was standing, who threw the chair. I remember taking my sister to the emergency room, my father driving there like a maniac. My sister remembers it differently. She says I was the one who landed in the ER. She also remembers the ambulance arriving at the house.

Whether you remember the details accurately or not, the *emotional* impact is reliably recorded in the amygdala. The fear and other feelings you experienced at the time conditioned you to react to sensory data—

sights and smells associated with the crisis, much like the way the sound of a bell triggered salivation in Pavlov's dogs. Two other clients summed up their own triggers:

I always get uptight during Christmas...and sad. It brings me back.

I smelled the decaying autumn leaves underfoot, and it brought back feelings from my childhood all in one whiff...

Your oldest feelings, both pleasurable and painful, can be brought to the fore by things happening in the here and now. Anything reminiscent of an old loss—a sight, smell, or sound—can trigger an emotional glimpse of the past. And we feel it in the now. Sometimes it's a vague undercurrent and sometimes a sharp pang. Sometimes it's nothing less than an emotional storm.

No matter how intense or unwelcome the feelings, they are not the problem. It's the way we cope with those feelings that makes the difference. Outer Child's impulse is to act on them defensively rather than allow us to feel our feelings, accept them, and work them through. Separation therapy provides the tools to help us finally deal with emotions from the past.

When you write a dialogue, Big You promises to take exquisite care of the tender, precious, wee child within you. This prevents that pesky Outer from acting out your long-standing needs automatically, impulsively, repetitively, or unconsciously. The dialogue is effective in taking care of your long-neglected needs, irrespective of what may have happened in your childhood to create them. It isn't necessary to remember the specific traumas from your past. Instead you address the feelings that rise to the surface in the here and now and provide emotional healing to forgotten events.

USING THE PRESENT TO HEAL THE PAST

A new romance, job, or other venture may send you on an emotional roller coaster, to be sure, but no matter. It isn't all bad; there are a few ups that come with the downs. You can use the ride to develop a stronger Adult Self. Applying the program enables you to look after your own emotional needs so you won't look to a partner, boss, or new romantic interest for security. When you're feeling alone, worried, or insecure, get out your notebook and ask Little to talk to you about it. The more self-compassion you inculcate, the more emotionally self-reliant you become.

Many years ago, a woman, Marie, came to me following a traumatic breakup. Her husband of 20 years had suddenly left her for another woman. After working through abandonment fears triggered from her troubling childhood and dealing with the intense crisis of adult separation, she was able to find love again and ultimately remarry. Unfortunately, as I later learned, she'd lost her second husband—a man of 50—to cancer. Following his death, and after six years of being alone, she met someone interesting. But she was extremely anxious, almost panicky around him. Her knee-jerk responses were threatening the budding relationship, and this brought her back into therapy with me.

Marie's earlier losses emotionally conditioned her amygdala to hit the panic button when the possibility of a new relationship moved into view. Her self-sabotaging response was to turn away and isolate. It was an unconscious response, of course, and meant to protect her from a future hurt, as self-abandonment almost always is.

I convinced Marie that writing dialogues could help her give love directly to herself instead of leaving this important need exclusively in the hands of her new romantic interest. She had unwittingly made him a replacement for the husband she'd lost, placing all of her emotional needs at his feet, handing over her grief to him along with her power, and then running from him to preserve herself.

Here is a sample of her dialogues:

BIG MARIE: Why are you so frightened around Gil?

LITTLE MARIE: Nobody's ever going to keep me. Nobody loves me. I feel bad inside.

BIG MARIE: Why do you feel nobody loves you? I'll love you forever.

LITTLE: All you care about is him.

BIG: No, I care about you too Little.

LITTLE: No you don't. You'll leave me again. Because I'm not enough. He's more important.

BIG: I love you and will never leave you again.

LITTLE: Yes you will. You'll leave me as soon as Gil comes around. You only worry about him.

BIG: I'll stay right by your side, even when I'm with him.
LITTLE: I'm too scared.

Little Me was really upset and I knew I had to calm her down—I just didn't know how!

Marie's was a common dilemma. When you get Little to express the depths of her emotions, the next step is to assure her that you are capable of taking care of her needs, which can seem nearly impossible. Your effort to do so is a real stretch for your Adult Self and provides good mental therapy for your developing brain—all to the good. I showed Marie how to use a new application of the dialogue, which I call "Turn Around," that facilitates this stretch and gets you through the impasse. Imagery is an important component of this technique. You've been using your imagination to *personify* and *relate* to the three parts of your personality—Inner Child, Outer Child, and Adult Self—as well as to create a Future Vision of yourself as you would like to be. These images provide focus, nourishment, and stimulation for your changing brain. With the Turn Around exercise, I offer another image to keep front and center.

TURN AROUND

First, I want you to imagine that all of these years, Outer Child has had its back to your Inner Child, so that it could fend off attacks from the outside world. Outer has been walking the perimeter surrounding your Inner Child. Its fists are up and ready for action. Outer's constant patrol around the perimeter has enclosed your Inner Child—your feelings—in an isolated bubble.

Second, imagine that Little, enclosed inside the circle, has been pulsating with primal feelings that are regularly triggered by events in your daily life. The dialogues are helping you develop empathy for this long-neglected emotional center. But Little needs something more.

When Outer does encounter a negative trigger—anything that can make you feel what you don't what to feel—it acts out your Inner Child's feelings in its usual knee-jerk ways. Outer's defenses might include *passive* ones, like avoiding a new relationship or procrastinating about asking for a raise; or *active* ones, like yelling at a loved one or shoveling down a second bowl of pasta. Outer, remember, is a glutton for immediate gratification and uses Inner's feelings as a primary source to fuel its mammalian impulses.

The key image in the Turn Around exercise is, simply, to visualize Big You asking Outer Child to *turn around* and face Little You. From this new position, Little You is going to express its feelings directly to Outer. One more thing: Your stronger Adult Self is still in charge, in fact acts as a compassionate mediator between your Inner and Outer. Not only that, Big You is going to bestow a reward upon Outer Child for complying with the Turn Around request. The reward is a promise to find some healthy, productive, fun things to do to release Outer's energy, rather than let it run around loose, acting out protective responses (unhelpful ones) to Little's feelings. Your Adult Self feels compassion for all of your parts.

By turning around to face your Inner Child, Outer is forced to fully separate from Inner. When its back had been turned, Outer was able to stay enmeshed with Inner's feelings (like a parasite usurping the host's blood supply). When Outer comes *face-to-face* with Inner, these Mutt and Jeff parts become separate entities who oppose each other with separate agendas: Inner's emotional and Outer's behavioral. Turn Around uncouples the symbiotic twins, another step in the process of separating feelings from behavior. This separation is the crux of change.

Here's Big Marie laying out the ground rules to her Outer Child:

> BIG MARIE: Outer, I know you want to run from Gil, but I'm in charge and I want something different, which is to somehow find a way to work it out with this guy. I know you'd prefer to just talk to friends on the phone all night, then read until I fall asleep. You're trying to keep it safe, to protect Little Marie from going through another loss, but I will stay with her now, Outer. Little is scared, because she needs *me,* the adult, to keep her tucked in close when I'm with Gil. Yet she needs love from other people (like Gil) too. So you have to stop all of your antics and step aside.

Remember Bob, whose goal was to make more money? He shares the note he wrote from his Adult Self to his Outer Child:

> BIG BOB: Outer, I know I've left you on your own and I know how hard you've been at it to protect the little guy. I appreciate how

quick you are to stick up for him but I'm asking for a change. I'm asking you to turn around and face Little. Stop walking the perimeter and listen to his feelings instead of trying to protect him.

Carla's goal was to advance in her career.

BIG CARLA: I know I have neglected you, Outer, but now I'm changing that. From now on, I'm going to be your parent and take you under my wing and find things that you enjoy doing to release some of that energy of yours. I need you to help me take better care of Little—*my* way, please. You are important to me, Outer, but Little has to come first, because she's so small and helpless. You don't have to protect her anymore; that's my job. I need you to help me do constructive things to make our lives better.

YOUR TURN

Why not start the writing part of this exercise as Bob, Carla, and Marie did: Embed this message in your imagination with a similar note—your Adult Self to Outer Child—in your notebook, using your own words and sentiment, beginning with today's date.

Dear Outer,
    I know you mean well when you _____. But it's time for me to take charge of Little's needs. I'm going to _____ from now on. So it's time for you to turn around and face Little.
Your Caring Parent,
Big

Finally, create an image of a Big You who is wise and powerful enough to make Little feel connected rather than isolated within its incubation chamber. Imagine that this enhanced version of your Adult Self is capable of helping Little You feel safe during Outer's momentous turn around. Big You will now encourage Little to confront its gatekeeper and express its resentment, anger, and fear toward Outer. Little doesn't have to be afraid anymore, because Big You will be right there to offer love and support and will not abandon Little You this time (or ever again).

Here's how Bob did it:

Dear Little Bob,

    I'm going to take charge of Outer now, Little. So you are free to express your feelings to him. As your protector and advocate, I will never leave you. I will be right here so you can feel safe.

Again, to reinforce this message, you can write a similar note—Big to Little—in your Outer Child notebook, using your own words, feelings, and details about what's happening in your own life.

Dear Little,

    Outer is going to turn around and face you. I want to reassure you that you can express your feelings to Outer, because I promise to

_____.

Your Loving Parent,
Big

Once you send this critical message to your imagination—that it is the Adult's job (that's you) to nurture your Inner Child as well as to parent your Outer Child—you'll immediately begin reaping the benefits of this exercise. You're redefining the relationship between Inner Child and Outer Child. What begins in your imagination, with enough practice, manifests in the form of growth.

Next, Little talks directly to Outer, its meddling older sibling, but never without the protective presence of Big. Little's job here is to tell Outer, *"Stop trying to protect me."* Generally, Outer responds by saying something like, *"But I thought they were coming to get you."* To which Little should reply, *"I'm afraid sometimes, but I'm feeling close to Big now. I don't want your help anymore. Big has a whole new plan for us and I want you to get out of the way."*

Gerard, someone who came to my workshop dressed in a business suit, provides a powerful example, which he allowed me to reprint here. He didn't have to think long before coming up with an issue that would be the focus of this exercise. His marriage had just fallen apart. His wife had recently said five words that made his heart stop and his mouth go dry: *I want a legal separation.* His reaction was the universal human reaction any of us have when we feel the threat of abandonment: emotional crisis!

> I felt like a small child who'd just lost his mother. Worse: banished from the household. I had it rough as a kid and now I was reliving my worst nightmare. I married Margaret 30 years ago. And all those years I'd been driven to earn a good living, to give her everything she could ever need or want. That was what got me out of bed in the morning and motivated me to work day and night to make my business a success. I was a man on a mission: to support the wife I deeply loved and give her and the kids financial security, something I never had growing up. So when she said, "We don't have a connection anymore, the passion is gone," the bottom dropped out of my world.

In the course of ongoing conversations with his wife, she uttered the awful words, *I love you but I'm not in love with you*—a cliché that has devastated many a love-stricken partner. If I had a nickel for every time a client or friend recounted these words, I'd actually be able to build my Dream House! These words compounded Gerard's abandonment fears and led him to do what most of us would—commit a whole new level of self-abandonment. He began imagining that he wasn't good enough: not a good enough lover, not compelling or charismatic enough, not young or trim or sexy enough. He was weak, needy, and dependent—and that's why she didn't want him anymore. His ragged state of anxiety, triggered by primal abandonment, sent his stress hormones through the roof. Like most other people struggling with abandonment, it wreaked havoc with his sense of personal power, self-confidence, and self-esteem. He continues:

> I took a friend's advice and went to an abandonment-recovery workshop, where I learned the Turn Around exercise. Initially I didn't believe writing these dialogues could possibly help, but I was perfectly compliant and did them all; after all, my way clearly hadn't worked.
>
> Prior to the workshop, I'd been acting out my devastation in every way imaginable. My Outer Child had taken over, and I was a basket case. I'd been apologizing to Margaret for things that weren't my fault, wearing my desperation and self-loathing on my sleeve.

At times I also raged at her. Under the influence of a drink or two (something uncharacteristic for me), my anger overflowed. I would have these emotional meltdowns—my Outer Child trying ever more desperate measures. I became an obsessed, deranged man trying to cope with abandonment and win back my wife's love at the same time. As I wrote about it I could see that these things were at odds with each other, at least the way my Outer Child was handling it. I was acting like a dependent, overgrown child instead of the strong, valuable adult my wife first fell in love with. I hated my Outer Child for making me act like this.

Before you put pen to paper, first think of an issue you're grappling with, this time a relationship issue, and get in touch with your goal around this issue—something you've been struggling to achieve. Are you pining for an old love? Smarting from a recent rejection by a colleague or friend? Samples of the kinds of issues and goals workshop attendees focused on:

I have a goal to inspire more romance and passion in my relationship with my wife.

I have a goal to let go of my relationship with Katy; she's never going to be able to give me what I want.

Write this goal in your Outer Child notebook along with today's date. Then start a dialogue with your Inner Child: How might Little feel about Outer's constant interference in this goal? Next, get Little You to express your true emotional response to your worst self-defeating behaviors, and aim those feelings at the culprit: Outer Child. Just imagine how it has felt for Little You to have had this annoying older sibling around, trampling on its feelings, using them for fodder, making things worse. Imagine how frustrated Little must be that your most urgent needs have been neglected for so long.

You might begin the Turn Around exercise by having Little You say to Outer You: *"I'm mad, Outer! I'm mad at you because _____."* Imagine Big's hand resting protectively on Little's shoulder as Outer turns around to listen.

Gerard describes his first Turn Around effort:

I got Outer to turn around and let Little Gerard speak his mind. Much to my surprise, all of this hatred and rage spewed forth. Since my higher self was writing the dialogue, I (Adult Self) never felt personally attacked. The anger was directed at my Outer Child. My Inner guy told my Outer guy to stop acting like such a desperate wreck. He told Outer things like, "I can't stand you. You're making me look and act like a fool. I want Gerard (Big Gerard) to take care of me, not you. You're an idiot!"

It took a whole page for Little Gerard to get all that anger out, and when it was over I was drained. But I was also CLEAR. It was as if there really were these separate creatures—an Inner Child speaking to an Outer Child, and an Adult Self who was calmly in control of the situation. It was a strange feeling. I recognized these different parts of myself but instead of it making me feel crazy— like I had multiple personalities—I felt saner than I had for months. And beyond that, it gave me ideas about how to better handle things with my wife. For one thing, I needed to get my Outer Child to stop begging her for love. I also felt protective of my Inner Child—of my feelings. Suddenly I counted again.

Susan warned me that Outer was not done with me yet, but at least I had a useful tool to get me back on track.

Let words flow from Little You and aim them at your interfering, self-rebellious Outer Child. Don't censor yourself. Your higher self is the one who's writing the dialogue and creating and speaking for all three parts of your psyche: Inner, Outer, and Adult. You have complete control. If the feelings become too overwhelming, you have two options: The first is to stop the dialogue and pick it up later when you feel you have greater emotional resources. The second is to have Big You reach in deeper to find more reassuring ways to calm and nurture Little You. This mental reaching is good physical therapy for the brain. Stretching to increase self-compassion strengthens the muscle of the Adult Self, along with the cognitive, mediating regions of your brain.

The Turn Around exercise manages primal fear by giving voice to your feelings—to your inner self. When your Inner Child confronts your over-protective, bungling Outer Child, Inner feels less helpless and more powerful. This releases Little You from its incubation chamber. The exercise provides your emotional self with the sense of entitlement, openness, and courage it needs to be able to uncouple itself from your Outer Child's reflexive patterns.

Performing separation therapy once or twice is not sufficient to eliminate your deep-seated anxiety or deeply entrenched patterns, but incorporating Turn Around and the other dialogues into an *ongoing* regimen will certainly move you forward. Gerard, though, was amazed at a subtle change that occurred after his very first attempt:

> When I got home from the workshop, I noticed a change in my attitude toward my wife. The self-apologizing, the begging—it all felt alien to me. I suddenly realized how self-sabotaging it was. How could I have behaved like that? There were other ways, I just had to find them. Creating a Future Vision helped. I imagined myself being self-contained and able to get real with my wife. And I found that I could (sometimes). When I felt like lashing out at her, I would stop and soothe myself before trying to respond. I was no longer acting like a supplicant. I was taking care of the little guy now. I became a man who could contain his needs and assure himself, someone I could respect.

This was a huge step for Gerard, as it is for anyone who struggles with primal abandonment fear within a relationship. What Gerard now had going for him were three things: greater emotional self-reliance, Future Vision, and tools for getting stronger every day.

When you feel uncertain in a relationship, use Turn Around to turn the tables. It allows you to take complete responsibility for your most vulnerable feelings. You don't need to look to an external source (another person!) for your emotional sustenance. When someone triggers your anxiety, hurt, or panic, just attribute the feelings to Little and use the Outer Child dialogues to administer to those feelings yourself. What you want to avoid at all costs is leaving Little's care to someone else. That's like dropping Little You at the street corner and waiting for someone else to adopt him.

Turn Around is a step toward permanently installing your Adult Self in the role of compassionate CEO of your own life, but it doesn't work by magic—especially when you're working on something as monumental as personal change. To strengthen your mental muscles, go beyond reading about them and actually *do* the written dialogues regularly. Incorporate them into your daily journaling. Repetition of constructive mental exercises, not a single experiment, is what guarantees forward motion.

When you sense your old patterns trying to get in the way, turn to the tools you now have at your disposal. As you practice, your Adult Self gets stronger and more responsible and you inch closer to reaching your higher self. Eventually what begins in your mind's powerful eye—a stronger Adult Self, a contented Inner Child, and a tamed Outer Child—becomes real.

EIGHT

Outer Child, Your Stress, and Trauma

In previous chapters we explored how *past* emotional experiences can affect *current* emotional responses. In this chapter we examine where Outer Child behaviors overlap with post-traumatic stress response. Specifically, we'll look at concepts developed in the study of trauma to help us better understand where Outer Child behavior comes from and how to change it.

I'm not suggesting that we're all victims of post-traumatic stress disorder. Even so, the study of trauma provides valuable insights into Outer Child behaviors, whether they stem from events we would usually classify as traumas or not.

In truth, stress and trauma are part of everyday life. Any experience that leaves a footprint of fear can be called "traumatic." These experiences are part of learning. They condition us to develop an essential repertoire of learned defenses. Many of them serve us well throughout life; some become maladaptive. When stressful events are severe or protracted enough, they become a breeding ground for some of our most entrenched Outer Child behaviors.

We humans all react to intense emotions in highly patterned ways whose roots may reach deep into our past—some as far back as the womb. As discussed in Chapter Four, the memory of your birth is known to be preserved in the amygdala, which means the sensations you experienced can be triggered by current life-situations, especially those bearing a resemblance to being thrust out of a secure, comfortable place—such as when you lose a loved one, job, or home. When you lose someone or something important to you, a different kind of umbilical cord is cut. You are suddenly disconnected from your primary source of sustenance. An infant stops crying when Mommy picks it up and cuddles it; the enclosing warmth of her arms reminds the infant of the womb. We seek that same kind of connection in the wake of loss our whole lives. Our oldest, most helpless, newborn feelings of dependency have been reactivated.

Birth trauma, the seminal place of abandonment fear, creates the emotional template upon which later traumas are layered. As new stressful experiences accumulate, they nurture the development of the three major post-traumatic symptoms:

1. Heightened emotional arousal
2. Memory lapses of earlier traumas
3. The development of repetitive behaviors

If these symptoms sound familiar, it is because they are identical to what drives a lot of Outer Child's behavior. People with active Outer Children (most of us) exhibit the same three components of the post-traumatic syndrome. To wit:

1. We overreact to hidden emotional triggers.
2. We have gaping holes in our childhood memories.
3. We repeat self-defeating behaviors.

In the previous chapters, we provided some theoretical background for the first two symptoms of the Outer Child syndrome—hidden emotional triggers and memory gaps. In this chapter we'll zero in on the third—repetitive behavior. Looking at our Outer Child patterns through the lens of trauma helps us see many of them in a whole new light—and it is an empowering illumination. The field of trauma recovery calls them "repetition compulsions." And they are doozies!

ONLY THE PLAYERS HAVE CHANGED

Repetition compulsions are exactly what the name suggests: behaviors we feel compelled to repeat. Nothing new there. Of special interest to our work is the idea that we repeat these behaviors compulsively to *re-create the original trauma*. As one former client explained about his own circumstances:

> My father was my hero, but one day when I was eight, he walked out of the house with a suitcase, waved good-bye, and never came back. When my fiancée gets upset, she doesn't explain anything, just packs a bag and walks out. I somehow managed to fall in love with a woman who brings that agonizing walking-out scene back to life over and over again. Why?

Repetition compulsions are well known to psychotherapists because they are rich in clues about an individual's emotional history—events that are often lost to conscious memory. Gilbert Kliman, MD, trauma specialist, explains that by reenacting an earlier traumatic experience, we unwittingly reconstruct an emotionally rich history about which we may have little or no contextual memory. Repetition compulsion provides a kind of behavioral pantomime—a post-traumatic behavioral narrative of the original trauma.

Most of us perform repetition compulsions without realizing it and without knowing how to break the patterns, but it doesn't have to stay that way. I'm going to show you how to identify these *retraumatizing patterns* to free yourself from their stronghold.

Katherine, a workshop member, offers an example of her own repetition compulsion:

> My uncle sexually abused me throughout my early teens. I felt degraded and worthless. When he finally left me alone, I picked up where he left off and started seducing older guys. I had no idea why I felt compelled to do this. These relationships always ended badly, with me feeling used and getting dumped in the end. But I didn't waste any time before finding the next guy and doing the whole thing all over again.

Why would this woman repeat something that had hurt her so deeply in the past? When you learn how to identify some of your own repetition compulsions, you may ask yourself the same question.

When another woman, Patricia, was a child, her mother was confined to bed due to multiple sclerosis. Her father had long since "abandoned ship." As her mother's illness progressed, Patricia took over more and more of her mother's care, forgoing her own social life. Ultimately she quit school and got a job to support them both. After Patricia's mother died, she married Barry. Within a few years Barry's weekend partying had progressed into full-blown alcoholism. He could barely hold down a job.

> I had to support us. Every time he picked up a drink, I felt aban-
> doned—he was choosing that drink over ME. It was just like my
> father choosing to leave when we needed him most. In another way
> I was also reliving life with my mother. She was the parent but
> needed ME to take care of HER instead of the other way around. I
> felt I was in the same role reversal with Barry.

Our repetition compulsions unwittingly replicate scenes from our childhood. The dynamics remain the same, even some of our behaviors are the same—only the players have changed.

PATTERNS IN YOUR PERSONAL HISTORY

See if you can identify a repetition compulsion of your own. Let's say one of your Outer Child patterns is procrastination. Consider whether procrastinating makes you feel bad about yourself. Does this bad feeling remind you of times in your childhood when perhaps you didn't live up to your parents' expectations? Could your tendency to procrastinate be re-creating the emotional climate of your childhood?

Or maybe your Outer Child tends to *avoid confrontation*. You let people walk all over you. Do you remember times when you couldn't stand up for yourself? Maybe your parents, siblings, or someone else victimized you or bullied you. In avoiding confrontation in your current life, are you retraumatizing yourself?

Or maybe you're in a *no-win position* in your marriage. No matter what you do, it's never enough to please your partner. Were you in a no-win situation in your nuclear family? Maybe no matter how perfect you tried to be, your parents always found an excuse to get angry with you. Did you marry someone who would keep you in the same double bind?

Or maybe you *overspend*. Does it make you feel irresponsible? Indulgent? Do these feelings resuscitate emotions from your childhood when you felt foolish or guilty for creating a problem? Does your overspending send you back to the same old bad feelings?

Listen to Bruce, a man from one of my workshops:

My father used to go into alcoholic rages and attack my mother. I hated him for it, but ironically I became an adult with my own whopping anger-management problem. Here was history repeating itself. My explosive anger wrecked my marriage and all of my subsequent relationships with women. The Outer Child paradigm is the first to help me pinpoint this out-of-control piece of me. Now that I have a firm grasp of what it's all about—the fear and helplessness and hurt—I can finally stop acting it out. Why should I keep creating this drama of violence in my life?

Bruce knew his rage-reactions stemmed from his father's violence, but he couldn't get a handle on how to change it until he understood the Outer Child mechanics that caused him to retraumatize himself.

And then there's Rita:

I was a perfect Catholic girl with perfect grades, and then shamed my whole family by becoming pregnant at 16—this was back in the 1960's. I cried for months when I had to give the baby up for adoption. Having caused such shame and grief, I vowed to redeem myself in the eyes of my family. But I kept getting in my own way. Though a top grade-getter, I never managed to finish college. And then I married a guy who did not fit in with my family at all. He turned out to be a complete loser. I divorced him eventually, but since then I've been with other guys who were even worse. I'm terribly self-conscious whenever I introduce them to anyone. These choices put me back into my past when I felt so ashamed and exposed.

Why would we do things that bring us back in touch with the worst feelings? Why would Rita keep choosing people who make her feel ashamed? *Why don't we avoid doing these things?*

Here's another example, this one from Sarah, a woman we met in Chapter Two who struggled to lose weight.

> I had low self-esteem as a child. My parents were both alcoholics and alcohol was their primary focus—never me. As an adult I've been a compulsive overeater, which means that I'm addicted, just like my parents; only, food is my Number One. But what really kills me is that being overweight relegates me to the background, where no one pays me any attention, especially not guys. By overeating, I've cast myself in shadow, re-creating my own worst nightmare.

So what's really going on here?

I believe these repetitive behaviors scratch an itch, the itch of an aroused emotional memory. And I believe that you find ways to arouse your old emotional memories so that you *can* scratch the itch. Yes indeed, this one can be filed under vicious cycles. Fortunately the Outer Child program can help you override the mechanism that has you chasing your own tail.

HOW THE HURT KEEPS HURTING

We can begin to short-circuit repetition compulsions by understanding their internal dynamics. Similar to the way you can learn to use biofeedback to control your blood pressure, or neurofeedback to control your brain's alpha waves, you can train your cognitive resources to commandeer the apparatus that has you reliving the most emotionally fraught pieces of your personal history.

To explain how the dynamics of post-trauma work, I'm going to break it down into a few digestible parts.

No control

The first component of post-trauma is stress, especially the stress produced by *helplessness*. When you feel truly helpless, you are suffused with fear and the sense that you have no control over the circumstances causing that fear.

Helplessness is a key ingredient in creating repetition compulsions and one that is prevalent in childhood. You'll notice that in most of the examples above, the original traumatic experiences involved helplessness—a child raped by her uncle, a little boy who witnessed his father beating his mother, a girl whose parents were alcoholics.

Daniel Schiele, a trauma expert, says that if an event is stressful enough, it overwhelms your mental capacity to cope with it. It's too large and unfamiliar to be mapped onto the template of your ordinary experience; it doesn't fit with any of your prior knowledge about the world. In short, you simply haven't learned how to handle such things, so you're *helpless*. The traumatic scenario is etched in the amygdala, and its central alarm system remains on constant surveillance for any hint of potential recurrence.

In Jeannette Walls's memoir, *The Glass Castle*, she describes exactly this kind of compulsion. As a young child the author suffered terrible third-degree burns that nearly killed her. Yet when she's released from the hospital after an extended stay, she becomes inexorably attracted to the very thing that nearly killed her: fire. She's mesmerized by bigger and bigger flames, and then full-blown fires. She's drawn toward more heat, more danger, more risk as time goes by.

Helplessness frustrates the need for control, and my interpretation of Walls' fire-setting was that it was a repetition compulsion driven by this primal need. By repeating the traumatic condition, she was practicing to master it, unconsciously trying to get it right. Reliving a trauma, as I wrote above, scratches an itch. And if the itch is helplessness, the scratch is the brain's attempt to grab control, to regain its balance. But the itching comes back, thus the repetition.

The stress of helplessness, of having no control over what's happening to you, has been the subject of decades of rigorous research, and the findings are extremely valuable to our work. Countless laboratory animals and human subjects have been subjected to mild shocks, loud noises, or carefully monitored social deprivations. If that strikes you as alarming, know that the more painful experiments were performed decades ago and have been substituted for less invasive ones due to ethical concerns for the well-being of the subjects! Nevertheless, researchers have carefully observed the subjects' stress hormone levels, behaviors, and memory performance (memory deficits are a strong indicator of stress). The results: Stress hormones produced by helplessness alter the way the minds works. Stress hormones impact learning, cognition, attention span, emotional reactivity, memory of early childhood events, short-term memory, the ability to regulate one's emotions, and, of course, behavior patterns.

Robert Sapolsky, a neurobiologist who has devoted his career to studying corticoid stress hormones, provides a gem of insight in his book *Why Zebras Don't Get Ulcers* that forms the basis of an extremely effective Outer Child tool. He describes experiments in which the subjects were divided into two groups, and each group subjected to mild but inescapable shocks or loud, unexpected noises to simulate helplessness. One group was given a lever to hold with no explanation about its function. The other group was given nothing. The findings were significant. The group *with* the lever produced fewer stress hormones than the group *without,* and performed better on a post-memory test. What is most striking is that the lever group performs better even when they are *explicitly told* that the lever is not connected to anything. These experiments support Sapolsky's important conclusion, that just having a lever of control—a psychological handle—reduces the stress of having no control.

The experiment has been repeated by multiple researchers from multiple disciplines, in a variety of settings and conditions, with both humans and other mammals as subjects. And the findings are consistent: A lever of control (even if it is only symbolic) reduces the impact of helplessness on brain functioning. Later in this chapter, we will take advantage of this finding and bring levers of control into our lives.

Loss of social support

People living alone (and possibly suffering the stress of separation or abandonment) produce higher levels of stress hormones, which compromises their immune system, cognitive functioning, and overall health. Conversely people with social support (and *lower* stress hormones) are known to suffer fewer cancers and heart attacks, and live longer. Additionally lab rats, baboons, human children, and adults who have a companion with them when they perform a stressful task have lower stress hormones and perform better on the post-memory test than control-group members who go through the experiment on their own. The support of a companion (analogous to a "lever of control") helped reduce their stress.

The belief that things are only going to get worse

Another stressor is the perception of life worsening. Research shows that when we've given up (we feel helpless), we produce higher stress hormones than when we're still fighting (or exercising a lever of control). Psychologist Martin Seligman, an expert on *learned helplessness*, has shown that children who've been traumatized have a tendency to give up easily. And as counselors can attest, these children try to get us to give up on them too (by trying our patience). It's one of their repetition compulsions.

Believing we should be able to change the unchangeable

Another stressor is the idea that we should be able to control something that we simply can't. For example, the child of an alcoholic may think, *"I'm being perfect so Mommy will stop drinking. So why is she drunk again?"*

Some people believe they caused their own cancer or that they should be able to cure it through positive thinking. In presuming themselves responsible for their illness they compound the problem—they condemn themselves for getting cancer in the first place and for being unable to control it. If cancer does go into remission and then returns, they beat themselves up all over again.

Stressors appear at random

Unpredictability is a significant factor in helplessness. If experimental shocks come at random rather than at predictable intervals, subjects produce higher levels of stress hormones and do poorer on memory tests. Research into stress response during WWII bomb raids shows that attacks coming at regular intervals over London produced less stress-related diseases than those occurring at random over the English countryside.

Even if the stimulus is a *pleasurable* one (like eating), subjects will produce higher stress hormones if it comes at random, rather than predictable, intervals. The stress wrought by unpredicted pleasure (a rapid rise to stardom or winning the lottery) is known as *eustress*. Being unable to predict a windfall ultimately threatens one's sense of control. You wonder why you're on edge and can't sleep, so you surmise "something must be wrong" when actually it's just the opposite. Something is right—you just didn't expect it!

Frustration with no place to go

Another stressor is a lack of outlets for frustration. When a baboon is stressed he generally takes it out on another baboon of lower social standing. If he's the low man on the totem pole, he produces higher stress hormones, gets ulcers, and can't learn. The message here isn't to find someone to take your stress out on, but to understand that mammals use "scape-goats" to reduce their stress and restore their sense of balance. This proba-bly helps explain the primitive dynamics behind war.

Many people (both adults and children) tend to pick on someone below them in the pecking order, unconsciously driven by the need to gain a lever of control. To reduce the stress of helplessness, they might take out their frustration on a child, a wife, a husband, a dog—any creature unlikely to effectively fight back. The Outer Child program provides more productive outlets for your frustration to help you lower your stress hormones and increase your adult functioning.

STRESS AND MEMORY

Stress interferes with memory—specifically (thanks to some of the stress hor-mones we discussed in Chapter Seven) with hippocampal context-memory,* which brings us to the memory lapses that often occur in the wake of traumatic events. The process through which we lose those memories is called "dissocia-tion" and it offers another clue about why we repeat certain behaviors.

Dissociation is really a shortened form of *dis*association and refers to intru-sive emotional memories that float free from their original context. You feel pervasive anxiety but don't know what you're anxious about. These free-floating feelings represent a disconnect between body and mind, between emotion and context—in other words, between amygdaloid emotional mem-ory and hippocampal informational memory. But wait, there's more. Dissoci-ated emotional memories are also *accompanied by the numbing and blunting of other sensations.* In the midst of trauma's anxiety people say they "don't feel like themselves." They may be surrounded by a spouse and children but are unable to take comfort in that. *"I just don't feel anything—not even love."*

Dissociation creates a disembodied state of emotional arousal. The numbing comes from our brain's internal supply of opiatelike substances, including *endorphins* (a contraction of endogenous and morphine). Endor-phins are chemically identical to medicinal or street opiates (morphine or heroin) and equally addictive.

---

* Children as well as adults experience the damaging impact of these stressors. Please visit outerchild.net under the topics section to download information on this issue: "The Impact of Stress on Cognitive and Emotional Development."

These opioid chemicals are released in the brain as analgesics—nature's way of killing pain and reducing anxiety. And while they're effective, the drug-induced haze creates its own set of problems. Dissociated feelings cause victims of post-traumatic stress to experience altered states of consciousness, sometimes referred to as "derealization" and "depersonalization." In derealization, you are blunted from feeling a sense of reality about the present. In depersonalization, you are blunted from feeling that you are fully participating in your experience. Since these mental states are opiate-induced, they're addictive states to which you return again and again. You experience chronic waves of aroused emotions (anxiety, sadness, panic) dissociated from the events that caused them, while at the same time you feel numb to life going on around you. You become an observer of your own life, unable to get inside the flow of your experience, trapped in an uncomfortable, post-traumatic, emotional stupor.

Remember Katherine, who was sexually assaulted by her uncle as a teen and later revisited that trauma with other older men?

> I never understood why I was doing the things I was doing. We read *Macbeth* in high school, and I totally identified with Lady Macbeth. She had blood on her hands and went walking about in a trance of guilt. It's just how I felt a lot of the time. I was watching someone else's life. I didn't feel like I was occupying my own body. I felt more like a robot. Nothing felt real. I didn't FEEL period. The world was going on around me, but it was no longer MY world, and the only way I could feel something again was to go out and find someone to MAKE me feel something—even if that something was to feel sexually abused and degraded. Those were the only feelings I could feel, the only sensations that felt real.

Katherine was reenacting her traumatic scenario to break through the layers of numbing and blunting caused by post-trauma stress—so she could feel again, even if the feelings were awful. It was a way to scratch the itch.

Does this provide a clue about why we tend to retraumatize ourselves? Is it our way of breaking through layers of numbing and blunting that prevent us from feeling life? Theories abound as neuroscientists continue researching the inner workings of the brain:

Stress hormone expert Robert Sapolsky says the biological benefit of repeating traumatic behaviors is that it lowers our stress response to the trauma.

Amygdala expert Joseph LeDoux says repetition compulsions are a kind of learned behavior that ultimately takes the amygdala out of the conditioning loop, bypassing the need for constant emergency fight-or-flight responses.

From Ann Graybiel's study of habit formation, we might conclude that repetitions become the domain of the basal ganglia and are dopamine-rewarded behaviors functioning similar to addictions.

Howard Hoffman and others who study endogenous opiates say that in fact the trauma-induced opioids are addictive—we repeat the trauma to keep getting the drug.

Trauma recovery specialist Bessel van der Kolk says a withdrawal phase, akin to heroin withdrawal, is incorporated into the reenactment, creating a vicious cycle of addiction to the full sequence of behaviors.

Daniel Schiele says we rechoreograph the roles of persecutor, victim, and rescuer over and over because we are addicted to the opioid-induced numbing and dissociation that accompany the drama.

Gilbert Kliman suggests that by producing an ongoing flow of opioid painkillers, repetitions prepare us for traumatic injuries that might be just around the corner. Reenacting the trauma also warns the tribe (gene pool): Don't go here!

And then there is psychology's old standby: We repeat trauma to try to get it right this time.

Most likely there is insight to be gained from all those propositions. Whatever the cause, our emotional responses to a traumatic event can become poorly integrated into our emotional and cognitive schemes and yield a repertoire of automatic (Outer Child) behaviors. These behaviors fall under the control of our autonomic (automatic) nervous system, rather than the cerebral, higher thinking brain. Fortunately the story doesn't end there. Thanks to the plasticity of the brain, you can change. The Outer Child exercises give you the ability to exercise mind over matter, and through repeated effort, help strengthen neural connections in regions that mediate emotions, reason, and behavior. In short, you can overcome these automatic behaviors.

Since we may have memory gaps and distortions about the very experiences that had the greatest impact upon our emotional conditioning, it's doubly important to use tools that deal directly with the emotions and behaviors of our *current* life. The Outer Child program offers techniques that do not rely upon remembering the events that caused primal fear to gather strength. Your emotional memory is nearly indelible; you have only to tap into the primordial emotions safely stored in your amygdala. Whether or not you remember your past, your oldest needs, yearnings, and vulnerabilities remain intact in the here and now. You don't need to know which trauma led to which particular repetition compulsion to free yourself of self-sabotaging behaviors. And you don't need to blame anyone from your past. The Outer Child program gives you direct access to the full breadth and depth of your feelings so you can take responsibility for your own life. It puts tools in your hands for bringing your higher thinking skills to the table so you can stop responding automatically.

In short, biology is not destiny. We can overrule our patterns—replace old ones, even the most persistent ones, with healthy new ones.

TAKING ACTION IN THE REAL WORLD

As discussed earlier, the Outer Child program is a three-pronged approach, consisting of separation therapy, guided visualization, and goal-fulfilling behaviors. The first prong is using Outer Child dialogues to gain access to our feelings, name them, and give them voice, all of which help us tame our emotional brain. The second prong is nurturing our mindscapes by enhancing our Future Visions. Now we focus on the third—taking behavioral steps. You'll learn to express your Future Vision and your growing relationship with yourself by taking action, not with pen and paper, but out in the world. Remember those rewards you promised to your Outer Child during the Turn Around exercise? Well here they come: Action steps use Outer's outbound energy constructively.

Action steps provide an antidote—a lever of control—to the helplessness you've internalized from stressful childhood events both large and small. You'll find that they are easy to perform and help you reestablish a sense of control over your destiny. The levers are designed to break through the numbing and dissociation of past traumas by bringing you into the moment with your feelings intact. You gain incremental emotional, spiritual, and behavioral healing with each consciously chosen action.

What do I mean by *action*? I mean a small step, something simple that only takes a few minutes to accomplish. The actions you're about to choose involve doing something positive for yourself—simple acts of self-kindness.

Remember what Sapolsky's experiments taught us: Levers don't need to control the stressor (the shock or loud noise) to lower your stress response; having a lever to hold improves conditions even when the subjects are told explicitly that it isn't connected to anything. The lever provides an emblem of control—a *psychological* handle. Likewise the action steps you choose do not need to be directly connected to your goal—especially in the beginning. As long as you hold the conscious intention to achieve your goal as you commence each action, it will help move you in that direction.

Remember too that unpredictability is another stressor. Making the commitment to take a simple, positive action and then carrying it out creates predictable structure, where before there had been only random emotional arousal. You'll be using predictability as an antidote to helplessness. You'll also be administering self-love—Big You to Little You—in a *behavioral* way, with actions, not just words. You'll gain forward momentum by accumulating these action steps, eventually taking real strides toward your intended goals.

BABY STEPS

In the dialogue process, your Adult Self's empathetic responses to your Inner Child's needs has helped get you partway there. Now Big must promise to take specific behavioral steps aimed at addressing Little's expressed needs. These promised actions are qualitatively different from your Outer Child behaviors—different from Outer's primitive grabs for control. The individual writing the dialogue (your *higher Adult Self*) chooses the actions you're going to take, not Outer.

The idea is to choose an action that will bring Little You into the moment with you, while beholding your goal in your mind's eye. Big You promises to take this action and then *carries it out during that very same day* (within 24 hours). Again, the chosen action can be a brief, easy activity that lasts only five minutes. The key is the conscious intention with which you choose it and then carry it out.

For instance, if your goal is to lose weight, your first action might be to leaf through some of your favorite photographs. Though seemingly not related to weight loss, your conscious intention is to perform an act that nurtures your Inner Child in a healthy way. You're holding the image of yourself losing weight in your mind all the while. Or if your goal is to feel more secure with your new girlfriend, your action step might be to take a solo drive to your favorite park. The bottom line is that you are doing something to nurture your emotionally self-reliant self. The actions work cumulatively to strengthen your ability to cope with current stressors and acquire new "learned behaviors."

Don't let the modest scope of these action steps fool you—they represent powerful devices that give you forward motion. Eventually they fall into step with your goals and help you take consciously chosen strides toward achieving them.

While you are carrying out this deed, hold both your Future Vision and Little You in mind. You must make the mental connection—by energetic use of your imagination—between your intended goals, Little's needs, and the action step you are taking. Hold this mental link in your mind's eye (at least for a few seconds) while you are making the promise and again while you are carrying out the action step. This mental link strengthens your intention, which in turn creates the change. When you carry out the action, however small and irrelevant it may seem to your goal, do it with the conscious intention of helping Little feel secure in your care. This brings you into the moment and stimulates your cerebral energy to gain enough strength to ultimately overcome your repetition compulsions.

Why such small actions? Because big steps are daunting. If you choose too big an action, like "Start my diet today," Outer Child might try to avoid doing it. Big steps can seem like work—more punishment than reward. With action steps, you choose steps small enough to make them feel effortless, even pleasurable, to carry out, because they're things you're doing to nurture Little You and reward Outer Child for being cooperative (for a change).

LEVERS OF CONTROL

Workshop members who shared their repetition compulsions earlier provide examples on the following pages of how they motivated themselves into action. Remember Patricia who had taken care of her mother and later married an alcoholic? She wanted to turn her life around.

In dialoguing with her Inner Child, Patricia confronted her primary emotional dilemma—that she spent most of her emotional energy on Barry. She knew she needed to make amends to Little Patricia for neglecting her needs. "You waited long enough," she wrote, "I'm going to change this, one small step at a time." She promised to take Little Patricia on a walk through the fall foliage after work, to which Little responded, *"How is that supposed to help!"* *"I don't have all the answers yet,"* replied Big Patricia, *"but I want to show you I'm working on a new life and that I'm true to my word. This is only a first step, and the best one I can think of right now. The walk is for us."*

Patricia was skeptical about the baby steps. She'd been traumatically bonded to Barry and (Little Patricia) felt helpless and hopeless about ever finding a way out of her stressful life. She doubted that taking such seemingly insignificant steps would help, but once she got started, she noticed a shift almost immediately.

> If the actions had been big steps, I would have been too overwhelmed to go through with them. So I started taking baby steps. The first change I noticed was that doing them gave me a purpose; I never broke a promise to my new adoptee: Little Me. At first I had to remind myself that I was doing these things for Little. But whenever I did think of her, I'd feel more present in the activity. This took me out of my worries and into my own life, instead of obsessing about what Barry was doing or not doing.
>
> The first few actions I took didn't seem relevant to the problem, but after a while they began to point me in a new direction. After a few little outings, my next action step was to find out about Al-Anon [an international 12-step program for friends and families of alcoholics]. Then a few action steps later, I actually went to an Al-Anon meeting (Little and I). Later still, I joined a walking group that met on weekends and met more people. All of these interesting new people! Some of whom became my friends! I was building a new identity.

Remember Bruce, whose father attacked his mother during alcoholic rages, and who later developed his own anger-management problem? He described his Inner Child as desperately helpless and angry about how "messed up" his life had become. He started with a dialogue:

BIG BRUCE: Whenever you feel angry, Little, I admit I've let Outer get excited by that. He becomes a bully. You told him yourself to stop it during the Turn Around exercise, but now I know you are waiting for me to step up to the plate and take steps to stop Outer's old habits.

LITTLE BRUCE: But you never do anything about it, Big. Outer is just too strong.

BIG: I'm not going to let Outer do what he wants anymore. I'm going to find better things for him to do. For your sake, I'm getting stronger. I am going to stay close to you from now on so I can find out when you're feeling helpless or afraid and I'm going to take action...

LITTLE: Yeah, right, Big.

BIG: From now on, when you feel angry and scared, I'm going to do something for you.

LITTLE: What can you possibly do? You're just doing a stupid exercise and you'll forget all this stuff.

BIG: You know me pretty well, but I'm going to surprise you. I'm going to do something for you, like getting a really good DVD, a movie *you'd* like—and we can spend the evening taking a breather.

Bruce's schedule made it hard for him to write a dialogue every day, but he forced himself to "talk the dialogue" in the car during his long commutes. After following up on a few actions steps, he noticed a change.

Finding something to do each day to bring Little into the moment with me was a real effort! The only time I'd ever consciously tried to be in the moment was in a yoga class. These new actions—levers of control—were like taking yoga on the road. It changed everything. Every day I did something different for my Little guy. Sometimes I got Little to tell me what he wanted the action step to be, and he'd ask for really unexpected things. Once he wanted to go over to my brother Pete's house to roll around on the floor with the dog! Little and I, we became buddies and I became more active in my life.

What did this have to do with my anger problem? Everything. I'd already taken anger-management workshops, and I was seeing a therapist once a week. Since I didn't have a girlfriend at the time (no surprise), my actions focused on other things—like Pete's dog. I admit it took some time to see the connection between these "levers" and my goals. I kept my Future Vision in my mind and did something just about every day for my Inner Child, which kept Outer Child busy too. Eventually one of my action steps was to sign up for tango lessons (my brother's idea) and I danced with a very nice woman. Now that I'm taking care of myself like this, I'm in my first working relationship. I don't get angry as often, and if I do, I take care of it (my Inner Child) myself so Outer won't fall back into his old tricks.

Here's Paul, whose mother put him down all of the time, something he later did all by himself, though he knew it was a self-defeating pattern.

I kept dialoguing with Little Paul, letting him express his anger toward me. He didn't feel good about himself and didn't trust me to stop Outer from allowing people to put us down. I told him I'd do some things to build him up. And right there on the spot, I came up with an action step. I wrote, *"Maybe you'll feel better, Little, if you see how much I care about you. I'm going to get my father's gold watch that's been on the bureau since he died and have it repaired and polish it and wear it every day just for you."* My Inner Child replied with, "Now I really feel helpless, Big. That's not going to help!"

Paul experienced conflict with his Inner Child during his dialogues until he started accumulating a few of his promised action steps. Most days he found some way to show Little Paul he really did care; often he drove to the beach, windows down and music blasting from the radio. He also followed through on his promise to get his father's watch fixed, and when it was ready, he carried it in his breast pocket. He'd told me, "Patting that pocket felt like patting Little Me." Paul's Inner Child began to seem like something very precious to him, like the gold watch. Soon he made a habit of patting his pocket watch (Little Paul) every time he took another action step. And things began to change for Paul. His Outer Child stopped interfering so much and he noticed people reacting differently to him. In his own words, "I never would have believed this was possible."

I know what you're thinking. These action steps are symbolic—not "real" steps toward your goals. And for the most part they are, but they're just what you need to get you moving. The action steps bring your unconscious feelings into the moment with you, where they can dissipate into the larger reality of your life, if only for a few moments at a time.

Choosing and carrying out these actions give your Adult Self the active role of guide. By following through behaviorally, you become a person your Inner Child can finally trust (and your Outer Child can obey). Creating this expanded role for Big You uses your imagination to increase your intention and engages multiple areas of your brain in a coordinated, constructive way.

Action steps work in tandem with your Future Vision. You've been giving your mind a pleasurable image of how good it would feel to have your problems behind you, your goals achieved. By holding that vision and focusing your action steps on Little's need for fulfillment, your actions bring you closer to reaching your vision. Notice that action steps are similar in structure to Future Visions in that they are both easy to perform, self-soothing, and pleasurable—in short, brain-rewarding. Coupling your Future Vision with your action steps allows you to reward your new action (with a squirt of endorphin, or perhaps dopamine). Science has shown that reward reinforces new behavior better than punishment, so when you take each rewarding baby step, take heart in the fact that you are reinforcing healthy new learned behaviors.

When you're ready to follow through with bigger steps—things that seem more directly related to a goal—you're going to do just that. On the other hand, there may be times when you need to commit to smaller steps, steps so easy and pleasurable that you can get one of them done each day, no sweat. When you find that you're not following through regularly enough to make a difference, scale it back to even smaller steps. The idea is to overcome inertia, develop sustainable forward motion. As long as you consciously dedicate each action to reaching your goals, your baby steps accumulate and eventually get you where you *intend* to go.

No matter if these actions seem to come from left field, no matter how unrelated they seem to the patterns you're trying to break, they get you to act with the conscious intention to reach your goals (even if for only a few moments a day). Taking baby steps creates incremental change in the area on which you focus your mental energy. So if your intention is to overcome a particular repetitive behavior, your actions will ultimately dismantle that pattern. If your intention is to meet someone special, your actions will build toward finding someone. Just conjure up an image of your Future Vision and take an action every day that brings you into the moment in a self-nurturing, pleasurable way, always keeping your innermost self in mind. Don't worry if you're a skeptic; skepticism will not hinder the results. You don't have to believe the "levers" will work. You only have to follow through.

WRITE IT DOWN, MAKE IT HAPPEN

The only way to appreciate the benefit of this exercise is to experience it yourself. First create an image of yourself in the future as you would like to be and then get your notebook and write an Outer Child dialogue. Zero in on how your repetitive behaviors interfere with your goals and how your Inner Child feels about it. Big You should empathize with Little You's feelings and use that empathy to follow through with an action of self-compassion that very same day.

Remember, action steps do not need to last more than a few minutes. If you get stumped coming up with one, let the following list inspire your ideas:

1. Promise to organize a drawer full of things your Inner Child will enjoy having easy access to.
2. Buy an extremely comfortable pair of shoes, always thinking of the comfort you're providing Little when you put them on.
3. Take photos around your neighborhood. Looking through a camera lens helps you attend to things you might not ordinarily notice—things that might delight your Inner Child—bringing you into the moment. Maybe later compile the photos in your Outer Child notebook.
4. Cut out pictures from magazines that capture details of your Dream House. Later, make a collage.
5. Take the long way home from work so you can consciously take in a new scene, keeping Little You in mind.
6. Draw or paint a stick figure of Little You in a happy setting.
7. Call a friend you haven't spoken to in a while and talk about your feelings and future plans. Be sure to also ask about his!
8. Make a call to find out about a local adult education program, support group, or volunteer program.
9. Browse in a flower shop and ask Little You what her favorite flower is that day (whether you buy one or not).

10. Show your pet some love; devote the affectionate cuddling to your intention to reach your goals.

Just make sure to choose an action that is readily accomplished within the day. Paramount in all this is keeping your promise to Little You. Breaking it would retraumatize Little, so commit to something so small, you *know* you can get it done. Go back to your Outer Child notebook to record each action step taken, with a check for the date completed. This small gesture of self-recognition gives you yet another reward. Remember, these rewards work cumulatively to inculcate new behavior.

If you haven't already done so, now's the time to put that pen to paper. Take the step you've committed to within the next 24 hours. Then do it again tomorrow, and the next day, and the next.

BE IN THE NOW

Levers of control channel your energy toward your Future Vision by bringing you and your feelings (Little You) into the moment with you. When you make contact with your oldest, most important tender feelings, you do this in the now. You feel and take actions now, because the present moment is where all of your consciousness and power reside. Now is the modality for change, for healing your wounds, for redirecting Outer's energy, for dealing with life. Now is when the Adult assumes responsibility for your Inner Child's needs and takes the reins from that overgrown, out-of-control kid of yours—Outer Child. Now is when you act.

With this tool in hand, you don't have to leave your primal needs unattended, where they can subversively motivate your Outer Child's old behaviors. You, your Adult Self, can learn to administer *behaviorally* to these feelings and exercise healthy conscious control. You no longer have to live in the past, but are free to be in the moment.

One caveat: Under enough stress, some of our conditioned behavioral responses can rebound. When a life crisis is sudden, unexpected, or extreme, you can revert to an old repetition compulsion. Conditioning, after all, is a powerful mechanism—that's why we've been struggling with these patterns for so long. If it were easy to override, you wouldn't need this book! But as Big You gets stronger and begins to take more constructive actions, it takes more and more stress to trigger an old pattern. And if you should slip back, you don't have to stay there. You have specialized tools to get you back on track.

The Outer Child program heals your deepest emotional issues, including primal abandonment. It does this not by looking backward at your past, but by using your imagination to look forward toward a future of self-acceptance, self-mastering, and self-love. Don't expect to eliminate your issues in a one-shot emotional breakthrough; instead prepare to take things step by step, building a stronger relationship with yourself along the way. You will get plenty of opportunity to continue practicing the steps as you continue through the book.

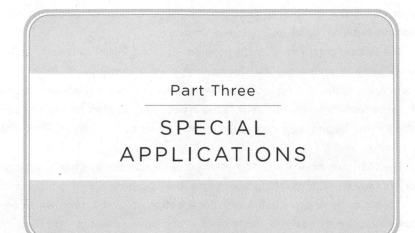

Part Three

SPECIAL
APPLICATIONS

In the following chapters we'll explore the everyday challenges people face (such as managing their weight, finances, and relationships) and what role your Outer Child might play in those dramas. Along the way I'll introduce special applications of tools you've already learned, applications that can help you conquer each of them. I encourage you to stay with me through each of the succeeding chapters even if you don't feel the particular topic is an issue for you. If you cherry-pick the ones you think are most relevant, you're likely to miss important information, handy shortcuts and tools that can help you with other areas in your life.

Throughout the program you'll find the approach to be more like tai chi than armed combat. If you try going head-to-head with Outer Child, Outer just responds by becoming more argumentative. Trying to control Outer's habits only intensifies the power struggle. Outer excels at strategies for resisting change. Locking horns with Outer keeps you at the level of the problem. To resolve thorny issues you need to aim higher, focusing on the vision of a better future, on self-compassion, and on follow-through.

All three components of the program—dialoguing, guided visualizations, and action steps—support the work of separation therapy. Its primary exercise involves separating the three functional parts of the psyche and giving them voice. Isolating your Outer Child from your Inner Child allows you to finally give yourself unconditional self-love. This reduces the impetus for Outer Child to act out your neglected needs inappropriately and places your drive energy in the hands of a stronger Adult Self. The problem was never about the *di*chotomy between head and heart, but about the *tri*chotomy between head, heart, and *behavior*.

The second component of the program—guided visualization—complements separation therapy by distinguishing your current self from your future Adult Self. Creating a conceptual distance between them allows you to take a leap forward into your highest potential, at least in your imagination. What begins as a conceptual image incrementally manifests in the real world.

The third component—taking action steps—also complements separation therapy by distinguishing your old automatic behaviors from a set of new consciously chosen behaviors. Each action step you take with conscious intention brings you closer to reaching your potential. The tools of the program provide physical therapy for the brain, gradually strengthening the muscle of the higher self. As you continue through the chapters, you spotlight your vision, plumb your emotions, commit to new goals, reintegrate the parts, and take actions to reach your dreams.

NINE

Outer Child and Diet

Defining what constitutes a healthy diet is an increasingly complex challenge in our society of plenty. What kind of food should we eat? How often, and how much? Outer Child has a veritable heyday when our Adult Selves are faced with quandaries like these. Outer knows a chance to step in and take control when it sees one. Outer's motto is: When in Doubt, Eat Whatever You Want, Whenever You Want, and as Much as You Want.

When it comes to eating, I know I'm not alone as I struggle with this thing called "moderation." A fellow Outer Child foodie once marveled, "I actually know someone who is satisfied with having a single cookie! For the life of me, I can't figure out what makes him tick."

Of human addictions, obsessions, and bad habits, food addiction might be the most difficult to overcome. After all, we have to eat. It isn't something we can just abstain from. So Outer Child always has access to food. If we limit ourselves too much, Outer just sneaks cookies from the cookie jar.

FOOD IS LIFE—AND YOUR BODY KNOWS IT

We have a primal connection to food—we need it to survive. But what's more, our earliest experience of sublime oneness involved being fed at our mother's breast or hand. The mouth is the original site of pleasure. And throughout life food stimulates highly tactile, sensory-rich areas of the mouth, such as your lips, tongue, and internal palate. The mechanism that urges you to consume goes back even further, because the sucking reflex was established prenatally. Your oral urges hearken back to when you were still in the womb. Food represents succor, nurture, and life itself.

Outer Child seems to have transmuted the sucking reflex into a chowing-down reflex. When Outer is in control, you feed both physical and *emotional* hungers with food—sweet, salty, or savory food.

Food is the ultimate quick fix. You don't have to wait to get "high." When you pop a piece of chocolate into your mouth, it gives you *instantaneous* gratification. You taste it and smell it immediately; and then chew it, swallow it, and feel it going down. You feel satisfaction grow inside your stomach with each bite. Your body's neurochemistry gets in on the act, releasing feel-good neurotransmitters that tell your body, *"Hey, let's do this some more!"* What could be more reinforcing?

While food addiction is driven by forces on the inside, we wear it *outwardly* in the form of excess weight. We can often hide most other vices from public view, but if we gain 20 or 30 pounds we might as well wear a flashing lightbulb at the end of our nose, or wear a sandwich board proclaiming, *"I overeat."* Indeed, overeating is one of Outer Child's most conspicuous habits.

Many of us use food as a panacea, especially when we're under excessive stress. But not everyone who is overweight overeats. Out of compassion for those who have trouble losing weight regardless of their diet, I want to state for the record that metabolism can be slowed by neurobiological conditions. Certain viruses and microbes that live in the human gut are known to promote excessive fat storage. Some antidepressants and steroids list weight gain as a possible side effect and it's common to put on extra weight during menopause. Of course, there are also a number of other reasons you might gain weight—a genetic predisposition, a disproportion of white fat cells to brown ones, and unbalanced chemicals produced in the body (such as leptin) that increase appetite and promote fat storage. Fortunately the program provides effective tools for remaining trim and fit, regardless of your biological predispositions.*

PUTTING THE PROGRAM TO WORK ON YOUR WEIGHT PROBLEM

Whether the causes for your weight problems are primarily psychological or physiological, the Outer Child program is remarkably effective in overcoming any internal resistance you have. Using separation therapy, visualization, and action steps, you gain control over your oral needs. When you control what goes into your mouth, you feel in control of your life.

THE INVISIBLE WOMAN: ME

When I hit menopause, I gained a lot of weight and had to work harder than I ever had before to lose it. It took serious wrestling with my own food urges, and I didn't really get on top of it until I honed new tools for the Outer Child program. Once I learned to separate out my Outer Child, talk to her directly, and listen to what was going on underneath, I finally succeeded.

Prior to developing the program, my willpower had failed me over and over again. Given the hormonal shift that goes with menopause, weight loss was more challenging than ever, and required strict adherence to a calorie-restricted diet. It was too stringent for me and at times I simply broke down and binged. My metabolism had slowed and I could no longer get away with a big meal. If I gained a few pounds, I couldn't slough it off the way I had in my twenties and thirties. No, getting rid of the extra pounds involved hard labor.

Gaining Outer Child awareness was a game changer. Little Me told me how awful she felt about being overweight and this mobilized Big Me to help her. But Outer Child was beastly strong when it came to food and fought my efforts tooth and nail. For worse and better, I had an extra spur—the disheartening realization that the extra 35 pounds had made me invisible.

People (mostly male) had stopped looking at me. I had never thought

---

* For more information about factors interfering in weight loss, please see the note section and alternatively visit outerchild.net and click on "topics" to download information on this subject.

much about whether men were looking at me or not—until suddenly they weren't. And it hurt.

I'd become a phantom. I noticed that men no longer bothered opening doors for me. They began clearing their throats and spitting on the sidewalk right in front of me, or belching, or doing other unattractive things, as if I weren't there. In my thinner days, men must have been holding back, waiting for the attractive-enough women to leave the scene before belching and scratching to their hearts' content.

I realized that I'd lost attractive-enough status. And my weight was the problem. It had gone straight to my face, and then doubled back to widen my hips, aging me overnight. I'd become a rounder, asexual version of myself. But it seemed that along with the sexual power I'd lost, I'd also lost my willpower. I couldn't stick to a diet the way I used to.

I took stock of the situation. Secure people can handle this, I reminded myself. The obsession with having to stay thin and attractive is a sign of insecurity. Right? Well, guilty as charged. I had been an obese child and this caused me to experience rejection, isolation, and shame. Menopause brought me back into that fat body and all of the abandonment feelings that went with it. I didn't want to stay there.

Willpower had not failed me earlier when I'd wanted to lose a few pounds. In fact, in my forties I'd gone on a liquid diet for 365 days. I didn't chew for a whole year; the only kitchen appliance I used was a blender. This diet succeeded at making me rail thin, but it also drastically lowered my metabolism and raised my set point, forcing me to eat like a bird to maintain my figure.

Thanks to my year on the unhealthy liquid diet, when I returned to eating my appetite had become more like a truck driver's than a bird's. I couldn't always hold back—when I binged, I went whole hog and didn't care who saw me. I could have charged admission for the spectacle because I had no shame (except for the weight gain).

THE DANGERS OF DEPRIVATION

Why does the power struggle with food have to be so intense? And why does food so often win?

For me (and possibly for you), it has to do with *deprivation*. I'd been dieting all of my life to stay thin. Like novelist Helen Fielding's fictional character Bridget Jones, I've lost at least 1,000 pounds over my lifetime—

losing 10 to 15 pounds and gaining them back over and over again. When I'd learned about fear conditioning, I finally understood how dieting had turned me into an overeater. Here's my take on how it works:

Let's say your eating habits have at one time or another caused a problem; for instance, eating too much made you fat. During that time your mammalian brain forged an emotional connection between food and weight gain—and not a good one. The result is that when you get hungry, it triggers subliminal anxiety.

Taking it a step further, when you try to limit food and withstand hunger pangs, it sets off your body's innate fear of starvation; but when you consume food, it sets off your fear of losing your attractiveness, which in turn arouses your fear of abandonment. So your amygdala gets fear-conditioned to couple hunger with starvation and food with danger. The more you diet, the more complicated your relationship with food becomes.

The result is that you overreact to your own appetite. Instead of your appetite being a background feeling, one that allows you to delay gratification and take care of other issues at hand, for you a little hunger sets off starvation alarms and the specter of food glows in your mind in neon lights. This rivets your attention on all things related to food consumption— hunger pangs, the smell of food, stomach rumblings, and, of course, eating itself.

If you have a tendency to store fat, you're primed to react to food as a powerful substance, a seductive lover you adore but know can hurt you. The more delicious and irresistible the food, the more dangerous it seems and the more hypervigilant you become toward it.

On the other hand, if food has never done a bad thing to you—it never raised your cholesterol or made you fat—then your (lucky) emotional brain would *not* have a heightened response to it. When the amygdala is kept out of the loop, food is just food. Eating holds no special power over you. While it might be sustaining, sometimes pleasurable, and enhance social interactions, it remains part of life, not an addiction. You would eat until you feel satisfied and then turn your attention to other things. If you're one of those lucky people, it might be hard to imagine why anyone (me, for instance) would obsess about food, create elaborate fantasies about it, and go on restrictive diets.

For those of us who have been directly affected by food's power as a romance repellant, food indeed arouses the emotional brain, giving rise to Outer Child's food-seeking patterns. Furthermore, the anxiety around food triggers the chronic release of cortisol, a long-acting stress hormone known to enhance appetites, slow metabolism, and promote storage of visceral fat. That's the fat that attaches itself to our internal organs and increases our risk of heart disease and diabetes. Visceral fat has its own hormonal effect, which can cause a second cycle of weight gain. So getting all hopped up over food "feeds on itself" hormonally and traps us in a vicious cycle.

Depending on your fat-storage history, you can develop a love-hate reaction to food—similar to the reaction you might have to an old lover who left you. Despite what you know, you only want it (him) more. Desire and deprivation become intimately linked in the emotional brain—you *want* something you don't *want* to *want*. You'd think that something (or someone) that once hurt you would take on the aura of poisonous gas. Instead food and old flames become all the more desirable. Our approach-avoidance behaviors around food and lovers are prime examples of repetition compulsions. We keep setting ourselves up to feel needy and undesirable.

A HOUSE DIVIDED

Why do these patterns have such power over us? The metabolism can be slowed by neurobiological conditions. The neuronal circuits leading *from* the amygdala to the higher thinking centers of your brain are faster, thicker, and stronger than the circuits leading from thinking centers to your emotional brain. In other words, your higher brain takes orders from the amygdala, not the other way around (unless you use our special tools for overriding it). That's why people can recite a long list of reasons why they shouldn't smoke or drink or eat so much but do so all the same.

Dieting creates a state of chronic self-willed deprivation. Suppressing your food cravings turns you into a house divided against itself, increasing your desire for what you can't have. Dieting (enduring chronic, subliminal hunger pangs) plays with the on-off switch controlling your fear of starvation, which has a powerful pleasure-pain conditioning impact on the brain. Deprivation makes food ever more desirable, a principle that holds true for any other addiction. For example, alcohol addiction progresses during periods of abstinence; when alcoholics relapse, they drink more than ever before.

For people whose emotional brains have *not* been conditioned to react to food this way (imagine, there are naturally thin people who don't need to go on diets!)—a little food deprivation is no problem. Their bodies know they won't starve to death if they have to skip lunch occasionally.

In contrast, if you're an inveterate dieter, you feel subliminal anxiety if a sudden work emergency means you'll miss a meal. It triggers the primal fear of starvation, along with the stress hormone cortisol, which in turn lowers your metabolism and increases your appetite to protect you from losing your fat stores (heaven forbid). Your Outer Child acts out in response, by overeating.

Have we had enough of what brought us to this place? It's time to do something about it. When I started honing the Outer Child tools, my need to overcome my heightened amygdala-related response to food was one of my greatest incentives. The challenge required specialized tools but I finally had my hands on them and I put them to the test. And they worked! A variation of separation therapy I call "Radical Listening" helped me get on top of my love-hate affair with food. Let me show you how it can work for you.

FOCUS BEYOND FOOD

Radical Listening gets us to do something radically different. We're *not* going to try talking Outer Child out of food. Outer responds with extra force if we become too confrontational about its primary pleasure. Instead we're going to approach the problem indirectly, side-stepping Outer's resistance, to get to the source of the internal drives—the animal drives of appetite, tension reduction, and pleasure. It's a three-step process that starts with holding a clear mental image of how you'd like to look and feel. Next you'll use Radical Listening to delve into your Outer Child's food urges. The idea of deeply examining these urges may sound counterintuitive, but the truth is, the best way to deal with overeating is to become conscious of what you're up against. Finally, you'll take brief pleasurable action steps every day that bring you into the moment with conscious intention to reach your weight management and other goals.

Back to the beginning. The first step is to hone a vision of yourself as you would like to look and feel. This places your mental energy at the space *beyond* your stumbling blocks—a hallowed ground where Outer has no turf to dig in its heels. Like karate masters who break cinder blocks with their bare hands, you're going to focus your energy not on the cinder block itself, but on the space *beyond* the cinder block. This trajectory helps you *focus through* the barrier and arrive at that space of achievement—the new you.

So let's go for it. Use your imagination to create a vision of your future self as you would realistically like to be, imbued with all of the health, beauty, and well-being you desire. For added mental therapy, imagine feeling gratitude for the blessings this brings you, *as if* you already enjoy them. Keep this image in your mind's eye so that you can refer to it at every possible opportunity.

To increase your imagination's power, you can install this image of yourself in your Dream House, sitting before your dream view, enjoying your dream life. Weave this image of yourself into your conscious thoughts whenever possible. Imagine writing this new self into a better script for your life.

RADICAL LISTENING

The next step involves listening to your Outer Child's food behaviors in a way you've never listened to your thought processes before. It's a multilayered process involving careful and patient listening on your part. Along the way you'll be attending closely to:

> your food urges
> Outer Child's denials and rationalizations
> the reality facing you
> Outer Child's attempts to protest that reality
> the challenge before you

The idea is to give full vent to your Outer Child's food desires, allowing your hedonistic pleasures to express themselves freely and without shame. This allows you to zero in on the inner workings of the pleasure-pain conditioning that have led to Outer's food-seeking patterns. Through this process you transform what was automatic and unconscious into empowering adult awareness.

You must grant your Outer Child complete immunity to speak openly and confess all its dirty little food secrets, so that you can learn exactly what you're up against. One of the reasons diets fail is that people don't listen to how potent their food obsessions and compulsions truly are. They underestimate the strength of the beast they are fighting! Through Radical Listening you can tame this beast by recognizing it for what it truly is—a now fully exposed part of you just waiting to be redirected.

Ready? Get your Outer Child notebook, because you're going to start a food journal like no other food journal you've kept before. Keep a daily journal until things change. And they will.

YOUR FOOD URGES

Here's a sample journal entry from someone I'm close to who shall remain nameless. Never mind the suspiciously familiar writing style. She's sharing this in the hope that it will inspire you to be as honest about your own urges and feelings about food.

> Last night I learned that risotto is a dangerous food for me. I relished each bite and working the food's rich, gummy, crunchy textures and flavors into all the nooks and crannies of my mouth. I chewed and swallowed, chewed and swallowed, experiencing mouthful after mouthful of pleasure. I felt full and hungry-for-more all at the same time—such wonderfully opposing sensations! There was never a point at which I had enough—I just ate until the supply was finished.
>
> I can't imagine stopping myself in the middle of such sensual reverie—such ecstatic mastication. How could I turn away from anything that delicious? I wanted it to go on forever, forking in mouthfuls of pleasure, feeding the insatiable hunger.

The next day, she wrote another entry, which helped her uncover more layers of truth about her Outer Child's food tendencies.

> Why did I eat so much so fast? I realize I don't chew food thoroughly. I'd rather crunch it with my teeth just once so that the splash of flavors can shoot into my mouth and hit my tongue and I can taste it all the way up to my gums and the roof of my mouth. And then I swallow it quickly to make room for more. That's why I binged on that risotto. It didn't require a lot of chewing.
>
> I've learned to swallow huge bites. Chewing is just a way for me to release the flavors and to break the food down into small enough chunks to get it down my throat. I'm hopelessly in love

with chewing, tasting, swallowing, gulping, and feeling food go down.

The writer was initially shocked by what she wrote, but later accepted it as the simple truth: She had a gluttonous monster living within her whose food passions were ferocious enough to make her fat.

The kind of listening I'm talking about here fosters a profound level of consciousness. When Outer Child uses food as a source of immediate gratification, it encourages a loss of consciousness. You've no doubt noticed that having a full belly creates a drugged feeling and that obsessing about your next meal takes you out of the moment. Radical Listening restores this consciousness so you don't have to robotically succumb to your eating addiction. Zeroing in on your food urges takes you off automatic pilot.

To help you get started, you can use the questions below as prompts to get your Outer Child to open up a little more with each new journal entry. You can spend a day, a week, or a month exploring that question—or switch back and forth among them, depending upon new challenges you may face: holidays, buffets, and life-dilemmas for which food provides self-medication or a quick fix. You can subtitle your entries so you can reference them later on. They provide fascinating reading material as you work toward your goal.

I've provided sample responses from people in my workshops who were kind enough to share them. Please note that these folks give Outer the floor to describe the urge to overindulge without imposing judgment upon those urges. I hope these contributions encourage you to do the same. Breaking the shame barrier will set you free.

Does your Outer Child have Full Belly syndrome?
I love having a full belly. I love to eat until I have a stuffed feeling, until my stomach is stretched to the max. I like the feeling even when it's painful.

How does food feel in your digestive tract?
The whole thing from my mouth, down my throat, and into my stomach gives me tremendous pleasure! But it stops when the food hits my intestines. I'm not into that intestinal thing—it's a different body function. I like it coming in, but could care less about it going out, as long as it eventually does, to make more room in my stomach.

Does your Outer Child use food as a tranquilizer?
My life is stressful because I'm alone and don't like the way I look. That makes me isolate and overeat. My only pleasure is food. What a vicious cycle. Help!

How does your Outer Child react to hunger?
I don't like feeling hungry. When I stuff something in my mouth, it's my Outer Child trying to protect Little Me. Little hates feeling hungry and hates feeling fat and ugly! Those feelings are at war. They say "Feed me!" and "Don't eat!" at the same time. When I don't know what to do, Outer wins by eating. Right now, I am not even hungry, but I sense myself looking forward to getting hungry so that I can enjoy the next meal.

How does Outer react to hunger pangs? How do they make you feel?
Yesterday I felt myself losing weight. I had that hungry feeling where you can actually feel your body burning its own fat supply... But instead of letting it happen, I fed the feeling... I (Outer) spent the whole day popping food into my mouth. I told myself, "DON'T stuff the feeling," but I kept eating anyway because I didn't like the hungry feeling.

Why does your Outer Child keep eating even when you are full?
I'm never quenched by food, I'm inspired by it. Outer knows just how to egg me on: *"You don't have to deprive yourself now, Donnie, go ahead and have more. You can diet tomorrow. Eat now, weigh later." This is why I'm the size of a house and why I have no life.*

Radical Listening shows respect for Outer's food urges. It helps you accept Outer as a real presence within you—a part that must be unconditionally loved before it can be redirected toward healthier patterns. It brings you to a turning point in your life—the equivalent of Step 1 of Alcoholics Anonymous—by getting you to accept your *powerlessness* over your food urges. That said, remember that you are *not* powerless over your behavior, just over the fact that you have urges.

When it comes to any compulsion or addiction, denial is your enemy— honesty about those urges befriends you. Conversely addiction means lying to yourself. Radical Listening keeps you fully conscious, rigorously honest, and in a state of sublime acceptance.

As you're writing your food entries, you are likely to find Outer's rationalizations convoluted. So be it, and by the way, that's an excellent observation! By giving full vent to them, you have a chance to listen to them like never before and clearly see the challenges you face. Changing that behavior involves moving a muscle, even if the first muscle you move is your hand pushing the pen. Remember, making frequent food entries—at least daily—will give you the best results. Here are some more prompts to get the ink flowing:

How does Outer Child sabotage you with food?
I seem to break my diet at a moment's notice. My resolve is strong in the morning, but if you offer me cake at night, Outer says yes and the binge begins.

Are you in food denial? What lies does Outer tell you about food?
Outer tries to convince me that I can somehow lose weight without reducing portions. All I have to do is eat diet food—all I want of it—and still lose weight.

Does alcohol ever play a role when you overindulge?
I have to be careful of wine. One glass makes me want another, and then I forget all about my diet—it lowers my willpower and impairs my judgment, not to mention that booze is itself fattening.

What does it feel like when you break the overindulgence cycle?
I've had no bread since last Thursday and I finally stopped craving it.

How does Outer sabotage your diet?
I hate exercise so much that when I go to the gym, I manage to avoid pushing myself. I use the equipment just enough to say I've exercised. Big Sarah is trying to burn fat and my lovely Outer Child is trying twice as hard to preserve it.

IT'S A GIVEN

Listening to your rationalizations leads directly to facing reality. You discover the givens you are faced with. Once again, Alcoholics Anonymous Step 1 is in force: You are powerless over the intensity of your food urges. You are *not* powerless over your behavior. You can't stop your emotions or your food urges by willing them away. They are real, at least for now. Radical Listening allows you to own up to them, which positions you to dismantle their destructive power. The old way—trying to ignore, suppress, dismiss, or deny them—hasn't been effective. The new strategy—Radical Listening—gets you to see what you are truly up against so you can focus your energy on what you can control—your behavior. Let your responses to the questions below nudge your Adult Self to focus on changing things.

Is your addiction to food progressive?
I no longer stop when I'm full, I seem to have developed a separate bread stomach.

Which is really more important to you? Getting fit or enjoying the immediate gratification of food?
My Outer Child wants food more than I want a thin body. *"Okay, Sarah, it's time. I have been indulgent. I overeat. My hunger won't stop but you must. Eat slowly and take small bites. Swallow before cutting a new piece."*

What are the givens of your food urges?
I am clear: I am addicted to food and I am in denial most of the time, and I'm not ready to quit. Just hearing me write this makes me want to change.

Can you withstand the discomfort of sticking to a food plan?
The rewards will be to feel more comfortable in my own body, but I'm fighting it. I am determined to overcome Outer's sabotage!

What other needs is food a substitute for?
I started taking bowls of ice cream to bed for comfort after Sam died. Now I don't feel good enough about my expanding body to meet a new person. But when I deprive myself, that empty feeling reminds me of what Sam's death took from me.

LISTENING TO THE PROTEST

Most people try to protest their food urges, dismiss them, and talk themselves out of them. Protesting a reality doesn't change it. Radical Listening snaps you out of protest mode. You can't move things forward while you're still in protest.

Many people prefer to stay in denial rather than accept the givens of their situation. They try to change the unchangeable. Protesting reality only squanders precious time and energy. Railing against the unchangeable is just spinning your wheels—you don't gain any traction. On the other hand listening to your protest makes you conscious of a background noise—the sound of you banging your head against that wall of protest. You gain radical acceptance, the kind of acceptance expressed in the serenity prayer from Alcoholics Anonymous. You learn to accept the things you can't change and focus your energy on changing the things you can. When you finally accept the unchangeable, you arrive at the fulcrum of change.

Once you come out of food protest, you're primed to deal with the realities facing you. These realities include your own unique metabolic issues and food proclivities—the way you've been conditioned to respond to food. By accepting *what is,* you're empowered to take it from there. Use the questions below to encourage Adult resolve:

What are your givens?
In order to overcome, I must face that I have a broken appetite shut-off valve. I can't stay in denial about it, or food will win.

What would happen if you stopped protesting and accepted the challenge?
I become more ravenous the more I eat. Okay, so now that I've taken that into account, now what? Before taking the first bite, I must remind myself: "This food will make me hungry." I have to prepare myself for it. Then I need to eat it slowly and experience the food as a quality thing rather than a quantity thing. Yes, I can picture myself doing that, me, Donnie, a thinner version of myself.

Why do you fight the solution? What can you do about it?
I know that my overeating is not about hunger. Yes, I eat way too much when I'm hungry and I eat to avoid hunger, also. Hunger is a given. The solution? Welcome hunger. Hunger means my body machine is burning calories. I must welcome hunger.

I would have to tell myself BEFORE sitting down to eat that I will limit my portions for this meal. Only an overlarge portion will make me feel "full." So during this meal, "full" is not my goal. I must set my sights not on "full," but on enjoying the eating experience. I must be willing to walk away still hungry. It might take an hour or more for the hunger to dissipate, but the feeling will eventually go away. It won't be easy, but if I don't accept the challenge, I could become one of those people who have to be moved with a derrick. I'm holding a picture of a thinner Donnie in my mind.

Food fulfills the desire to feel connected. I have to find ways to nurture my emotional hunger that won't make me fat, like joining new activities or meeting new people. This is my challenge and my goal.

As you face your givens and resolve to take action, you see how transformative Radical Listening can be. Remember, no one ever has to see your Outer Child notebook. In complete privacy, tune in and listen to the rationalizations that correspond to your overeating. By writing, you discover sensations, desires, and beliefs you were barely conscious of. You have a relationship with food and being rigorously honest finally gives you a clue about that relationship. The self-disclosure is cleansing, healing, and motivating.

Additional prompts to guide you through the Radical Listening process:

Prompts for Outer Child

- Outer, as you tune in to the sensations of your mouth and gut, what are your guilty pleasures about food?
- Outer, when you start eating, why don't you want to stop?
- Outer, what is your favorite part of eating? Chewing? Holding the food in your mouth? Swallowing? Describe.
- Outer, do you like to eat slow or fast? Why? Describe the sensations.
- Outer, which do you enjoy the most—chewing or swallowing? Describe.
- Outer, do you like to chew food thoroughly or partially? What kinds of pleasure does chewing bring? Where do you feel the pleasure? In your mouth, tongue, throat going down, belly? Describe.
- Outer, do you like the feeling of digesting food? Describe.
- Outer, how do you react to hunger pangs?
- Outer, how do you use food to cope with uncomfortable feelings? Describe.

- Outer, can you feel your body trying to burn calories? Do you eat something to get rid of the feeling? Describe.
- Outer, do you get antsy when you start to lose weight? Do you eat more to stop burning fat? Describe.

Prompts for your Adult Self

- Adult Self, does overindulging harm your relationship with yourself? Explain.
- Adult Self, if food is a substitute for a deeper pleasure you want, describe what you believe you really want underneath the food.
- Adult Self, does overeating make your Inner Child feel abandoned all over again? Explain.
- Adult Self, what can you do differently with regard to your eating habits to improve your life?

After a month or so of writing your food entries, you will discover it's nearly impossible to return to your former state of unconsciousness. Even if you were to succumb to another binge, you would remain more aware of your actions. Of course, if you were to keep bingeing you would eventually lose consciousness once again and go back on automatic food-pilot. But you can use Radical Listening as a power-lift tool to get back on track.

OPENING A DIALOGUE

So far in this chapter we've kept your Inner Child out of earshot because Little feels helpless and scared when it hears how tenacious Outer's overeating tendencies are. But now it's time to use a dialogue exercise to respond to Little's feelings—the ones underlying Outer's binges.

The dialogues you've written in previous chapters have increased your empathy and compassion for your Inner Child. Through Radical Listening, you've gained some empathy for Outer's food urges as well. As leader of the team, you must be in empathy with all the members to be able to integrate your approach. The leader must pay special attention to the member least capable of acting on its own behalf. In the construction of your psyche, this helpless part is, of course, your Inner Child. So your Adult Self must act as your Inner Child's advocate and protector.

When your Adult Self gets your Inner Child to open up, you zero in on the source of Outer's food habits— -your long-frustrated emotional needs. It's not really cake your Inner Child is after. Cake is a meager substitute for what Little really wants: the pleasure and tension-reduction that come from more basic things, like love, comfort, and security. Your Adult Self is going to check in with Little You to establish what, beyond food, can emotionally satisfy you. This takes Outer Child out of the loop.

Here is a sample from Sarah's first dialogue:

LITTLE: I hate to be fat. I want to be beautiful again, Big. I'd have a really beautiful body thin. I'd feel powerful thin. I feel really bad fat. Really bad. Really really bad.

BIG: I know you do and I want to help you. There's a part of me (Oh, hello, Outer) that loves to stuff herself, Little. But I'm getting stronger. I'm working on getting beautiful.

LITTLE: You always say you'll fix it, and then you let Outer eat too much. I feel sad because I want a boyfriend and nobody likes me.

BIG: I'm going to do a dialogue with you every day to help me stop overeating.

LITTLE: But when you go on a diet, it just makes me scared because you always let Outer break it.

BIG: You can tell me your feelings every day. It will make me stronger.

LITTLE: It won't help. I'm hungry all the time. I feel so helpless. I want to look beautiful like I used to.

BIG: Today I'll do something different, Little. At dinner I'll walk away from the table before I'm full. I'm going to eat to eat, not to get full. Maybe you won't feel so helpless tomorrow. In fact, I'm going to make it my action step for the day.

LITTLE: You'll just break the diet again.

BIG: Not if we stay in touch with each other every day and you tell me how you feel about it. I'm going to do something every day to make a change.

Through writing the dialogue your Adult Self gets stronger and more able to balance Inner Child's desires with Outer Child's tendency to grab for the solution at hand (food). It becomes crystal clear that Little wants pleasure, but the more Outer eats, the less pleasure Little gets, at least of the kind she really wants. You realize how negligent your Adult Self has been in the past and what your stronger Adult Self must do to set it right. Here's how Donnie described the process:

> In my dialogue, Little Me spewed anger at Big Me for getting so huge. I realized I was listening to my own self-hatred. It was real. It made me really conscious of what I was doing to myself. Beyond the anger there was fear. Little told me he didn't want us to die early. He wanted us to be healthy.

Here's Sarah after a month of dialoguing:

> When I dialogue, Little Me lets me know how frantic she is. She wants to look great. I'd been pushing it down for so long—her desires to be beautiful and her feeling bad about herself—stuffing it down. No more. I've become too conscious of it. Getting in touch keeps me on track. I'm really losing weight.

Writing the dialogue helps you resolve a conflict between two things: Little's urgent need to feel pleasure and Outer's penchant to use food to gratify it. Practicing helps you reach to a higher self, who can get you out of this double bind.

Higher selves often seek higher powers. You might consider reaching out to weight-management experts, spiritual leaders, wellness programs, Overeaters Anonymous, therapists, weight-loss doctors, nutritionists, Outer Child workshops, fitness literature, life coaches, sponsors, and friends to support your journey. Your stronger Adult Self needs to adopt the motto If It's Going to Help, *Get* Help. A word of warning: You'll probably have to stand up to Outer—you know how much Outer hates to ask for help.

TURN AROUND AGAIN

In a three-way dialogue, you can interact with Outer directly. First envision your Outer Child turning around to face Inner so that Outer can hear exactly what Inner is feeling. Just make sure Big stands protectively by your Inner Child's side.

The individual writing the dialogue (your higher self) knows that Little craves pleasure, but the pleasure isn't about food. Little wants deep pleasure, the pleasure that comes from feeling more healthy or desirable—things for which food is merely a quick fix. So Little begins with:

> LITTLE: You make me fat, Outer. Stay away, I hate you.
>
> OUTER: But when you feel empty and hungry I want to do something about it, so I eat. I'm only doing what you want.
>
> LITTLE: I want Big to help me, not you.
>
> BIG (to Outer): It's my responsibility to deal with Little's needs, not yours, Outer. You can let go. I'll find other more constructive things for you to do.

Here are a few workshop members describing their Turn Around dialogues:

> I told Outer that all he had to do was step aside *[turn around]* when I asked, so that Little could tell us both what he wants. I promised to do things every day to improve Outer's life and keep him distracted from food cravings. Outer needed to hear that food isn't the only pleasure out there.

> When Outer pitches one of his rationalizations, my Inner Child gets agitated. Outer wants to eat now and diet tomorrow. Little gets upset by how manipulative Outer is, afraid Outer will win again. Sometimes Outer does win, and I have hell to pay when I write the next dialogue with Little. If Little's rage about being betrayed doesn't motivate me, nothing will. Actually, it DOES motivate me. I'm doing better than ever before.

> When my Inner Child senses that my Outer Child is about to overeat, she starts tugging at me. She wants Big Sarah to be strong and stick to the diet—to free her from the bondage of fat.

DAILY ACTION STEPS

As the individual speaking for the three voices of your psyche, you become acutely conscious of the intensity of your internal struggle over food and motivated to transform the image you hold of yourself into reality. Your next task is to follow through with action steps.

Every day commit to an action, even if for only five minutes, that brings you into the moment. Taking an action means moving your muscles. Hold a mental vision of yourself as you would ideally like to be so that when you take the action, you do so with *conscious intention* to nurture your emotional needs and reach your goals. This gives Little, who desperately wants to be healthy and trim, a lever of control. When Little feels hopeful instead of helpless, Outer's impulse to overeat is dampened. Notice I said "dampened," not extinguished. Remember, you are dealing with behavior patterns that are embedded in the conditioning of your mammalian brain.

The actions you choose can be as simple as promising Little that tonight you will revisit him in your food journal, or you will attend a weight management meeting fully attentive and conscious, or you will take a walk and take in the sensations of the moment, or you will roast vegetables with only a drop of oil or salt and eat them slowly and consciously, or you will go to the bookstore and seek a diet or nutrition book to increase your consciousness about what food choices to make.

Your daily actions do not always need to be directly related to getting fit. You might choose an action entirely unrelated, like taking a drive along a beautiful back road to tune in to the season. As long as your conscious intention is to lose weight and your imagination remains focused on the space beyond the cinder block (your future image of yourself), rest assured that as you take your drive, your brain will actively work toward your goal.

Every day commit to an action, however small, that reassures Little You that you are attending to its desires to be fit, healthy, and beautiful. These brief pleasurable actions channel Outer's energy constructively.

To make substantial changes, you need to perform these exercises daily for about three months. The Outer Child program is a layered approach to recovery. Stay focused on your Future Vision. Use separation therapy to personify the working parts of the personality to manage the dynamics of your psyche. Radically listen to your Outer Child's food urges. Radically listen to your Inner Child's deepest desires—the ones underlying the food urges. And follow through with brief, pleasurable action steps that bring you into the moment with the conscious intention to incrementally reach your goal.

I can personally attest that the Outer Child tools are the fastest and most effective approach to modifying old stimulus-response conditioning and stimulating the basal ganglia's and limbic system's capacity to learn new behaviors. Outer, who springs from subcortical regions in your brain, is a sly fox when it comes to food. Outer is a master rationalizer, a force to be reckoned with. So you must deal with it strategically, compassionately, and systematically through an ever more powerful Adult Self. Incrementally, you recondition your brain and inculcate healthy new automatic behaviors.

As you move your muscles with conscious intention, you exercise the master muscle of your mind, strengthening the circuits of higher brain centers; you reduce your amygdala's heightened response to food; you nurture your Inner Child; you tame your Outer Child and you reach to your higher self to achieve your goals.

From here on in, you will use all three prongs of the program—separation therapy, visualization, and action steps—to tackle your issues one by one.

TEN

Outer Child and Procrastination

Procrastination is the most pervasive and insidious stumbling block to success. Just when you're all fired up to take action steps toward your goals, Outer Child tries to pull its favorite ploy: procrastination. In fact, one of Outer's most energetic pastimes is "not doing." Some voices from my workshops bear this out:

> I could win a procrastination contest. Just give me a task and I will find a way to put it off. I had a paper to finish over the weekend but instead of writing it, I embarked on cleaning my apartment, which I'd put off for over six months.

> I'm a hoarder. I procrastinate about throwing stuff out. I spend my whole life dealing with clutter. I never invite people over for dinner even if I've been a guest at their homes a dozen times. I can't let anyone see my squalor, so I concoct elaborate excuses about why we always go to THEIR place. When I finally reciprocate, I invent pretences about why I'm treating them at a restaurant, which they

know I really can't afford. After the charade, I go home and climb over stacks of stuff and swing from chandeliers to get to my bed.

Overdue deadlines pull us backward, entangling us in the past. According to motivational speaker Wayne Dyer, procrastination is "the art of keeping up with yesterday and avoiding today."

Everybody procrastinates about something. Even task-focused people admit that in spite of the things they regularly *do* accomplish, there are important things they neglect. They have a sound financial life, but procrastinate about starting a weight-loss program. They're rock stars at work, but have been meaning to write an online dating profile for a year.

One of Outer's favorite ploys is to bury its head in the sand. Picture a giant python slowly slithering toward you. Your solution? Stick your head in a hole instead of hightailing it out of there.

My best friends moved away. Bottom line, I needed to make new friends. But instead of reaching out, I threw myself into my job. I had a two-week vacation coming up and no one to go anywhere with. The sense of loneliness almost killed me. How had I let myself get so isolated? It's not like I didn't see it coming.

I hang around watching TV while my to-do list gets longer and more nightmarish.

Burying your head is an imaginative coping strategy, just not a productive one. You *imagine* that if you ignore something unpleasant, it will go away. Acting like an ostrich is Outer Child's shortsighted idea of stress reduction, but as the problem grows, your stress only *increases*. A dirty diaper needs changing, not ignoring.

THE SAME OLD GAME

I believe that procrastination is an adult form of peekaboo, that game we learned at our mother's knee. As newborns, when Mommy walked away from the crib, we panicked. To our infant brains a mommy we couldn't sense was a mommy who had ceased to exist. She had to be standing by the crib for us to know that our source of survival was ensured. Mothers help their children manage these primal abandonment fears by teaching them to play peekaboo. Your own mother probably did this instinctively: She smiled playfully as she disappeared and then reappeared behind her hands. At first your laugher may have been nervous, but as you got the hang of it, those were big belly laughs of relief over the fact that Mommy always came back again! *Ha-ha-ha.* You learned to make her go away again by covering your own eyes, and then when you couldn't stand it one more second, *pop,* you made her come back again. Hilarious! Through this game you were able to manage your primal fear. You gained a lever of control by making Mommy disappear and reappear at will.

Soon you played peekaboo with other things. You threw toys out of the playpen and retrieved them again (or had Mommy retrieve them for you). You shut the world out by hiding under the blanket and then pulled it off to make the world come back. You cranked the jack-in-the-box. Where is Jack? Oops! He was here before, but now you can't see him! *Pop!* Oh, *there* he is!

When you learned to walk, you ventured away from Mommy's lap into different rooms. Then you came right back to make sure she was where you left her. These playful repetition compulsions helped you inculcate the message that Mommy was a retrievable source of nurture. This strengthened networks in the developing brain that coordinate emotional, behavioral, and cognitive activities.

As you grew a little older, what if there was something in the outside world you didn't want to see, like a dead squirrel? You learned you could play peekaboo in reverse; you could make it go away by tuning it out. Could you make other unpleasant things go away by blocking them out? What if you had a difficult homework assignment? Could you make it go away by simply not doing it?

As you continued developing, you learned to play peekaboo in other situations. Through trial and error, you learned what you could get away with. In adulthood, what if the boss treats you unfairly? Can you make the conflict go away by avoiding it?

People who harbor a lot of negative feelings about themselves tend to avoid their responsibilities and become inured to extremely negative consequences. Things have to reach catastrophic proportions before they are "forced" to finally do something about it. They avoid a weight problem for decades until finally the doctor says, "Lose weight, or die."

Making believe things will go away if you simply avoid, ignore, or hide from them involves an automatic, unconscious use of your imagination. In other words, it's done without well-thought-out conscious intention. Denial involves using your imagination to suspend rational judgment, pretend the problem isn't there, and fool yourself. The Outer Child exercises throughout the book help you use your imagination more consciously to intentionally target your goals. With these tools, you no longer need to play unconscious games of peekaboo with your life.

CAN'T SOMEONE ELSE TAKE CARE OF THAT?

The more we observe children, the more we learn about procrastination.

They can leave toys on the floor when they lose interest in a game, throw a tantrum, and generally act out—leaving their parents to deal with the consequences. They don't have to take care of things. They can let things fall where they may because they know it will be taken care of *for* them.

Does that sound familiar? Have you ever avoided a necessary task because you assumed things would get taken care of...somehow? Rather than take action, have you ever opted to suffer the consequences of not doing anything and been surprised by the big mess, embarrassment, or inconvenience that resulted? Dylan, a workshop attendee, describes his predicament:

> My school district told us teachers that we had two years to comply with new state education requirements for certification, and I put off completing the papers until the last minute. When I finally did them, it was too late! I lost my certification and my job! How could I have been so negligent?

How does a rational adult justify avoiding important responsibilities that have inevitable consequences?

We developed a desire to take care of things for ourselves at the age of autonomy—during the terrible twos. To assert our separateness from our parents' control, we said, *"No!"* to just about everything. *"Honey, would you like to get up from your nap?"* "No." *"Would you like to stay in your crib?"* "No." *"Would you like to go to Grandma's?"* "No."

Into adulthood, your Outer Child can use these learned oppositional tendencies to self-sabotage through procrastination. Procrastination combines the autonomous obstinacy of a two-year-old with the passive idea that someone else can take care of things. *"I've got to work on those taxes,"* thinks your Adult Self; *"Not yet!"* says Outer Child.

What a combination! Outer asserts its will by not doing and unconsciously assumes things will get taken care of…somehow.

OUTER CHILD THE PERFECTIONIST

When it comes to procrastination, Outer Child can be a perfectionist. You don't act because you're waiting for perfect conditions. You want to do it perfectly or not at all. Nothing meets your standards of perfection, so you postpone things indefinitely.

> I needed business cards. I was doing a lot of networking, but when people asked me for my card, I had nothing to give them. As an artistic person, I couldn't hand out just ANY card. It had to have just the right esthetic and message to properly represent my unique style. No card ever fit that bill, so I never got one.

Procrastination is a primitive way to ward off discomfort, no matter how sophisticated its embellishments:

> I procrastinate by sipping an exquisite glass of wine and reading something of high literary value, trying to feel virtuous when I should be looking for a job.

NO ONE CAN SEE ME

Procrastination can sometimes stem from a tacit belief that if no one can see what you're doing (or not doing), then it's not real. This belief developed in early childhood when you were able to sit with your back turned to your parents and do something naughty—something you thought you weren't supposed to do (like play with your diaper or scribble on the wall)—and think you were getting away with it. You couldn't see your parents watching you because your back was turned, so you imagined your parents couldn't see you either. Your brain had not yet developed the ability to realize that the outside world continued to exist even if you couldn't see it. In deconstructing people's procrastination I've learned that they often hold on to this primitive belief: that we can make a particular reality cease to exist by not looking at it. It's another example of peekaboo in reverse.

> I stuck to my diet all day, but alone at night when no one was watching, I tripled the portions.

COMPELLED TO DO NOTHING

Procrastination in the extreme is a symptom of obsessive compulsive disorder (OCD). Many people think of OCD as compulsively washing your hands until they bleed or checking dozens of times before leaving the house that the oven has been turned off. But some people's compulsion is expressed through the *inhibition* of action.

> I found a woman's wallet on the road, filled with credit cards, money, all sorts of important things—and it had her name, address, and phone number. I couldn't wait to call her. I just knew how heartened she would feel to find out that there were honest people left in the world. But my OCD kicked in and I kept NOT calling her. I'd never think of spending a penny of this woman's money, but I just couldn't make myself call her. It wasn't about feeling afraid of her reaction or anything. It was just something I badly wanted to do and the OCD wouldn't let me do it. My therapist said, "If you can't call her, mail it," but I couldn't force myself to do that either. I obsessed about this for weeks, felt sick over it, wanted to send it, but never did.

Procrastination—whether occasional, chronic, or severe—is partially mediated by a chemical in the brain called "dopamine." Dopamine is involved in your reward/addiction system and very relevant to our work here. In laboratories, depending upon whether researchers turn the gene for dopamine receptors *on* or *off,* monkeys either lazily put off a task or work at it nonstop. The Outer Child program uses your imagination to override the glitches in your wiring, providing incentives and rewards to enhance dopamine so that your new habits will be positive ones.

PROCRASTINATORS HAVE FEELINGS

Procrastinators are engaged in repetition compulsions where they abandon themselves over and over by not taking care of their needs. As this would suggest, procrastinators have important but neglected feelings.

How does it make Inner Child feel when you procrastinate? Dialogues with Little provide the answer.

My Inner Child hates it when messes pile up. She gets mad at me for making her feel ashamed.

Little gets anxious when things have to get done, knowing I'm probably going to let it go and get in trouble.

In radically listening to their Inner Child, workshop members were able to see their patterns:

I get a lot done on a daily basis, but there are certain things I keep putting off, like phone calls I should be making to promote my business. The contacts I avoid are the people I think are somehow better than me, like extremely successful or extremely confident people—people who could potentially make me feel less-than. It's all about Little Me—the feelings going on inside me. These feelings are blocking me, but I've been avoiding feeling them by avoiding the phone calls.

I'm only motivated to do things when I'm with other people. Completely alone, I just laze around waiting for someone to do something with me. Otherwise, I "don't do." Loneliness blocks me from getting anything done.

I resent having no one to take care of me, so I waste a lot of energy NOT taking care of things. I didn't get around to renewing my car registration, so when I parked it in the city, they impounded it. It took days of wrangling and tons of money to get it back.

In the last chapter you may have faced some of your own procrastination as you began applying the Outer Child program to your diet. Maybe you put off joining a health club or have yet to start a new healthy-eating plan. The chapter discussed in depth a method for taking charge of overeating, but it's all just words unless you follow through. If you procrastinate and do nothing, your body won't change.

To improve your love life, waistline, career, living environment, bank account, or self-image, you need to change behavior. If you lead your life exactly the way you did before, things will stay the same, unless manna falls from heaven or you win the Powerball. If you don't want to leave your fortune to chance, you must follow through, and the first thing you come up against is procrastination.

So let's use the three prongs of the Outer Child program—dialogues, visualization, action steps—to dismantle it. First, the dialogues. Where there is procrastination, there is a frustrated, helpless, neglected, abandoned Inner Child waiting for your compassionate attention.

Joyce, an attorney and chronic procrastinator, exhibited the full complement of its symptoms, including the tendency to:

- avoid acting on her good intentions
- invest her time in menial tasks
- downplay her true abilities
- manage her time poorly (chronically late)
- accumulate overdue tasks that keep her stuck in the past

Like most chronic procrastinators, Joyce has low self-esteem, poor self-control, low self-confidence, and she's also a perfectionist.

Joyce's close friend Doug—a fellow attorney—had given her referrals from his overflowing law practice. But after collecting people's retainers, their cases remained untouched on her desk. She was wracked with guilt and exasperated with her own inertia. To get herself going, she asked Little how she felt about it.

LITTLE JOYCE: When everything gets backed up it makes me so upset.

BIG JOYCE: I know, Little. The longer I wait to call people back, the madder they get, and the more upset *you* get. I'm going to change that.

LITTLE JOYCE: I want to feel peaceful. You always give in to Outer and play Sudoku and knit afghans and take naps. If you cared about me, you'd get things done so I wouldn't feel so bad.

BIG JOYCE: Little, I want you to feel better. We have done a lot of dawdling.

LITTLE JOYCE: If you'd get things done, I wouldn't worry. I want to be free.

BIG JOYCE: To help you feel free, let's get some ocean air. We'll go to the beach this afternoon.

LITTLE JOYCE: But I won't enjoy it because there's still too much to do. I won't feel relaxed. I hate you for that.

BIG JOYCE: Okay, then I will call at least one client before we go. And another tomorrow…until I catch up, and then we'll go to the beach and relax.

LITTLE JOYCE: You said that before and you let Outer goof off again.

BIG JOYCE: Then I'll have to show you.

That day, she called one of her clients and felt better, so she called two more, then packed for the beach—it was a start. Joyce committed herself to ongoing dialogues until things changed. She recognized that she would need some help, so at first she hired a "coach" to sit with her and goad her into writing them. In fact, calling that coach was one of her first action steps.

Now it's your turn. Get your Outer Child notebook and open a dialogue with Little You. How does Little feel when you put things off?

PICTURE LIVING THAT LIFE

The Outer Child exercises help you overcome two levels of procrastination. One involves in-your-face issues like *not* doing your taxes, *not* cleaning your house, *not* returning a library book, *not* getting your license renewed, *not* going to the gym—the *overt* procrastinations that nag at you and make Little You feel guilty and anxious. The other level involves things you don't realize you're procrastinating about, the things you avoid *thinking* about—perhaps an abandoned goal or dream.

Consider one of your dreams. Have you scaled down your goals to avoid disappointment? Which ones have you avoided thinking about because you feel their time has expired? Give yourself permission to conjure up an abandoned dream—even if it seems out of reach—so you can use it to expand your Future Vision. Can you think of one? Guess who would know if you can't? Little You. Little has been waiting a long time for you to ask about it. (Outer has been busy keeping you distracted.) Deborah, a former client, had always wanted to be a veterinarian:

> I got married and other things came up and going to vet school went on the back burner. Then I had to earn a living so I became a real-estate agent. I loved caring for animals, so I had a dog and a cat and went horseback riding at a friend's stable whenever she invited me. But my life felt bumpy and I wasn't sure why my energy was always so low.
>
> Big Me tried to get Little Me to talk about what the problem was, but Little wouldn't say much. Then, when Big asked just the right question, Little finally admitted she was only really happy when she was with the horses. This wasn't a shock, but I had no way of doing anything about it at the time, so I just listened and told her I understood and left it at that. It felt good at least to acknowledge an unlived life that had been silently haunting me.
>
> Then a few days later I asked Little if she was mad at me about it and she said yes, and out came a stream of accusations. She said I let Outer Child sit around and watch TV instead of doing important things.
>
> The dialoguing helped me see that I wasn't living my dream. Little wouldn't let go of what she wanted. She had become fierce on the subject. In responding to Little, I began to take actions to change things.

Maybe your dream is to write a book, start your own business, improve your social life, or live in a foreign country. Consider what you do in your current life to avoid living that dream. What are you doing instead of writing that book or learning a second language? Ask yourself if the lifestyle you currently live is one you would have designed intentionally. Or did it just fall into place through a serious of defaults, happenstances, expediencies, necessities, and old habits? Rebecca shares her story:

> I have a personal shopping–errand business. Some of my clients were taking outrageous advantage of me, expecting me to do all of these extra things for nothing. They were running me ragged. If only I felt as entitled to my time as they did. I grumbled under my

breath a lot, but I didn't say "*No!*" to their demands. Somewhere in the back of my mind, I knew I was being remiss about something. I knew I needed to expand my vision. Then, just to comply with a workshop assignment, I asked Little Me what she'd like to be doing if we weren't always running all over kingdom come for other people. Little said she wanted to feel close to Antonia (my daughter) and her baby. She reminded me that we hardly ever see her.

I was really surprised that Little Me wanted to get close to my daughter. It hadn't occurred to me that all of the running I was doing was a way to avoid her. Our personalities always clashed; and there'd been major battles in her teens. Now she was a single parent, working odd jobs, and only nice to me when she needed a handout. I picked up her son from his nursery every Wednesday to help out, so I got to see him—but not her.

Staying busy distracted me from feeling the growing distance between us. It had been easier taking orders from strangers—my clients—than dealing with my daughter's "tude" toward me.

The dialogue got me to tune in to how I wanted to connect with her and how helpless I felt about it. Outer had been mindlessly running around for my clients, and now I needed to free up time to reestablish our relationship. It meant I had to say no to my clients. Wanting time for Antonia gave me the incentive to make my own life come first.

Is it possible that you unknowingly set up your current life to distract you from working on your personal issues and goals? Does your Outer Child use procrastination to block you from fulfilling your greatest desires? Why let Outer Child defeat you? Now that you have tools to change things incrementally, all excuses have expired. Deborah's experience:

I started visualizing. I created a Future Vision of myself on a big piece of property, caring for a whole variety of animals, riding horses, feeling connected. In my real life, my daily activities began with baby steps, like volunteering on Saturdays at an animal shelter. Then one day I drove to a horse ranch after work, and on another, I inquired about costs of renting stables. These were things I could have been doing all along, but I'd been too busy and too unconscious to get the ball rolling.

STEPS TOWARD SELF-DISCIPLINE

Remember Dylan, who let his teaching license lapse?

> Little was so mad at me for losing my job, there was no making it up to him except to get another job, but no one was hiring. I'd curled into a ball of depression and self-loathing. I knew I had to get out of that hole, so I signed up for an Outer Child workshop.
>
> I hated what my Outer Child had done—I'd lost my job! I learned how to radically listen to Outer's procrastination and give myself (my Inner Child) unconditional love—at least while I was writing a dialogue. I learned new things about myself I didn't know before, like that I didn't feel important enough to take better care of myself.
>
> I started doing small things to try to break the mold. Those small things became big things. They added up to a new teaching job—not the perfect job, but something that positioned me to restart my career. Most importantly, I became more self-disciplined. I knew my pattern and what was behind it and how to get past it. Putting it all on paper made me so conscious of it, I did what I had to do.

How wonderfully put. After all, what is self-discipline but the act of taking conscious control of your mind?

What role does procrastination play in your own life? What internal resistance do you face? What productive activities could you add to your life—activities aimed at achieving your goals? How might you eliminate less productive activities—activities that spin your wheels? When in doubt, radically listen to your Inner Child to dig down and get at the emotional truth.

You are not going to defeat Outer Child's tendency to procrastinate by snapping your fingers and bidding it good riddance. You will defeat procrastination only by staying focused on your goals, making a deeper personal connection, and taking baby steps that eventually overtake your self-defeating behaviors.

Outer Child likes things the way they are. To the extent that your current life affords immediate gratifications (like having a six-pack of beer or a shopping spree at the mall), Outer will balk at change. This is why this program is designed to be practical and realistic. Baby steps are realistic. Baby steps are practical. Baby steps get the job done. No magical thinking here. Just easy to accomplish, painless actions that when taken with conscious intention, work incrementally and inevitably to achieve far-reaching goals.

As realistic and practical as the Outer Child program is, it doesn't skimp on substance, because the impetus and drive required for such momentous change comes from tapping into your primal feelings and core needs.

False promises about instant remedies sound good on paper, but in practice only increase self-disillusionment, self-disappointment, and self-blame when you fall back into old patterns of procrastination. I encourage you to stay focused on your goals—large-scale visions of change—but know that the road to success involves not a magic carpet, but action steps—incremental, forward-moving actions.

So get confident. You can change. The broken record in me is here to remind you that change involves more than thought, it involves behavior. And behavior involves first moving your mental muscles, then writing muscles, then your whole physical self forward.

Just remember:

1) **Keep holding your Future Vision in your mind.** Make this image a mental refuge of peace, calm, beauty, and forward motion.

2) **You're a work in progress.** With each baby step you take toward your goals, consider yourself in *process*; you're growing.

3) **Stop and smell the roses.** Take in this moment; find the joy in each forward step. Reward yourself with the knowledge that you're moving in the right direction.

4) **It's Outer Child's mess.** Continue attributing your resistance to your Outer Child to prevent self-anger and self-hatred from infiltrating your newly emerging, still fragile sense of self. Just blame your old habits on Outer and then work to improve your love relationship with yourself. You need a tight coalition between Big You and Little You to keep Outer constructively occupied.

5) **Your Adult Self is in charge.** When you take a baby step, take it as your *volitional* self—your higher Self. A stronger Adult Self is able to make peace with your Outer Child and use its energy to get your life in order.

ELEVEN

Outer Child and Love Relationships

In this chapter we apply the Outer Child program to issues that may be interfering in your love life. You may be alone and feeling concerned that you'll never find a relationship. Or perhaps you're mired in a relationship that just isn't working. Or you're part of a couple but feel a lack of passion toward your partner. Or you love someone who doesn't love you back. Or you keep going through cycles of breakups and can't seem to get a relationship to last. Whatever has been getting in the way, there's a good chance Outer Child is at the bottom of it. Dealing with this hidden culprit helps you break through your most difficult, persistent love barriers.

Outer's bungling defensive maneuvers are at their most disruptive when it comes to intimate relationships. Stealthy and quick, Outer intercepts love before you realize what happened. In fact, the struggle for satisfying relationships is so fraught with Outer Child interference, we'll be exploring the antidote for the next several chapters.

As you may have noticed, Outer's love patterns are extremely resistant to conventional psychotherapy and defy the dictates of your conscious will. This is because they are implanted in your limbic brain wiring. Seemingly insignificant events can trigger instant stimulus-response networks of conditioned Outer Child behaviors. Case in point: Your partner makes an offhand remark and you cop an attitude you can't shake, ruining an otherwise pleasant evening.

THE EMOTIONAL PENDULUM

One of the reasons Outer Child runs rampant over your conscious will has to do with a mechanism that governs our attachments—an emotional pendulum that swings between *fear of abandonment* and *fear of engulfment*. For many people this pendulum doesn't rest in the middle long enough for them to establish ongoing healthy attachments; instead they swing back and forth from one extreme to the other.

As discussed earlier, *fear of abandonment* is fear of someone withdrawing love and support from you. Outer's most deeply ingrained defenses are the ones that try to defend against this primal fear. Prominent among Outer's maneuvers are avoidance and projection: You *avoid* intimacy to avoid the risk of rejection. Or you *project* your needs into the relationship and make more emotional demands than your partner can handle.

Fear of engulfment occurs when someone's desire for you makes you feel trapped. As you grow emotionally closer, you start feeling responsible for her needs and lose your romantic feelings toward her. You feel engulfed— threatened, lest your autonomy be taken away. You fear you'll have to abandon yourself.

Both fears can drive us into isolation. In fact, fear of engulfment is merely the flip side of fear of abandonment. That's why most people experience each of them at one time or another. Think about it. Has someone's keen interest in you ever made you feel smothered? Or on the flip side, when someone you like fails to return your kiss, does it send you into a tailspin? If your emotional pendulum swings wildly between those fears, you are probably seeing evidence of unresolved abandonment. Unresolved feelings from earlier losses, disconnections, and disappointments tend to accumulate and make you more prone to abandonment fear.

Fear itself is not the problem—we are emotionally conditioned to feel that. It's the primitive patterns of avoidance and projection that create the problem. When Outer Child erects defenses against your fear, it undermines your ability to form stable, mutual relationships. Over the next few chapters I'll show you how to take the reins away from this mammal-self—your reactionary Outer Child—and deal with your fear constructively.

TRAUMATIC BONDS

Let's take a moment to appreciate the impact fear has on the mammalian brain—the part of your brain involved in forming attachments. For one thing, abandonment fear leads to the ultimate paradox of attachment: The more somebody hurts you, the harder it is to let go. Why should this be so?

The answer has to do with traumatic bonding. When someone's behavior causes you emotional or physical pain, it creates fear, and this fear intensifies the bond. A perfect example is the woman who knows her husband is cheating on her, but feels all the more in love with him and can't leave.

You'd think that when someone causes pain, it would weaken your bond to that person. But it does just the opposite: It strengthens the attachment. Millions of people are traumatically bonded to their partners (and children to abusive parents), yet remain unaware of the role pain has played in the force of their attachment. This pain we are talking about here is mostly emotional pain. It can range from mild anxiety—waiting for the phone to ring or feeling uncertain about the other person's love—all the way to full-blown panic about being left all alone.

A traumatic bond can set in insidiously. Let's say you've started dating someone. You're not sure you're interested in her, but when she doesn't call back, you feel concerned that she might be blowing you off. This is the first time you experience any concern about her interest in you. Your ego is momentarily ruffled. This mild discomfort silently implants an expectation —a *desire* for her to call. When she finally does call, you feel somewhat relieved. What happens in the meantime? Your mammalian emotional brain "remembers" the anxiety of waiting, as well as the relief you felt when the phone rang. Fear conditioning has begun.

Now you have a subliminal emotional response to any new sign that she might be unavailable; and conversely you're relieved when she seems fully present. You are slowly, insidiously becoming hooked. And it has nothing to do with whether she's "the one." It's a trick your emotional brain is playing on you. You anxiously wait for the next call or chance to see her, and confuse this expectant feeling with being interested. If she's fickle, you churn through the anxiety-relief cycle repeatedly, strengthening your traumatic bond to her each time.

When you are unwittingly caught up in a traumatic bond, your friends can quickly lose patience with you and come right out with the question on everyone's mind: *"How can you stay with someone who jerks you around like that?"*

A painful breakup creates another traumatic bonding condition. When someone leaves you, the pain of rejection traumatically bonds you to him, intensifying your desire for him, the more so because of the pain of loss. The emotional crisis of abandonment is as intense as it is bewildering. Your friends' song remains the same: *"How can you pine for someone who treated you so badly in the end?"*

That, of course, is the point. You desire him more because his absence causes pain; and his loving presence would extinguish it: He has become all-powerful. A love connection that triggers abandonment fear—whether the relationship has ended or is still intact—is harder to break out of than one that allows you to feel safe and secure.

Depending on your life experiences (and the way they've conditioned your emotional brain), you might be more susceptible to abandonment fear and therefore more likely to form traumatic bonds. This could happen whether the person you're interested in is *actually* rejecting you or whether you are being hypersensitive due to your own abandonment history.

HURTS SO GOOD

Why would pain make a bond stronger? The answer may seem preposterous but it has been scientifically demonstrated by countless studies: Fear-based attachments are physically addictive.

I have to back up to explain. Fear and pain are powerful reinforcers. They condition you to salivate (like Pavlov's proverbial dogs again) with emotional hunger when someone presses your insecurity button. The head honcho controlling the insecurity button is, of course, abandonment. When someone you love triggers this primal fear, your body releases a cascade of neurochemicals, which includes a category known as *opioids*. Opioids mediate attachments and are highly addictive. They physically addict you to certain relationships.

Opioids are natural tranquilizers and painkillers produced within the body. An opioid many are familiar with is endorphin, the basis for runner's high. Endorphins (a contraction between *endogenous* and *morphine*) are bio-identical to heroin, morphine, codeine, OxyContin, and other opiate-based drugs. When someone causes you to feel emotional pain (fear, anxiety, hurt), it triggers the release of these potent chemicals, which make the attachment more physically addictive and therefore harder to break. Traumatic bonds are especially prevalent among people with early histories of loss and abandonment whose fears can be easily triggered.

Traumatic bonds are found throughout the animal kingdom. The fact that pain strengthens attachment has been scientifically verified through countless observations and research with many species. For instance, when a researcher inflicts mild pain to a duckling's foot, it imprints (follows) him more closely than before.

Another piece of evidence comes from the hazing ritual involved in joining fraternities. Fraternity brothers inflict emotional and physical pain on the new pledges—beating them up, yelling at them, urging them to drink toxic levels of alcohol, etc. This distressing treatment triggers opiates and leads to traumatic bonding conditions, which *increases* rather than *decreases* the pledges' loyalty to the fraternal order. The Stockholm syndrome is another example of this kind of bond. It is based on an incident in which hostages, after experiencing the hair-raising ordeal, displayed overtly loyal, protective behaviors toward their captors. They had become traumatically bonded.

Take Patty Hearst, for example: When she was still a teenager, the Symbionese Liberation Army took her out of her bedroom in the middle of the night, holding her hostage at gunpoint. The experience was so terrifying, she soon entered into a traumatic bond with her captors, and joined them in committing serious crimes, for which she was later convicted. The court hadn't understood the mechanism of traumatic bonding or its biochemical imperatives and found her to be a "voluntary participant" in the crimes committed.

UNDER HIS THUMB

Research into the startle response provides additional insight into traumatic bonding. Startling is an involuntary fear response. Some people are more prone to obeying verbal commands immediately after being startled. The squirt of endogenous opiates (along with other neurochemicals) induced by the startle apparently contributes to instant traumatic bonding conditions.

A certain Malaysian subculture has a special term—*latah*—for people who startle easily and are prone to obeying any commands that follow. In some circles, it is acceptable social amusement to startle these people and then issue absurd directives. Repeated teasing strengthens latahs' automatic responses, which can leave them vulnerable to potential exploitation. For instance, a man startled a latah and gave her a command to stab to death the person next to her, which she did immediately. When the case went to trial, the judge created a test to see if the latah could be held legally responsible for the murder. The judge startled the latah and told her to bring her hand down upon a nail-studded stick. She obeyed instantly, impaling her hand. The verdict: The man who startled her was guilty, while the latah was exonerated. Unlike the American legal rationale that convicted Patty Hearst, Malaysian courts unwittingly acknowledged the power of traumatic bonding to directly affect one's behavior.

What this extreme example shows is *not* that we shouldn't be held accountable for our actions, but that pain and fear tend to make us more susceptible to falling under someone's power and control. Fear and insecurity can cause you to emotionally surrender to that person due to the powerful opiate-induced bond that is created. You lose volition. The Outer Child program is, of course, designed to reverse this self-abdication—another common, if virulent, form of self-abandonment.

RUNNING HOT AND COLD

The kind of insecurity we've been exploring doesn't occur in a burst the way it does when you've been startled. Insecurity acts more like a continuous wave of pulsating fear and anxiety over a considerable span of time. Its ongoing, pervasive nature accounts for the loss of emotional control you feel when your partner's rejection, drinking, gambling, or philandering become chronic sources of pain.

Intermittent reinforcement intensifies the traumatic-bonding process. If your partner is occasionally loving, sober, or gainfully employed—this intermittent reinforcement makes the emotional conditioning that much more powerful. Patricia, a woman we met in Chapter Eight whose husband was alcoholic, illustrates:

> Barry picked on me all the time, but then every once in a while he'd become tender and caring. He'd always revert back to blaming all of his failures on me. I was always looking for crumbs of respect or appreciation or reprieve. I know I should have left him, but I was hopelessly hooked.

Intermittent reinforcement creates a stronger bond than steady reinforcement, and the conditioning occurs unconsciously. Occasional acts of kindness or bouts of sobriety elicit intense feelings of relief and create a strong pull toward the other person, which we mistakenly interpret as love.

HEARTACHE

In a traumatic bond, love is infused with emotional pain. Painful love feelings are more intense and harder to ignore than feelings of safety and security—the latter can easily move to the background, even be blissfully taken for granted. When love hurts, it becomes intrusive and we feel its presence keenly.

If you're questioning for the first time whether your relationship might not be a healthy love, but a fear-conditioned bond, that alone is a big first step. It is a revelation to behold the possibility that your love connection may be reinforced through fear (*"You mean it's not really love? It's just addiction?"*). Simply acknowledging that has helped many of my readers, clients, and workshop attendees release themselves from bondage.

ABANDOHOLISM

Let's explore a subtype of traumatic bond—an Outer Child pattern so prevalent, it wins the hit parade on my website: *abando*holism. Abandoholism is the tendency to be attracted to the hard-to-get. It's like other kinds of addictions, but instead of being addicted to alcohol or narcotics you're addicted to the high stakes drama of abandonment and the neurochemicals that go with it.

*Abando*holics pursue emotionally unavailable partners to keep the body's addictive analgesics (opioids), stimulants (dopamine, norepinephrine, adrenaline), and other love chemicals (oxytocin, vasopressin) flowing. It sets in when you've been hurt enough times for your emotional brain to associate love with insecurity. In other words, you've been conditioned to think that unless you're feeling insecure, you're not in love. Conversely when someone comes along who wants to be with you, that person's availability fails to arouse the level of pain that would trigger your body to jump-start production of those yummy neurochemicals. If you can't feel those addictive, yearning, lovesick feelings, then you don't feel attracted.

Abandoholics swing between the extreme poles of *fear of abandonment* and *fear of engulfment*. You're either pursuing hard-to-get-lovers or feeling turned off by someone who is interested in you.

You become a rat in a cage, seeking crumbs of love by re-creating the unequal dynamics you may have had with parents or peers. Abandoholics tend to choreograph this scenario over and over. In their repetition compulsion, they are unable to feel anything when someone freely admires or appreciates them because it doesn't scratch the itch.

> She's so in love with me, there's not enough challenge for me to feel sexual energy. She has to be aloof for me to get turned on.

CARRYING A TORCH

Traumatic bonding helps us understand why you might pine over someone who broke your heart. Someone who activated your primal abandonment fear by leaving you has become a powerful figure to your mammalian brain. The pain conditioned you to have an ongoing emotional reactivity toward him—as well as an opioid-induced pull, something we commonly call "carrying a torch." You have a heightened response when you see him or think about him and this confuses you into assuming that he must have been very special to have created such an ongoing emotional charge. In fact, your ex may have been nothing special at all. S/he only seems so because s/he triggered your primal fear. What you are experiencing is *traumatic bonding*. This bond was reinforced by *separation anxiety*—a natural biological attendant to breaking an attachment and dealing with the ego-wound and ongoing rigors of being alone.

> I went through hell after Vince and I broke up and now I can't find anyone who makes me feel like I did with him.

INFATUATION

Traumatic bonding also explains why you can become more infatuated the more someone makes you question their interest in you. Insecurity (anxiety) triggers adrenaline surges combined with other stress hormones and opioids that create that special biochemical kick of infatuation. Infatuation is a cocaine-opiate-like emotional high that intensifies sexuality and engenders the body heat of chemically induced passion.

To stay high, abandoholics keep seeking uncommitted partners. When someone becomes available, your body doesn't produce the love chemicals it needs to maintain this high. You experience this letdown as "feeling no chemistry" toward the person and you go into withdrawal, craving a love fix from someone who's better at stimulating the chemical flow. Like a junkie desperate for a love fix, you search for another lover who arouses just the right amount of insecurity to get you emotionally loaded. When your body is "attracted" (addicted), it tells you you're "in love." When your partner ceases to be an emotional challenge, your opioids and other love-chemicals stop flowing and suddenly the thrill is gone. Hard-core abandoholics find it hard to tolerate the ambivalence and intimacy of an emotionally sober relationship.

The tendency to idealize those who trigger insecurity sets the stage for developing not only abandoholism, but other less-than-ideal intimacy patterns. Whether you're a hard-core love junkie or a garden variety abandoholic, your Outer Child tries to hide the real problem by telling your friends, *"I know she seems ideal for me, but there isn't any chemistry,"* or *"He's a nice guy, but I'm not attracted to him."* Your friends tend to believe in the mythology of "the right chemistry" and accept the explanations at face value—in fact, so do many therapists. Your Outer Child manipulates them into saying, *"You're right, don't settle,"* or *"You just need to find the right person."** To break these patterns, sometimes you need to reprogram yourself and your friends.

BUILDING A TOWER OF LOVE

The abandonment compulsion is insidious. You didn't notice it was developing. Its mechanism was unconscious. Until now you didn't have a name for it. You have been in a dense fog of denial. For you the fog is lifting.

Taming your Outer Child means building a better relationship with yourself, and you're well on your way. As your Adult Self gets stronger, you are better able to examine your values as they relate to your choices in partners, which means reexamining deeply held beliefs, questioning their merit, actively refuting their assumptions, and substituting more realistic ones. Your task is to stay grounded in self-awareness and focus your need

---

* Go to outerchild.net to find the "Outer Child Love Survey." Click on "topics" to download the survey.

for connection not on hard-to-get lovers, but on those who engender mutual trust. What if, for example, you have a weakness for men with an air of detachment or a big ego whose attitude sends your self-esteem into a nosedive? What to do? You can choose to abstain from these types of men. As you revamp your values and beliefs about love, you gain emotional sobriety.

Gaining insight into the whys and wherefores of your counterintimacy patterns is a start, but to actually overcome them involves more than awareness. It requires the specialized power tools that only the Outer Child program has to offer.

The first step in overcoming is to develop a vivid mental image of yourself participating in your love life as you would like it to be. Any great endeavor begins with a clear vision. Remember Eiffel, who transformed his Future Vision into the Eiffel Tower? That's what we are doing.

Hone your visual image of a future successful love life. To reinforce it you can go "back to the future" and imagine that it's approximately two years from now, that your Future Vision is a reality. You're feeling at peace, fulfilled, and happy because you have successfully overcome the patterns and obstacles blocking you from love. To stimulate your imaginative powers further, imbed this image in your Dream House. Imagine that you have the connection to life and to others you have always longed for. Imagine how good you feel about yourself for having accomplished this.

You don't have to believe it, just imagine it. And keep throwing this mental image on the screen of your mind—a snapshot of it—as you go through your day. Don't fret about how you are going to make this vision a reality, just take daily action steps to create momentum. As long as you hold your mental image, your daily actions will help you move your life incrementally in that direction. In the next two relationship chapters, you'll learn how to jump-start this change by applying the dialogues and other tools to your relationship issues. Chapter Twelve deals with how to overcome when you lose passion toward your partner and Chapter Thirteen deals with the other side of the seesaw—how to overcome when you're isolated from love relationships or sense your partner pulling away.

TWELVE

Outer Child and Losing Passion

The tendency to shut down romantically when you become too sure of your partner is a dilemma shared by millions of people. Even if you don't have problems in this area, read on, because this chapter reveals insights that apply to other important areas of your love life.

Our partners do all kinds of things that can jeopardize the romance. For example, they can change—change their personality, physical appearance, or conduct toward you. You committed to one person and find yourself confronted with someone who's developed certain love-killing traits—someone you wouldn't have chosen to be with if you had been forewarned.

But this chapter focuses on the more common cause of love-loss in a relationship—situations where it's not your partner's fault, it's something going on (or not going on) within *you*. Although you'd love to blame it on him or her, you know it's you. You're having trouble loving her the way you used to but you're not sure why. You wonder if it has to do with familiarity, which has bred a kind of complacency and boredom. You consider that you might be *love-challenged*.

BRAD AND DOTTIE

A couple, Brad and Dottie, illustrates this problem well. Brad was more or less dragged into couple's therapy by Dottie. In a nutshell, he felt no passion toward Dottie, which left her understandably feeling hurt, angry, and unsatisfied. Brad is a nice-looking guy, confident, forthright, and personable. But "I can't help feeling a lack of passion toward my wife," he told me during an individual session, "it just happened." He felt awful about it on one level and blamed her for it on another.

Dottie was a great mother, successful in her career, attractive, and outgoing. She freely admitted that Brad's withholding made her "want to lash out at him all of the time." And when she did, Brad used it as an excuse to blame her for the situation. Needless to say, Brad's indifference toward her as a sexual partner was doing nothing for her self-esteem.

The solution to the problem wasn't as simple as getting Dottie to become less needy and angry or getting Brad to become more understanding and sensitive. Better communication, better understanding, being kinder to each other—they'd worked with another therapist on those things for two years and their relationship still wasn't working.

In the meantime, Brad had turned his attentions elsewhere. He worked for a large corporation and frequently came in contact with attractive women. He had a tendency to construct fantasies about some of them, which made being at the office a lot more interesting. He felt most alive at work, and thrived on the challenge of attracting these women's attentions.

He engaged women in flirtatious ways, never crossing the line into the realm of infidelity, but he was sorely tempted with a particular woman, Lillian. His flirtations with Lillian had escalated to the brink of infidelity. Their mutual attraction was acknowledged, however, which is its own kind of cheating. During the workweek they spent time together as often as they could. Lillian was single—she wouldn't be risking a relationship by getting involved with Brad; she refused to move beyond flirting because Brad was not single. This kicked Brad's competitive charge up a notch or two.

Brad remained immersed in his obsession with Lillian even when at home, draining his emotional energy, leaving nothing for his family. Dottie remained unaware of his fantasy and thought he had become depressed. She pushed Brad to get help, and they came to see me.

During an individual session, under the protection of confidentiality rules, Brad told me he felt torn. Part of him wanted to leave his marriage so he could pursue a relationship with Lillian, and part resisted the idea of destroying the life he and Dottie had built together. This second part, although tenuous, held out hope that somehow he might be able to fall back in love with Dottie and live happily ever after.

Brad's history was significant: His mother died when he was 11. His father, a workaholic, later married a woman with three younger children of her own to dote on. Brad felt isolated. During grad school, Brad went through a traumatic abandonment. He'd been in love with the "woman of his dreams," who'd broken their engagement a month before the wedding.

In Brad's utter devastation, he'd built an image of himself as weak, damaged goods, emotionally unstable, unworthy, unlovable. It hadn't occurred to him that these feelings are universal—that everyone, including the strongest among us, feels emotionally overwhelmed when someone we love pulls away. Abandonment fear activates the autonomic nervous system, plunging us into a full-blown state of emergency. That reaction is no reflection on our competence or independence—it just happens.

It took a long time for Brad to get over the intense emotional crisis of abandonment and risk a new relationship. When he did, his strategy had unwittingly changed. He'd developed the defense mechanism of avoidance (his Outer Child had been busy at work). He took pains to stay out of harm's way by no longer pursuing women who might reject him in the end. Instead he focused on women over whom he was sure he had the "edge."

When he'd met Dottie, he felt this "edge." He deemed himself a better catch than she because though she was beautiful inside and out, he, being a financially successful man, felt he had more romantic options open to him than she did. She was destined to love him more than he would love her. In Brad's defense, let me say again that he wasn't conscious of the strategy he was employing. It was only through therapy that he could see that he'd chosen Dottie because she hadn't triggered his abandonment fears or any of his latent feelings about being weak or worthless, which he'd harbored as a result of his traumatic earlier breakup. Dottie made him feel valuable and special.

But clearly, Brad's need to have the edge had an undesired side effect: He needed to be in pursuit-mode (establishing his edge) to sustain his love interest. After a year of marriage, he felt completely secure with Dottie, and his passion for her started to seep away. It seemed he couldn't feel both passionate and completely secure at the same time.

Passion and pursuit are linked for most of us to some extent, but for Brad, like many others struggling with this abandoholic pattern, his passion was entirely *contingent upon* being in pursuit-mode. He *needed* the competitive challenge of the hunt to produce the right love-chemistry.

But whom did he hunt? To extend the metaphor, he hunted small game to avoid triggering the outright panic of being abandoned again. A further problem with his strategy was that after devouring his small prey, he was soon hungry for the next emotional meal.

Although rarely recognized, this pattern plagues countless lives. People choose partners over whom they have the edge and then lose interest when the challenge is won. This pattern saps the love and joy from their intimate relationships. People become *love-challenged* because they have difficulty feeling love toward a willing, available partner.

Like most love-challenged people, Brad also had abando*phobic* tendencies. In other words, he *avoided* relationships with women he perceived as equals to avoid the risk of having them fall out of love with him.

CHANGE BEGINS WITH INSIGHT

Brad was motivated to resolve this conflict. With effort, he gained insight into the fact that for him pursuit was linked to passion and that underneath lurked fear. Unfortunately his Outer Child didn't care much about insight. Brad's Outer Child didn't care *why* Brad didn't love Dottie; what mattered was the thought that he'd rather be with Lillian. Intellectually Brad knew that he might start a relationship with Lillian only to have it end the same way—with Brad losing interest in Lillian the way he had with Dottie— but his Outer Child wanted a love fix now.

Brad's higher self wanted something very different: He wanted his marriage to work out. He wanted to feel more attracted to Dottie so he could give her the love and affection she deserved and preserve the life they had built together—three children, a beautiful home, extended family gatherings, and hordes of close friends who came to dinner parties (mostly Dottie's doing). Not to mention that it would have cost him a fortune to divorce her.

It's important to point out that over the course of their relationship, Dottie had not changed. She'd even upheld her side of the sexual bargain. She'd taken great pains to make time for exercise to keep herself in good physical condition, both for her own well-being and with Brad in mind. A lot of people don't consider taking care of themselves an important part of maintaining a relationship. If they "let themselves go" (through various Outer Child indulgences), their partners can feel devastating loss and even abandonment, which can drastically reduce the passion quotient in the relationship. As one client put it, "My wife put on 50 pounds with the babies. She didn't even try to lose it and I felt betrayed." Not everyone cares about whether their partners take care of themselves in this way, but both Brad and Dottie did. Dotty had not defaulted.

Brad fully agreed that, *hypothetically speaking*, if Dottie were to meet someone else and make ready to leave him, the dynamics of the relationship would probably reverse. Dottie would almost certainly seem desirable again. And if Brad (hypothetically) succeeded in winning her back, he would probably remain amorous only for as long as it took to become sure of her again. Afterward the passion part of him would split off again in search of another challenge.

Brad found this insight extremely valuable. "I finally understand what's been going on with me." But, insight or no, his Outer Child continued to lobby for Lillian. Outer's obsession caused Brad to imagine that he would be happier outside of his marriage. Outer was even able to get Brad to imagine that his home life was *making* him unhappy. Outer tried to blame Brad's cold shoulder on Dottie's reactions, to absolve him from feeling responsible. Brad knew better. He knew he was giving Dottie short shrift, that his problem was *causing* her problem. The unconscious power struggle between Brad's Outer Child and his Adult Self was as exhausting as a real battle. At home he felt morose and anxious to escape.

When I asked him to use his imagination to visualize where he wanted to be in the end, he thought a minute and said he'd like a future in which he could fall back in love with Dottie. When I asked him to fill in more of the picture, he added, "I'd like to become best friends again, make each other laugh, help each other, have a good sex life, and grow old together, feeling settled, secure, and at peace."

That was enough. Despite his internal struggles I knew that if he could envision happily growing old with Dottie, his higher self could grow powerful enough to get the job done. It would require a specialized application of the Outer Child framework.

NOW FOR THE REAL WORK

Many of you out there struggle with this passion-pursuit dilemma, whether or not you have diagnosed it as such. In case there's any doubt, let me say that this is an incredibly challenging issue to overcome. Although your friends and therapists may be frustrated to see you sabotaging your relationships, rest reassured that if it were easy to resolve, you would have done so long ago. When passion is hardwired to pursuit, love and security become mutually exclusive.

To overcome, you need a stronger, wiser Adult Self who can take command. Otherwise, Outer Child will keep weaving this pattern until it destroys the passion or precipitates a crisis in your family (by having an affair or getting you to break away from your life partner).

Brad ultimately grasped the big picture—that his Outer Child strategy was flawed and he couldn't have it both ways: both passionate and secure. But like most of us, he didn't know how to *use* this insight to resolve the situation—how to reinvest his love energy into his marriage.

Brad had expected that gaining insight would automatically set him on the right path, spontaneously resolving the conflict as if by magic. Of course, the real solution involved work, the work of changing behavior.

Like Brad, many people think insight should be enough. But changing a pattern mediated by limbic-brain wiring involves adjusting the mechanism that makes it operate. So Brad and I worked to rebalance the working parts of his personality. Where there is a deeply entrenched pattern of self-sabotage, there is an Outer Child who is too strong, an Inner Child who is too needy and neglected, and an Adult Self who is too weak. These lopsided parts have to be realigned. This was crystal clear in Brad's case. His Adult Self (the beholder of the insight) needed to get stronger before it could change things.

Brad's Outer Child was completely enmeshed in his psyche, and didn't take kindly to our efforts, so I had to detour around this part of him. The first step was to explore what was going on in his Inner Child, another concept Brad unfortunately disdained. This made untangling these parts tricky, but I knew separation would be crucial to success.

Through careful prompting, Brad was able to describe his core emotions: He felt isolated, lonely, scared, and constantly worried about which side (his head or his heart) would win the contest. For instance, would it be the side that wanted to work things out in the marriage? Or the side that simply wanted *out*?

Brad made a few false starts before he was able to clearly express these feelings. His first stab had been predictable: He described his strong feelings for Lillian and how trapped he felt at home. That, of course, was the voice of his Outer Child. Underneath his attraction to Lillian were deeper needs that had nothing to do with her. Lillian was a substitute for something Brad had been searching for since childhood.

A WOLF IN SHEEP'S CLOTHING

This is where most people get stuck. They give voice to what their Outer Child wants, but never push past that. The key to overcoming your deeply entrenched patterns is to gain access to your innermost emotions (hosted by your Inner Child). To get there you must first remove the voice of Outer Child from the conversation. When given the opportunity, this bully will answer for your Inner Child, drowning out your deepest feelings. Remember the intensity of Outer Child's cake lust when you're on a diet? When you pose the question, *"What do you want, Little?"* and the answer comes back, *"Cupcakes,"* chances are that was your Outer Child in disguise. Underneath it all, Little You didn't really want cake. Little's needs are more generic. Little wanted what the cake was standing in for: pleasure, love, security. Cupcakes aren't a primal need—they're too specific an indulgence and typical of what you'll find on Outer Child's top ten list.

At the root of Brad's core emotional needs was something more basic than pursuing Lillian: He needed to feel loved and secure and sexual and peaceful and cherished and warm—basic human needs wrapped in one life-partner.

In trying to get to the bottom of your own feelings, remember that Inner Child is not attached to specific things like cupcakes or the latest model BMW, because Inner is not attached to *form*. That's *Outer Child*. Outer Child is impressed and even driven by form. When Little You gets too specific and seems stuck on things like knee-high suede boots or risotto, that's more than likely Outer Child speaking for Inner Child—your psyche's version of a wolf in sheep's clothing.

CHOOSING TO LIVE A CONSCIOUS LIFE

Outer forms a layer of calluses around Little's feelings, enclosing Little in an emotional incubation chamber. You have to remove the Outer Child crust to release Inner's pure emotional essence. Your emotional core is the part that gives you access to *consciousness*. At its highest level, consciousness is not about fear or pain, it just is. It's a pure feeling state that blends into the larger reality of existence.

Outer avoids this kind of consciousness because it doesn't want to feel. That's why it tries to keep its back turned on Inner. Its actions are defenses aimed at fending off feeling. Outer's emotional calluses prevent you from feeling your core, from being fully conscious, from entering a state of mindfulness. In Brad's case, he pursued other women to avoid feeling a core feeling of "not being good enough." His pattern was a repetition compulsion designed to scratch the itch of a constant need to prove himself.

Being attracted to things in the form world diverts your life's mission. These are illusions of fulfillment. And because Outer Child is basically disconnected from feeling, he's driven by false values. Outer Child has you lusting after cupcakes or Lillian, but cake and Lillian are false desires, counterfeit fulfillments, substitute pleasures.

Whether you do it consciously or unconsciously, if you remove yourself from your deepest feelings, you're committing to a misguided search for a form to fill the emptiness. Brad, you've undoubtedly noticed, had an unseparated Outer Child that thrived on his lack of consciousness. Outer was willing to jeopardize what Brad's higher Adult Self believed was best for him—his marriage and family—all for the substitute ego gratification of pursuing Lillian. His Outer Child wanted this, yes. We all have a part like this; the question is whether we want to put that part of ourselves in charge. Brad had another, higher, *conscious* part that sought something less ego-driven—to work things out in his marriage.

What was tripping Brad up was a mechanical glitch—his earlier emotional conditioning that had paired passion with pursuit. These cross-wires were depriving him of gaining fulfillment, even though mutual love was completely available to him: Dottie remained an open, willing partner.

I'm not moralizing here. It may sound so, but my thinking is practical. I fully concede that there are men and women in relationships with partners who are not willing to keep up their emotional end of the bargain. I'm not anti separation, I'm pro healthy choice. And since Brad deemed staying with Dottie to be his healthy choice, I was in full support of it.

A REBALANCING ACT

Brad, an intelligent guy, was able to benefit from our discussion about consciousness and look beneath his Outer Child encrustations to get in touch with some of his core needs. Many of you have used the dialogue exercises —including Radical Listening—to do just that. In case you missed it (see Chapter Nine), Radical Listening separates layer by crusty layer of Outer Child from the rest of your psyche; and writing dialogues with your Inner Child gives you access to your deepest, most tender feelings.

As Brad wasn't open to the dialogue exercise, I used role play—the next best thing—to separate the part of him that had fused passion to pursuit. Role-playing is not something you can do alone, so I urge you to write Outer Child dialogues. Writing stimulates more parts of the brain and facilitates the uncoupling process more efficiently.

What follows are highlights from one of the first role-playing sessions with Brad. His resistance isn't unusual; remember, we're talking about patterns of behavior that are both deep and complex. As you can see, procrastination is not the only way people resist change. Outer clamps down when it senses you're trying to take its candy away.

I told Brad I was going to try speaking the voice of the feelings going on inside him and that he could respond as his usual Adult Self. A preliminary step was to get Adult Brad to voice a different position from that of his Outer Child's Casanova self. He was indulging me as it was, so I had to coach him through it step by step.

SUSAN: Tell me what your Casanova guy is saying about the other woman. How is he rationalizing the flirtation?

BRAD: He's saying things would be great with Lillian.

SUSAN: What does your higher self say to challenge this thought?

BRAD: What's to challenge? I think it's right. I would probably be happier with Lillian.

SUSAN: If you had to play devil's advocate, which argument would you use against this?

BRAD: Okay...Maybe that things with Lillian would end the same way they did with Dottie, maybe I'd wind up losing interest.

SUSAN: What does your Casanova guy say to that?

BRAD: That Lillian is the right person and Dottie isn't.

SUSAN: What argument would you use against that?

BRAD: I'd say there's nothing wrong with Dottie. She doesn't deserve this.

SUSAN: And Casanova's response to that?

BRAD: That Dottie's nice and all, but I'm just not in love with her. She can't make me happy. I think Lillian would keep me interested.

SUSAN: What argument would your higher self use against that?

BRAD: That I might be wrong. Also, Lillian's faults would bother me if I lose interest in her. And who's to say she'd actually be with me in the end?

SUSAN: How does Casanova argue against that?

BRAD: That it would be worth it. If a relationship didn't work with Lillian, then there's someone else out there even better, that it will never work with Dottie.

SUSAN: What argument does your higher self use against the idea that you'd be happier without Dottie?

BRAD: That I originally chose Dottie. And that she loves me as I am. That I respect her. But I don't feel any chemistry with her.

SUSAN: Which side do you want to win—the Casanova or the Married Man?

BRAD: I know it would be better for all concerned to preserve the marriage. I just don't know if I can.

SUSAN: Which side do you *think* will win?

BRAD: Probably...maybe the same part that's winning now: staying with Dottie.

SUSAN: You're not winning if you're feeling morose, conflicted, and passionless when you're with your life-partner.

BRAD: But I can't have both—Dottie and passion.

SUSAN: You can if you emotionally reinvest in your marriage. Then you can put love and security into one package.

BRAD: That's why I'm here, but I said this at the beginning and nothing has changed.

SUSAN: Yes, but you had your parts all mixed up then. Now that you've sorted them out a bit, let's go for it.

If Brad had his parts completely separated, his higher Adult Self would be stronger, less muddled, and he'd gradually know exactly what he had to do. With his higher self focused steadfastly on his goal, he would be able to make an executive decision. He'd probably decide, for instance, to march right into work and set things straight with Lillian. After eliminating the flirtation's emotional drain, he could return home and fully engage himself in acts of love toward his family. But Brad was not yet ready. Like a lot of people, his higher self didn't have enough muscle to execute an executive decision of this order. He first needed a regimen of physical therapy for the brain. He needed to create new neural pathways between intention and passion.

CONSCIOUS LOVING ACTIONS

With the help of our work together, Brad was able to stay in touch with his core feelings. He was also able to create a degree of separation between his Outer Child, Inner Child, and Adult Self through role play. So we embarked on the next phase of the program—a course of daily action steps.

Did I ever say I had a magic bullet here? There are millions of men and women out there suffering from "passion erosion" and many have spent years in therapy trying to overcome it. There is no instant answer or sudden insight that can eliminate a pattern this deeply entrenched in the limbic brain. It takes the right tools and lots of elbow grease. At times you might feel as if you're pushing a boulder up a steep hill, but the journey is pleasurable when you keep your vision and purpose in mind. Emotional fulfillment awaits you.

Brad needed to take each action with the conscious intention of restoring love and passion in his marriage. And he needed to take those actions on behalf of his core needs; otherwise as he carried out these actions, he would feel he was performing them for Dottie's benefit rather than his own. Any resentment would work against his mission.

With a history like Brad's (in which loss and abandonment played a leading role in shaping behaviors), it was especially important to put the needs of his Inner Child first. It's important for all of us. When you change your life one action at a time, you must do so with conscious intention of meeting your deepest emotional needs. You must commit the actions self-*fully* as opposed to self*lessly*. This isn't about pleasing other people. To target your vision, you must take actions on your own behalf or risk losing touch with your emotional center—the source of your creative emotional energy—once again.

FIND THE JOY IN IT

When you carry out each act, you gain optimal growth if you can consciously and deliberately find the joy in it. This keeps the task-focused nature of the activity from feeling like work and channels the pleasure-seeking part of your psyche into a constructive, consciously chosen outlet.

To increase Brad's motivation to follow through with the action steps, he needed to square himself with his Future Vision each time he followed through with a daily activity. Each week I asked him to reiterate his answer to the question *What do you want in your wildest dreams?* He needed to be consistent in his answer, *"To feel passion for Dottie."* He also needed to touch base with his innermost emotional core to fuel his progress. So each week I asked him how it felt inside to be attracted to another woman who was not his wife. Sometimes Outer would answer for him, and I'd point out that his hidden Casanova had just taken over. With a little prompting, he'd come up with, "You want more basic feelings than that from me? Okay, I'm feeling lost, sad, and confused."

Since Brad's was a relationship goal, he needed to come up with an action step that would help him get into the moment with his chosen life-partner. He understood that this action was to be dedicated to his intention to invest love into his marriage as a way of fulfilling his innermost needs. To clarify, the action need not directly alleviate the problem, it just needed to be carried out with full consciousness and the intention to work toward his ultimate vision.

He thought for a long time before he described the first thing he would do:

> BRAD: I don't see how it will help, but maybe I could take Dottie out to dinner. We could do something a little different, maybe go to a nice place, or we could order an extra-nice bottle of wine— something she might notice was different.
>
> SUSAN: Is it realistic to think you can stay in the moment with Dottie for a whole dinner? Can you keep your Lillian-obsession at bay for that long?
>
> BRAD: Knowing me, I'd probably have trouble staying focused for ten minutes.

We revised his original idea. For five minutes he would be fully present and attentive to Dottie on their dinner date and exercise the conscious intention of practicing giving love to her—love as an *action*, not a feeling. He would commit this action on behalf of his own core needs rather than for Dottie's benefit—just five minutes of uncoupling his Outer Child, keeping the Casanova part of him separate. He would get into the moment with her—-deliberately and consciously taking in the sounds, feelings, sights, smells of the environment they were enjoying together—and also make a point to tune in to Dottie's special essence for five full minutes.

So Brad would spend five minutes that night being fully present with Dottie at a restaurant. No Outer Child hanging around. No triangle. Just the two of them. Not for Dottie's benefit but for his own. After completing the five minutes, he could consider his mission accomplished for the day.

Brad agreed to take one small action per day, although he couldn't imagine how it would change anything. He also agreed not to look for immediate results. He conceded that getting his higher self to strengthen its muscles five minutes a day *might eventually* add up to something good.

He decided that because of their busy workweek lives, Monday–Friday he would focus on actions he could take in bed. Sex or even physical affection was not required. He might even wait for Dottie to fall asleep so he could devote his five minutes to quietly and mindfully being with her with conscious intention. On weekends, he wanted to carry out the five-minute actions on planned outings with Dottie (and often the kids) and he dedicated five minutes of the time to being fully present with her.

Each action required preparation. First he conjured up his Future Vision and then tuned in to his innermost feelings, while beholding his conscious intention to restore passion in his marriage.

Here's what happened at a follow-up session:

BRAD: When I'm doing the action, I don't feel any passion or love feelings at all. It isn't helping.

SUSAN: Yes, but your goal isn't to feel passionate right away. That puts too much pressure on the situation. It doesn't work that way. You're just trying to get into the moment with positive intention. Just be fully conscious of your vision and your innermost needs as you take the action. Your Adult Self will slowly rise to power and take care of the obstacles in your way. This is about strengthening your higher self.

BRAD: Okay, I won't expect to feel anything new toward Dottie, and trust the process a little longer.

About a month down the road, Brad began to notice a difference, although he didn't initially attribute it to doing his daily action steps. He'd begun to stay in the moment for longer periods with Dottie and enjoy her company a little more, especially when the kids were around.

These moments with Dottie remained compartmentalized—he'd obsess about the other woman before and after. It would be unrealistic for Brad to expect to remain perpetually in the moment with Dottie, but he was feeling more goal-directed and purposeful when he took each action step, and at times, maybe a little closer to her. Brad said that although he didn't feel any progress, he felt he was engaging in a kind of physical exercise for the soul.

A few months later he was still attracted to Lillian but felt a little more emotional pleasure in his marriage—the accrual of those little five-minute segments of being in the moment with Dottie, no doubt. His higher self had incrementally strengthened and helped him gain some balance. From balance came perspective, and from perspective, resolution. In other words, his Adult Self was more in charge and able to exercise its cognitive abilities. Brad's Adult Self ultimately grew strong enough to realize that he could not continue to emotionally invest in the other woman and expect to feel any passion toward Dottie. This had been obvious to him for a while, but now he acknowledged it on a level that compelled him to take action. He had finally become powerful enough to make an executive Adult decision. In Brad's own words, "It was a no-brainer. I couldn't stay in a triangle for the rest of my life."

Brad broke away from his flirtation with Lillian (though he was still attracted to her) to let his need for passion build for Dottie. He wanted to devote his life to loving his family. It seemed to him like a long, rocky road ahead, but he resolved to keep his vision front and center and follow through with daily actions. He was a man on a mission, empowered with enough clarity and resolve to reach his goal. And he did. With the distraction of the third party eliminated, he began slowly building a richer connection with his wife.

He couldn't claim complete success at that point. There were dangers ahead. For instance, what would prevent him, under enough stress, from reverting to form? After all, he had that limbic-wiring glitch—that emotional conditioning in his limbic brain that linked passion to pursuit. It would also be easy for him to lose touch with his innermost needs (since he still avoided writing dialogues that would have otherwise kept his emotional awareness fresh). Losing touch with his emotional core would make it easy for his stealthy Outer Child to insinuate itself back into his Adult thinking and instigate a new self-defeating cycle.

But Brad committed to leading his life with the kind of love that comes from emotional wisdom and Adult vision. To keep the muscle of his Adult Self well exercised, he kept a weekly journal dedicated to strengthening his higher thinking self. His goal was to continue to exercise mind over matter, override his limbic glitch, and keep his love life on track. His ongoing work was surely changing his brain. He also agreed to return to therapy for periodic maintenance checks. The need for maintenance strategies comes up for all of us, even as we succeed at our goals.

MAKING THIS WORK FOR YOU

Enough about Brad. Make this work for you too. I've created a list below of advice for people who come to realize they are "love-challenged." By presenting this list, I'm not suggesting that anyone force him- or herself to stay in a relationship where there are no positive feelings. That's not the point. The list is helpful if you've recognized that you have a problem with love, and that it's worth focusing your love energy on a worthy person. If these two conditions fit, then following this path can help you build toward a love that has eluded you in the past.

1) The first step is to recognize that you have the problem. This is the most difficult step, due to layers of self-deceit and false attribution (such as blaming a passionless marriage on your mate's faults) that have been confusing you all along.
2) Redefine love. Love is not an absolute feeling, nor is it confined to infatuation. When it comes to love, one size doesn't fit all. Love is a set of feelings unique to the two people involved in creating a bond.
3) Commit to loving behaviors. Don't expect love to be a feeling you fall into, but a verb that you act out. Don't wait for the "feeling" to motivate you. Motivate yourself.
4) Recognize love as a creative process. Be open to discover your ability to create loving feelings.
5) Make the connection between self-discipline and love. Recognize that achieving love involves following through with loving actions on a consistent basis.

6) Care for your partner. The expression *Fake it till you make it* doesn't quite fit the bill here, but I am suggesting that even when you feel at a loss for romantic feelings, express care in your actions. There is no dishonesty here, as you will see in the next step.

7) Honestly talk about your feelings with your partner, even if this means explaining that you have a problem with feeling love or passion for him. It is best to talk about the difficulty, since it is real. Holding back only hurts your partner more as he senses your rejection and blames it on himself.

8) Take responsibility for your problem. Tell your partner that this is a problem you have and that you're working on it. Again, don't blame your love issues on your mate's inadequacies. Begin sentences with, "I'm dealing with something that has nothing to do with you..." when you bring up your issues about the relationship, so your mate won't feel he's responsible for your struggle with passion. Let your partner know that you are "holding the space" for these love feelings to grow within the relationship.

9) Make a plan to be completely in the moment with your partner. Show up not just physically, but emotionally, by carefully attending to everything he or she says and does. Create special moments of fun, communication, or intimacy. Find the joy in these activities. Build a legacy that belongs not to the two of you as individuals, but to the relationship.

10) Initiate conversations that get underneath the surface emotions. Draw your partner out by asking open-ended, caring questions to learn more about her emotional issues, especially as they relate to the relationship or her life, like *"How do you feel about us?"* Frequently discuss your relationship—don't try to "fix it," just create an open space for sharing. Show frequent curiosity about her feelings about it. Sharing relationship feelings builds intimacy and trust.

11) Be willing to create new feelings and a new level of communication in the relationship. Relate things from childhood; confide your current personal dilemmas; *radically listen* to your partner's issues. Risk admitting your vulnerabilities and secret feelings; dare to get close. This is just about sharing, not finding solutions. You're meeting each other's minds and hearts, building intimacy.

12) Ask follow-up questions the following week to show that your inter-

est in his feelings carries through —that your caring has trajectory. Be open to gentle waves of appreciation and sparks of excitement he sends back to you.

13) Make yourself sexually available. This is an important step. Understand that your sexuality may be specifically conditioned to respond only to someone who presents an emotional challenge. This is not that person, so be patient with yourself. Make allowances for the fact that insecurity is no longer serving as an aphrodisiac.

14) Share this sexual struggle openly with your partner. Neither partner should try to "fix it." Just sharing openly builds intimacy and relieves the pressure to perform. The old you used sex to consummate a love conquest. The new you is learning to consummate more substantial feelings, like mutuality, caring, and trust.

15) Be open to a new rainbow of feelings. Remember, sometimes it's hard to recognize love even when it's there working for you. Yes, feeling secure and comfortable might not be intoxicating, but that's the point—it's emotionally nourishing. Your old reference point for love was based on infatuation or love conquest. Your love gauge was skewed by the fact that you were used to pursuing unavailable partners. This new kind of love may feel different. Do you feel closeness, caring, trust, respect, security? Rather than dismiss these feelings as less than romantic, include them in your new definition of love. As for the calm, comfortable feelings of emotional nurturance, consider that this is what mutual love might feel like, unfamiliar though it is.

THIRTEEN

Outer Child and Feeling Unloved

We all know that for a love-connection to work, a delicate balance must be maintained. Without emotional symmetry the dynamics of the relationship become unstable. If one side loses passion, the other becomes insecure, and vise versa. It's a matter of relationship mechanics. If one partner pulls away, the other tends to push forward. One shuts down romantically, the other heats up.

The last chapter dealt with what it feels like to be on the "losing passion" side of the equation. This chapter explores what it feels like to be at the wanting end of love and what to do about it—how to prevent your clinging feelings from sabotaging your relationship.

DR. JEKYLL AND MR. SUCTION CUPS

Emotional suction cups rise to the surface involuntarily when someone triggers your abandonment fears. Some suction cups are huge and hairy and aim straight at your loved ones in an engulfing manner. Other suction cups make a more subtle appearance and are neatly trimmed and groomed; they might be disguised by nonchalant mannerisms your lovers can mistake for disinterest or anger. Emotional suction cups in whatever form are a primary source of conflict within relationships and the reason so many eligible, loving people remain single when they want nothing more than someone to love.

Case in point: Brad's unsuspecting wife, Dottie, had developed emotional suction cups when she felt him shutting her out. As anyone in her position would, she resorted to groveling for his attention at times and became the "push" in the push-pull dynamics.

In couples work with Brad and Dottie, I was in the therapist's position of having privileged information about Brad's obsession with Lillian, which affected Dottie but of which she remained unaware. My role was to help Dottie deal with her very human emotional reactions to her husband's emotional unavailability. Here is her testimonial:

> Brad was so detached; it turned me into someone I didn't like—a needy, demanding, angry person. It wasn't the real ME. The way I was acting was only driving him further away. It took a whole lot of work with the Outer Child program to turn things around in my life.

The institutions of marriage and children can sometimes keep couples bound together long enough to work through their emotional issues; but without these bonds, new relationships can fall apart precipitously.

As another client put it:

> My neediness scares people away and keeps me in a self-imposed prison of loneliness and I don't know how to escape it.

This self-imposed prison has a devastating impact on your self-esteem. The isolation makes you feel as if you're emotionally unfit to be in a relationship, unworthy of another person's love or respect. This is how Brad had felt when his fiancée left him. It is how Dottie felt when Brad became romantically indifferent to her.

AFRAID TO HOPE

Whether you are chronically single, going through a breakup, or feeling lovelorn in your relationship, you'll likely experience waves of anxiety about whether you'll ever feel loved again. Love becomes something you're almost afraid to hope for.

When fear gets attached to hope, it leaves its imprint in your limbic brain. The result: Hoping for love triggers anxiety, an anxiety of the what-if variety. What if I never find someone? What if I wind up alone? As time goes by and a new relationship fails to materialize, the "what if" begins to feel toxic. *"What if prospective partners can sense my 'what if'?"*

When you're feeling love-deprived, you aim the "what if" at your partner. *"What if he leaves me? What if I never win his love back?"*

Again, from Dottie:

I'm living one of those lives of "quiet desperation." Except I'm not so quiet. I'm volatile. I'm in love with my husband and he treats me like a piece of furniture—and I'm not taking that sitting down.

And from another client:

I've had this low-grade desperation oozing out of me for a while. Guys can read it, even though I've kept it really cool. I've never been in a long-term relationship—and I try to convince myself that I don't really want one. Actually, I'm happy and do a lot with my life. I go to friends' weddings and baby showers all the time, and have *passing* thoughts of "Why them, not me?" but I'm actually happy for them. Yet I know on some level they feel sorry for me.

When guys meet me, they see a positive person who loves life and has a fabulous career. But I'm sure it's clear to them—to everyone—that I'd prefer to be with someone. So guys are already wary of me. When I meet a guy I feel attracted to, that's when it gets really scary. I do everything imaginable not to aim my suction cups at them.

When you feel insecure, it wakes up the echoes of primal abandonment from the deep. You're anything but coolheaded when it comes to your relationship.

Many workshop attendees report that they lose equal footing if they start really liking someone:

When we'd start spending more time together or talk about commitment—that's when things always fell apart. I have no idea what I do that makes them lose interest. Am I too available? Do I expect too much too soon? I certainly try not to—I let them take the lead. Is it because they can tell I'm looking to settle down and that scares them? Am I just not good enough to be "the one" for them, or anyone? The most horrible thought of all is: Is there something repulsive about me that surfaces when I like someone?

Some people can't get a relationship started. They see someone they'd like to meet but they're so scared, they can't get beyond the first hello:

I've been alone for the past 20 years because I can't take the step to get to know someone. I'm so afraid of rejection; my Outer Child cripples me with it. It's why I'm here. I hate my Outer Child.

YOU BE THERE FOR YOU

Millions of people share these vexing dilemmas. Their reactions hearken back to primal abandonment experiences (we all have them) that accumulated within a deep emotional well. Although their circumstances vary, their problems can all be resolved the same way: Their Adult Self needs to get stronger so they can nurture their Inner Child's emotional needs rather than handing their vulnerable feelings over to someone else's care.

The misguided expectation that someone else should take care of your emotional needs is quintessential Outer Child manipulation. It can also be completely unconscious. When your Inner Child remains submerged within your Adult Self, its long-neglected needs incubate and Outer Child uses them as fodder to create a nuisance, projecting them onto your relationship:

My fear causes me to give all my power over to the woman, which freaks her out and makes her run from me like I'm Frankenstein. This puts me on the brink of emotional annihilation.

When you unwittingly hand your deepest longings over to your partner, you abandon your Inner Child all over again. You put Little You out there alone on a street corner and hope that someone else might soothe its anxiety and desperation.

Couples often trade responsibility for their Inner Children. They project their disowned feelings on each other and riddle the relationship with unrealistic expectations and displaced anger. There's nothing wrong with looking to your mate for nurturance, love, support, reassurance— providing he or she can give these things to you. But when your partner isn't able to, it is imperative to learn how to give love and security directly to yourself.

Through previous chapters, you've been writing dialogues to get in touch with your need to feel accepted and cherished. If performing the dialogues has helped you see the intensity of your long-neglected needs, then you can vividly imagine what happens when you unwittingly project them (thanks to your subversive, stealthy Outer Child) onto your love-mate. Your Inner Child's most pressing needs can potentially overwhelm the dynamics of an intimate relationship (or any relationship, for that matter).

Becoming emotionally self-reliant immediately changes the dynamics in your relationship. By becoming self-assuring and self-fulfilled, you take your partner out of the loop.

BEFORE LOVE, SELF-LOVE

The challenge, then, is to practice the skill of self-nurturance. A surprising number of people are wholly unfamiliar with this task. *"You should love yourself"* remains an abstract dictum they can only grasp at intellectually. Separation therapy makes all the difference. By separating the parts of your psyche, you position your higher self to administer feelings, words, and loving actions—behaviorally—to your inner self. You adopt your abandoned Inner Child; you rescue it from a life on the streets and hold true to your promise to take exquisite care of its needs. This releases your partner from the equation (reducing the suction in your cups!) and allows you to become a freestanding agent, master of your own destiny. Building a tight love-connection between Big You and Little You transforms you from an emotional supplicant into a self-reliant adult.

Let's check back in with Dottie:

The heartache started after Brad and I were married a year. We'd been tucked into each other's pockets, always reaching out to each other for a pat or a kiss. Then he started becoming less responsive and I grew desperate.

It is only natural to look for reassurance and love from one's partner—no one can blame Dottie or anyone else for expressing these needs. We are human as well as mammalian, and this is how we all react—until we realize (using our advanced cognitive brains) that turning to the withholder usually makes things worse for ourselves.

In a situation like this, it is in our best interests to remove ourselves from the demoralizing role of emotional beggar. We must transcend the need to look for validation from a withholding partner.

How to accomplish this? Use the dialogue process to transform your pulsating, throbbing suction cups into spurs of personal growth. Respond to your own primal needs. Remember that the relationship you build with yourself is the template on which all other relationships are built.

Unlike her husband, Dottie was willing to actually *write* Outer Child dialogues, so she experienced dramatic internal change. But I'm getting ahead of the story here. Her first task was to clarify her goal so she could best target her efforts. In her own words, this goal was to: "resolve my unhappiness in my marriage." She knew she couldn't change Brad or his feelings, but she could work on administering more lovingly to her own needs.

THAT MEDDLING KID

Dottie's next task was to identify Outer Child behaviors that interfered in achieving her goal. In her notebook she made an inventory of all of the self-defeating behaviors that kept her stuck on an unbalanced seesaw with Brad.

> The list goes on for three pages. In writing, I discovered my Outer Child has become clingy, suction-cuppy, angry, bitchy. My Outer Child yells and cries a lot—to try to squeeze some compassion out of Brad. My Outer Child can become passive-aggressive, as well as a nudge and a sniper when I get pushed too far. I also learned that when all else fails, I revert to guilting Brad. Guilt is a sort of booby prize for me—I can't get love from him, so I'll take a pound of flesh. My Outer Child doesn't want to change; she wants *him* to change. But I know I have no control over Brad.

Dottie's behaviors were natural reactions to feeling pushed away. I asked her if her Outer Child blamed *her* for Brad's withholding behavior, to which she responded, "When I feel the rejection, my Outer Child goes on the attack, and yes, sometimes the attack is against me—making it all *my* fault." I suggested she add "Dottie-bashing" to the top of her list of Outer Child behaviors and target it for removal.

Many people in Dottie's position tend to criticize themselves for being weak. When caught up in a situation like this, it's often difficult to let yourself off the hook for "being so emotional." Using the Outer Child concept helped Dottie avoid this bind. By attributing her self-defeating behaviors to Outer Child, Dottie sidestepped the common mistake of blaming her reactions on her feelings—on her beleaguered Inner Child. Communicating with your Inner Child is effective rather than destructive only when you separate your emotions from your behavior—Inner from Outer. By separating them, your Adult Self can moderate between them and finally address the needs of your helpless, blameless feelings, as well as place your behaviors in target range.

Dottie put it this way:

> I pictured my Outer Child doing all of these impulsive, annoying, clingy things to protect my Inner Child—all of it at odds with my own happiness. I imagined Big Me having enough stature and authority to tell Outer to stop, turn around, and *listen* to Little's feelings. I held on to the image and let it inspire my dialogues.

BEYOND BRAD

In writing the dialogues, Dottie coaxed a very mistrustful Inner Child to open up, using a gentle question-and-answer approach. Eventually Little Dottie articulated her most urgent fears and needs—feelings so basic they went beyond Brad and the circumstances of her marriage. This articulation empowered her Adult Self to administer directly to her own emotional core.

At first Dottie's Adult Self spent most of the time reassuring her Inner Child that she was listening and asking what she could do to help. To which Little responded with doubt that Dottie would actually do anything. But she persisted. Here's an excerpt from her first dialogue:

> BIG DOTTIE: I do care, Little. I want to know what you need.
> LITTLE DOTTIE: I want love. I want to be taken care of.

BIG DOTTIE: I love you, Little. I'll take care of you from now on.

LITTLE DOTTIE: You keep leaving me. You don't like me. I want to feel special and you make me feel bad because of the way Brad treats us. I'm mad because you keep doing this to me.

After a few dialogues, things became crystal clear to Dottie. Her Inner Child's needs were urgent and Dottie had neglected them. In her own words, "All along I had been placing her needs in Brad's hands and he couldn't take care of them!"

What Dottie is describing is exactly what happens on an unconscious level within most relationships when people project their Inner Child's most pressing needs onto their partners, abdicating personal responsibility. This handoff is the dastardly work of the Outer Child. When you turn to an external source for relief (to scratch that itch)—and if that source isn't forthcoming—you intensify the vicious cycle and unwittingly expose Little You to more deprivation.

By going to Brad with my Inner Child's needs, I was tormenting poor Little Dottie. I was reacting to Brad's neglect instead of helping her myself. I was doing nothing to take care of her! I'd been asleep at the wheel! I immediately changed that. For me, self-love came like a breath of fresh air. Little Me started opening up and Big Me started listening and responding and taking charge. I was actually doing things for her—practicing self-love!

With the Outer Child dialogue in hand, the path to healthy relationships is straightforward. Big You remains in tune with your emotional needs and takes responsibility for them. The stronger the connection between your Adult Self and Inner Child, the more you limit Outer Child. When your emotional needs are fulfilled, Outer no longer has grounds to act them out at the expense of your love-connections.

Listen to a bit more of one of Dottie's Outer Child dialogues. It starts at a point when she momentarily forgets to attribute a behavior to her Outer Child and instead blames it on her feelings.

BIG DOTTIE: I care about you, Little. But you need to stop groveling and being so needy and clingy.

LITTLE DOTTIE: I can't help feeling this way. I'm lonely. I need love.

BIG DOTTIE: You're right, Little, it's not you; it's me. I've been letting Outer do all of these self-defeating things, but I'm going to make this stop.

LITTLE DOTTIE: I don't trust you. You'll forget all about me. I'm not the one who yells and cries and spends the whole day trying to get Brad out of the house to do something. It makes me lonely and feel bad about myself. You care about Brad, not me. You'll just forget about me again. I'm all alone and scared. Nobody loves me.

BIG DOTTIE: Shush, shush, I love you, Little, and I'll never abandon you again.

This was a turning point for Dottie. She felt it—the emotional mechanics underlying her dilemma—the unhappier she'd become with Brad, the more she'd neglected her own feelings.

COMMIT TO YOUR INNER CHILD

Dottie gained the power of self-responsibility, but she didn't accomplish it overnight. It took vision, personal commitment, and consistency. She nurtured her Adult Self–Inner Child bond incrementally by diligently writing dialogues and following a daily action plan designed to satisfy Outer Child's need to release its energy.

I had to show Little Me how much I cared and I had to show Outer that I was in charge. I was willing to do anything to make Little Me feel better, now that I was assuming total responsibility for my own emotional needs—even if it meant doing something radical like maybe even leaving Brad . . . I wasn't sure. But I knew that I was in charge.

You, like Dottie, can improve your relationship with yourself, forming a tighter coalition between Big You and Little You, and bring Outer You under your conscious control. When you feel rejected in a love relationship, as painful as this is, it gives you an opportunity to transfer your needs for love and reassurance onto your own Adult Self. You can adopt your Inner Child and administer directly to its needs, leaving your partner out of the dependency loop so that you can ultimately enjoy a healthy, lasting, intimate adult-to-adult relationship, if that's what you choose.

I'M TOO AFRAID TO LOVE

In another client, Robert's case, abandonment fear had immobilized him. He'd developed abando*phobia*. He'd used avoidance as a strategy to side-step the possibility of being hurt, his fears incubating all the while. He'd gotten to the point where he was too *afraid* to risk even the first move. It was time to approach the problem in a new way. I walked him through the steps.

Step one was to clarify his vision. For those playing at home, use your Outer Child notebook to record an answer to the question "What's your ultimate relationship goal?" Robert's first attempt was: "To be at peace."

A little too vague. I encouraged him to be courageous and name the love goal he was afraid to hope for. This time I got a very different answer from the man who at 49 had never been close to anyone: "Find someone to love, have a family."

That was brave. And a real vision. Now his task was to hold on to that vision.

Step two is to ask yourself how your Outer Child interferes with that goal. Robert said that he already had a long inventory of the ways his Outer Child was ruining his life. So that part was in place. You, reader, might want to take this opportunity to inventory your own Outer Child behaviors in the context of relationships before moving on.

Step three is to Turn Around: Ask your Outer Child to stop defending Little You. Instead ask him to Turn Around and prepare to listen. Imagine the parts of your psyche as individuals and ask your Outer Child to face your Inner Child. Robert was able to quickly clarify that he needed his Outer Child to stop getting in the way and let his Inner Child speak up.

Step four is to discover how Little You feels about an unfulfilled dream of love. At this point Robert needed a little help to draw out those feelings:

> SUSAN: How does Little Rob feel about those 25 years without a lov-
> ing relationship, without a family?
> ROBERT: Upset.

SUSAN: Just upset? How about frustrated, desolate, needy, helpless, hopeless?

ROBERT: That too . . . oh, and terrified.

SUSAN: Why is the goal of having a family so important to you? Why does Little Rob need to find love and family in the first place?

ROBERT: Because he's lonely.

SUSAN: Any other feelings, Little Rob?

ROBERT: Because he feels bad that nobody wants him, nobody can love him. He's not important. Every day I'm alone, I feel like a failure, inadequate. And so afraid.

SUSAN: Would you say you feel bad about yourself for having these crippling fears?

ROBERT: Yes.

SUSAN: Do you realize how hurt and rejected Little Rob must feel to be resented for having these feelings—fears he can't help?

ROBERT: Yes. But what can I do about them?

Step five is for Big You to make amends to Little You for resenting his feelings and to accept them unconditionally. "Can Big Robert create a mental image of an Adult Self who is so competent and compassionate that he can fully embrace your Inner Child's fears? An Adult Self capable of loving this high-maintenance, terrified, lonely little kid? If you can accept and love him as he is, you'll come out of the self-anger and self-hatred. This alone would create change within you.

"In making amends, Big Robert must promise Little Rob that he will work on loving *all* of his feelings unconditionally—that he will practice loving his feelings until he gets it right."

When I asked Robert what Little Rob would say to that, he replied, "I don't trust Big Robert to do this."

So you see where Robert had (and you might have) work to do. Your relationship with yourself—Big to Little—is in conflict. The result: a lack of self-love. Big You needs to get stronger. You can begin to fix this with your imagination and reinforce it by writing dialogues in an ever more compassionate, commanding, adult voice—it's good practice.

Step six is for Little You to tell Big what he would like you to do for him. "If Little Rob learned to trust you, what might he ask you for?" Robert was quick to answer, "I'd want Big to be brave and to meet somebody." Fair enough.

Step seven is for Big to make a solemn commitment to Little. I explained that Big Robert could say something like: *"Little Me, I know how afraid you are and I'm going to get stronger so I can get you what you want. I'm going to help us meet somebody. I'm going to take new actions to change things—do something new every day."*

When Robert checked in with Little Rob we heard his doubts loud and clear: "He probably knows I can't follow through. Anyway, he knows I resent him too much because he's so afraid."

That self-rejection is what Robert and possibly you are working to resolve. A stronger Adult Self can respond by explaining that you accept those feelings, no matter how afraid your Inner Child is, and that you are working on getting stronger and braver every day.

Step eight is for Big You to promise to take at least one action a day. For Robert it could go something like this: *"Little, I'm going to put the vision of me with a loving family on the screen of my mind three times per day. I'm also going to check in with you (using the dialogue) every time you feel anxious. And I'm going to give you little levers of control—baby steps aimed at our goal to create a family. I'm going to find joy in these moments. In fact, tomorrow, I'm taking the following baby step: _____."* I waited for Robert to fill in the blank: "I'm going to a photography club meeting at the library," he said, "and sit through at least 15 minutes of it and check out all of the people who attend."

Step nine is dedicating this action to your consciously intended goal. Big Robert would promise: *"All the while I'm taking this baby step, Little Rob, I'm going to hold our dream of love and family, no matter how hopeless or afraid you may feel. I'm going to hold your fear and hold this vision for you, and never stop holding. With every baby step, I'm going to get stronger—strong enough to get you what you want, no matter how long it takes."*

Step ten is to follow through with little baby steps every day.

As you can see, Robert had a lot of work to do to build trust in his relationship with himself—his internal disconnect was cavernous. But now he had action tools with which to close the gap. By creating vision, writing dialogues, and following through with daily actions, he could get the ball rolling. His imagination now fixed on his vision, he could progress toward his goal incrementally and surely.

BELIEVE IT OR NOT

I asked Robert if he believed this plan could work and he emphatically said, "No, I'll be stuck in loneliness forever." I reassured him that feeling hopeless is to be expected, given what he'd experienced so far, but that being an unbeliever will not interfere with his progress. Unlike other motivational programs, this one's effectiveness does not depend on "believing" a possible future outcome will come true. If it did, it would alienate most of the people who need help with this issue! After all, hopelessness is the predominating feeling they report. The Outer Child exercises are specifically designed to work *with* self-doubt and hopelessness. It takes advantage of the feelings of "learned helplessness" to increase compassion in your internal connection and to motivate you to get moving toward your goals. To succeed, all Robert needed was to keep using his imagination to target a future vision, stay compassionately tuned in, and take consciously intended actions. A month later, he reported:

> After taking weeks of daily steps I got up the nerve to call a woman I'd met at a concert. I was cowering and shaking, but I did it as a baby step for Little Rob. For once, I made him come first. No act of bravery was too great to help this lonely, scared Inner Child of mine. It didn't matter how the woman reacted to me. I told Little Rob: "No matter how afraid you are, I'm not leaving your side for a minute. If you're scared, so be it, I won't leave you, it's you and me. That's all that counts. She's just a prop, an opportunity to show you that I'm going to be brave and take actions to get stronger."
>
> So I met her for coffee, quaking in my boots, but the whole time I stuck up for my fearful Little Kid instead of being ashamed of how terrified he was. My jaw was rigid from fear through the whole thing, so needless to say the conversation didn't flow too well. But at least I tried, and I told Little Rob things were going to get better as I got braver.

IT'S YOUR CHOICE

You cannot choose to stop having fears; they are involuntary. But you can choose whether or not to let those primal feelings interfere in your relationships. Whether the fears are triggered by another person or from old emotional wounds, you can use them as grist for developing self-reliance. Nurturing your own emotional core instead of seeking external nurturance helps you become a stronger Adult. In developing self-assurance, self-love, and self-reliance, your capacity for connection increases exponentially. Robert again, months later:

> A few women down the path—reaching out to each one was an act of true bravery—I finally met someone I could talk to a little bit— someone who'd also had a hard time like me, but in a different way. And you know what she asked? "Ever been married?" and I told her no. And then she asked, "How come you've been single this long?" I patted my shirt pocket where I imagined keeping Little Rob tucked in safely, and told her, "Because I have a lot of fear." Then she asked: "How about right now?" and I said, "I'm dealing with it."

When Robert shared this at a later workshop, the women universally found his admission of vulnerability to this woman appealing, insisting they would swoon if a man shared his feelings forthrightly like that. Robert hadn't been laying his fear at the woman's feet, expecting her to do something about it; he'd owned it and shared it openly with her without strings attached. Most recently, he reported this:

> This thing I've got with my Inner Child is really powerful. It's a tool I keep in my pocket. I use it to take care of my really intense Little Kid on a deep emotional level every day. This is making me a stronger adult. When the fear comes up, I know I have to get closer to Little and accept his feelings. I can't be ashamed anymore of how nervous he gets, even if he makes my mouth go dry when I try to speak. Likewise, if my hands shake, so be it. I have to put him first, no matter how foolish he makes me look.
>
> The dialogue keeps reminding me that it is not up to anyone else to make me feel secure. It's up to me. I'm getting better at it. I'm actually grateful when someone triggers my anxiety because it helps me appreciate how emotional and needy my little guy still is. I can't always calm him down, but at least I can stay by his side.

That last woman has become more than just a prop for me. So far, she hasn't run. Outer Child hasn't kicked up as much of a ruckus with her. Not that I don't have a lot of anxiety, but I'm patient with me and she's patient with me.

OUTER CHILD SIGHTINGS

Let's see how Dottie managed her situation. Remember the first action step Brad chose as his lever of control? He'd committed to getting into the moment with her for five minutes during dinner. Dottie said she'd felt a mixture of hope and anxiety when he'd ordered that special bottle of wine. "What's this? Are we celebrating or something?" she'd asked sarcastically. But she had been writing dialogues for a few weeks and was able to head off a potential self-defeating reaction:

> I did some mental work right there at the table. I put my Outer Child on notice. I told her to turn around and face me and listen. "I'm in charge," I told her silently. "I know you're trying to protect Little, and I appreciate that, but butt out and let me handle things. I'm taking care of Little now." And right there, as Brad was pouring the wine, Outer turned around and stood still. I had my parts in order and I was in charge. I was able to enjoy—no, savor—the very special wine.

As Brad continued working on emotionally reinvesting in his marriage, Dottie was doing her part, turning her attention toward nurturing herself. A few more weeks into this work, Dottie's posture toward Brad had changed and she told him she felt sad about the love that was lacking in their marriage:

> It's like an elephant in the living room, Brad. And my discomfort with it has made me think about which way to go with our marriage. In the past I tried to make you responsible for my needs. I'm changing that. I'm taking better care of myself now. You might still see the old Dottie once in a while—reacting to this love-loss between us—but I'm moving forward. The new Dottie has a lot more going for her. I've looked to you to make me feel better for too long. I'm feeling better about myself and trying to figure out what's in my best interest.

As the process unfolded, Dottie would still catch her Outer Child reverting to one of its old clinging behaviors, but she used each "Outer Child sighting" as a trigger to spur her growth in a self-loving, self-responsible direction. When she lapsed into an old pattern, she promptly recognized it, and observing that Brad remained emotionally unavailable, resolved each time to take charge of her own emotional needs.

The dynamics between Brad and Dottie were dramatically changing. They were in a new position to each other. I hope my readers can guess where all of their positive intentions eventually led. There was no instant cure here. It involved consistency of effort.

Remember, this program is about taking action. Actively use your imaginative powers to visualize yourself in the future as you'd like to be. Stay focused on your love goals. Use the dialogues to stay in touch with your emotional core—the source of your motivation to change. And perform the daily actions in the real world with conscious intention of reaching your goals. As another client, George, put it:

> When I became a wreck with my new partner, I thought, "This program isn't working." But then I realized this was just my Outer Child trying to get my partner to take my insecurity away. I'd been aiming this stuff at my lovers without knowing it, but doing the daily action steps changed things. Each action shows me that I can take care of me in a loving way. With my new partner I'm able to let my guard down and act more confident, because the risk doesn't feel as great. I have my own back. If things feel shaky, I have it covered. I just use the insecurity to get stronger and take self-loving actions.

BABY STEPS

As I've explained throughout this book, it doesn't matter whether each daily action you take relates directly to your goal. For example, if you're single, you might join a hiking club thinking it might be a great way to meet other single people. But when you go to the trailhead on your first "group" hike, it turns out you're the only one who showed! So much for romance on the trail. Okay, go for the hike alone. This builds toward your goal because you take this action with conscious intention to address your core needs. You *dedicate* it to your ultimate goal. As you hike alone you are exercising the muscles (neural connections) of your higher brain. When you "look for the joy in the activity," you're giving your brain an extra workout. The mental muscles ultimately help you overcome the obstacles blocking your love goal. Your immediate task is to use the hike to get into the moment on behalf of your Inner Child, not to meet Mr. Right. You are taking each action to provide a release for your Outer Child (after all, you're asking it to stop acting out your emotions) and on behalf of your Inner Child's constantly emerging needs—bestowing love upon yourself to go out and successfully create love with a willing partner.

FOURTEEN

Outer Child and Debt

A good way to strengthen your Adult Self is to focus on a very practical matter—your finances.

Some Outer Children hoard money. Others are underearners, sticking with jobs that pay far less than they're worth. Many have holes in their pockets when it comes to cash. And that hole can become a bottomless pit around credit. In fact, credit affects the brain differently from cash. There is a loss-aversion function in the brain. When you buy something with cash, it involves actual loss (your wallet is actually physically lighter); whereas paying with credit makes the transaction abstract and involves a different brain function. So plastic fundamentally changes the way we spend money.

BUY, BUY, BUY

Outer Child likes to wait until Adult Self isn't looking and then grab for your wallet. It can hijack your finances, tie up your assets, drain your bank accounts, and strap you with so much debt and worry, you can't enjoy life's day-to-day pleasures:

I don't let my Outer Child anywhere near my credit cards, especially not since I eyed that new boat. Buying it would put me under in more ways than one.

Some Outer Children spend money because the process of spending offers a kind of release itself... momentary happiness, regardless of what they purchased:

I have bags of things all over the house with the tags still on that I'll never use and yet I can't pay my oil bill this month.

Some Outer Children use money to pamper themselves. They buy things to replace the love they can't get from other people.

Outer Child identifies with the object: *"I can see myself in that house."*

Maybe we can't buy a sense of personal worth, but we can accumulate status symbols and impress friends and family. Outer Child is 100% behind the notion that *whoever dies with the most toys wins.* We obviously can't buy immortality, but we can buy things that outlive us, like boats, houses, cars, whose parts take longer to rot than ours.

Adult Self and Outer Child interpret the old adage that money is congealed life in different ways. Adult understands that a certain amount of money helps create lifestyle comforts and broadens your choices and experiences. Outer Child's take on it is more basic: More is better. The more you have, the happier you'll be. A research study in which psychologists collaborated with economists found that people with tons of money are no happier than people with just enough money to avoid having to worry about it. In fact, wealthier people experience social and occupational pressures that can increase rather than decrease their stress levels.

Unquestionably, life is even more stressful when you don't have enough money to pay your bills. The very real threat of canceled credit cards, collection agencies, and foreclosure notices keep more than a few people up at night. Which part of the personality was either compulsively underearning, overworking, overspending, or all of the above? Who was out there running amuck with the buck? Outer Child, of course.

Outer Child sabotages your finances through commissions and omissions—*commissions* like impulse buying; and *omissions* like procrastinating about finding a better job or saving for retirement. Outer is quick to embrace risks, like overmortgaging your house, yet uses procrastination and avoidance when it comes to taking positive steps toward improving your finances, like pursuing a new career path:

> My Outer Child has no problem shopping, but has a million excuses when it comes to following up on a job lead. I learned from doing dialogues that my Inner Child is afraid of the unknown—new work tasks, new settings, new people—but is equally afraid of being put out on the street because I can't pay my rent. My Outer Child responds by sleeping...and only gets up when there's another sale at Bloomingdales.

Outer's economic policy is Buy Now, Pay Later. It gets you to put your head in the sand while your financial issues silently escalate into catastrophes, and then goes on a spending spree or leverages what's left of your financial security when you should be finding the nearest Debtors Anonymous meeting.

ADDICTED TO BAD CHOICES

We've explored some of the brain areas involved in Outer Child's behaviors. Acting on those areas is a potent brew of brain chemicals that mediate Outer's impulsivity, risk-taking, bingeing, and gambling. Outer is especially susceptible to dopamine, the neurochemical we discussed in the chapter about procrastination. Dopamine facilitates motivation, feelings of pleasure, reward, and craving, and plays a major role in addiction. When researchers enhance dopamine in rats' brains, the animals eagerly run on wheels and press levers to get a reward—food. When their dopamine is blocked, the rats don't even bother to eat. Interestingly when force-fed the rats show they like the food. This is because the researchers had not blocked the rats' opiate, just their dopamine. *Liking* a reward is opiate-related, whereas *craving* the reward is dopamine-related.

Deregulated dopamine can shorten attention span, increase reward-seeking, and trigger the hyperactivity seen in attention-deficit hyperactivity disorder (ADHD). Cocaine and amphetamines increase dopamine transmission, which accounts for the reckless behaviors of cocaine addicts. Increased dopamine also accounts for the manic phase of bipolar disorder—when people become grandiose, do daring things (like try to fly off skyscrapers), and happily gamble away the farm. Schizophrenia, with its irrational thoughts and behavior, is believed to be caused by chronically high levels of dopamine in specific regions of the brain.

Blocking dopamine causes both rats and humans to lose motivation. For example, antipsychotic medications, which are dopamine blockers such as Haldol and Thorazine, help reduce people's delusions, but also reduce their volition and can produce lethargy.

Research shows that financial windfalls give you a greater dopamine rush than money acquired through steady accrual. Anticipating a pleasurable reward revs up the dopamine production even more. Depending upon how your brain processes dopamine, you can become instantly addicted to taking risks (like impulsive stock buying) that carry potential big rewards.

"Gambling is due to the frailty of our nervous system," explains science journalist Jonah Lehrer, "and exploits specific hiccups in our brain." One such hiccup is our tendency to become easily programmed by intermittent reinforcement. For instance, dopamine levels rapidly increase when you receive an unexpected reward, such as when you win at the slots. If you keep losing, you don't have great expectations that the next quarter will bring down the coins. When it does, it is an unexpected surprise, which triggers a surge of dopamine that instantly rewards you with pleasure, neurochemically encouraging you to stick with it.

Surging dopamine can heighten your awareness of particular things, planting them front and center in your consciousness. A multitude of ordinary things suddenly can take on "salience," acquiring an enhanced aura of meaning and significance. In trying to make sense of so many things calling out to you at once, the brain tends to organize the incoming data incorrectly, forming illogical assumptions, making irrational choices, prompting you to take foolhardy risks. The bombardment of information overwhelms the brain's ability to process it correctly, affecting its thought architecture, which leads to illogical thinking systems, delusions associated with schizophrenia, and mood disorders. This is the basis of some mental illnesses, but the occasional surge of dopamine can also explain why your Outer Child occasionally goes on eating binges at food banquets and shopping sprees at the mall:

> The other day I bought all of these things I didn't need. Yesterday in the store they were begging me to buy them. Today I don't know where to put them except in the garbage.

It's time to rise up to your current financial challenge. Tackling it will have a parallel benefit in all areas of your life, because along the way you'll strengthen your Adult Self. You'll be guiding the direction of your financial life rather than accepting your role as a rat in the cage programmed by intermittent reinforcement to repeat your old spending patterns. Rather than driven by internal fluctuations of dopamine, you can make conscious, informed choices. The rat running on the wheels to earn a token reward was your Outer Child. As your Adult Self gains control, your relationship to money changes—how you earn it, save it, spend it, borrow it, and invest it.

MANAGING FEAR

Making this change is not a superficial process. As always, it involves the primal. It involves dealing with fear:

I was afraid I'd never have enough, that I'd get left all alone with nothing and no one. So I filled my world with stuff.

The way we deal with fear absolutely affects our relationship with money. Fear can make us feel defeated too easily, overwhelm our creative thinking, and cause us to overlook financial opportunities other people snatch up. Fear itself isn't the problem. It's how we manage fear that makes the difference. The idea is to have your Adult Self face your fears rather than let your Outer Child act them out in mindless habits and defense mechanisms that have become counterproductive:

I hated my fear. It prevented me from establishing a name for myself. I was afraid to ask for anything, especially a raise. Fear was my enemy. But I learned how to blame my cowardly behavior on my Outer Child and to look at my fear as a part of me that needed acceptance. I used the dialogues to care for my fear like it was my little buddy. I learned to work with it instead of against it and push ahead in my career.

Fear is an intrusive emotion. When we lacked tools for dealing with it, our only recourse was to dismiss it, squelch it, ignore it, pretend it wasn't there, project it onto others, or numb ourselves. We may have acted *as if* we felt confident when we were anything but. These Outer Child defenses only served to drive fear in deeper, where it incubated and later interfered with extra force.

> My Outer Child was a miser. My kids thought I was cheap, but I couldn't convince myself that if I bought that deluxe swing set, we wouldn't starve to death ten years from now. When I asked Little Me about this, he was too afraid to talk. It took weeks to find what he wanted, and it was to feel secure enough to enjoy life with my family, so I learned to face the swing sets of life.

When you disown your fear, you're disconnecting from your emotional core. Of course, you don't do this intentionally, but by condemning your fear to the dungeon (your unconscious), you likewise send your Inner Child there. The more you suppress fear and abandon your Inner Child, the more powerful and subversive Outer Child becomes.

THE BIGGER PICTURE

History has provided vivid examples of what happens when major fear-provoking events cause people to act out collectively in self-sabotaging ways...what happens when Outer Child goes global.

We can look at the impact the attacks of September 11 had on the United States and the world for clues about which parts of our collective psyches took control in the wake of the event. The attacks created a heightened, sustained undercurrent of fear that triggered a lot of Outer Children to act out. We were shaken and looking for ways to feel secure again. So a huge number of Outer Children, eyeing easy credit, responded with, *"I'll give you security, I'll buy a McMansion."* When they couldn't pay the McMortgages, foreclosures gave their Inner Children something else to fear.

When Outer Children interact with other Outer Children, there are ripple effects, patterns of responses that permeate all levels of society— interpersonal, familial, governmental, and global. These ripples and patterns constitute an Outer Child culture that runs parallel to the larger culture. Part of Outer Child culture is out in the open, part is disguised, and part is underground. For instance, we can see people flashing credit cards, but we can't tell which ones can pay their bills. Yet we are affected by all levels of Outer Child culture.

Outer Child culture to some degree drives financial markets and governments—the hunger for money and power and the fear of losing it. Outer Children tend to get drunk on power. Politicians (who have active Outer Children) get quickly addicted to power and need more and more of it to feed their habit. They make decisions with the next campaign foremost in mind, not always what's in the best interest of their constituents. Leaders of all kinds can display the "form" of integrity, but lack the substance—like those TV evangelists whose own moral failings were exactly what they preached against.

When the recession hit, it hit hard. Lots of Outer Children had bought things they couldn't afford by borrowing money from lenders who couldn't afford to lend it. When enough people called in their cards (because they needed the cash), the house of cards collapsed.

Credit had turned dangerous in the hands of the Outer Child culture. To Outer Children, credit is high-carb food; bingeing on credit makes them hyperactive. And Outer Child culture is financed by credit. It probably started innocently enough, out of necessity, with people keeping tabs at the supermarket. Then they bought furniture on credit, took out car loans. Eventually they made smaller and smaller down payments and owed more and more. They took possession of things they couldn't afford. In a sense they owned nothing because it was all leveraged. Too many people did it. Eventually they couldn't sell assets to pay off debt. This is what happened to the mortgage industry with its variable interest rates, piled-on home equity loans, and subprime lending. When the real estate market bubble burst, it became a breaking point in a weak system and herniated the economy.

The collapse came as a shock, not only to the man on the street, but to the heads of our most esteemed financial institutions. In the height of the crisis, academics, economists, and investment experts were all at a loss, tripping over themselves trying to explain why they hadn't accurately and publically predicted this disaster. We'd thought the Adults were in charge, but it turned out that our leaders had just been well-dressed Outer Children. We realized too late that some had been operating on "presuming to know" and others on instincts of greed covered up by self-serving rationalizations, rather than acting like members of an evolved species.

FORM OVER SUBSTANCE

Outer Children are notoriously impressed with confidence—not just their own, but *other people's.* This is another example of Outer's attachment to form over substance. I'm talking here about confidence with little or nothing to back it up. Confidence is the glitter and bling of the personality. You probably know someone whose ideas are mediocre and sometimes completely wrongheaded and yet they exude supreme confidence in expressing their opinions and even impress other people with them. Conversely some of the world's most competent people can make a very different impression— they're humble, carefully qualify their claims, or even socially awkward. And as to the confidence they *do* exude—for instance, confidence in their convictions—if they can't convey their ideas charismatically and with aplomb, the general public tends to dismiss them.

In Outer Child culture, form is more important than substance. In fact, some Outer Children can't perceive substance at all. For instance, we didn't seem to notice that our financial leaders weren't investing in *real* assets, that they'd only been developing more sophisticated ways to put money at greater risk than ever before. Officials in corporate, government, and academic institutions had apparently conveyed impressive confidence. Certainly the system is complex and corruption in not unknown either. But the Outer Child culture, immersed in its love affair with form and lulled by false confidence, ignored the warning signs until it was too late.

BLIND FAITH

Outer Child culture thrives on blind faith. Outer Child doesn't want to know what it doesn't want to know. Blind faith is what led otherwise intelligent people to invest in grossly inflated assets and Ponzi schemes. They had blind faith in the integrity of the American and international banking industries. But as it turned out, rating organizations had not been scrutinizing the investment systems and in turn were not brought under scrutiny. There were no checks and balances. As Warren Buffet once famously remarked, as the tide went out you got to see who wasn't wearing his swimsuit. When its blind faith was shattered, Outer reverted to every-man-for-himself tactics, which led to the frenzied sell-offs that sank the market.

OUTER CHILD GOES EXTREME

Remember, your Inner Child is innocent in all of this. Little You feels bad when it doesn't have what other people have, and wants to be admired in the same way it admires other people for the beautiful things they have. Yes, Little You has *wants,* but it's the way Outer responds to those desires that creates the problem. Outer can be fiercely competitive and is sometimes willing to break the rules to win. For instance, at the Outer Child level of culture, it was commonplace for heads of financial institutions to make decisions that secured their personal assets in spite of tremendous losses suffered by their customers (the public was outraged by the Wall Street bonuses in the midst of recession). Outer Children want it all, even if it means other people have to do with less.

The bottom line is that many Outer Children try to get away with whatever they can. Subprime lending again provides the example. Local mortgage brokers and banks aggressively racked up as many contracts as possible—for the commissions involved—ignoring the homebuyers' financial wherewithal. Certain lenders must have known they weren't doing the individual homebuyers any favors, because they fraudulently modified buyers' financial data. But this fudging was easy for Outer Child to rationalize. Let's say you considered yourself an honest broker whose company sold subprime mortgages. When you signed up a new homebuyer, you thought, *"This guy won't be able to pay the mortgage in a few years, but I've told him the risks and he's not a child. He'll probably flip it before then anyway."* Although well-intentioned brokers did warn buyers about oversized payments, they couldn't predict that the house wouldn't be worth enough in three years to make a profit or break even. The culture of corruption was so pervasive, they'd unwittingly become part of the problem.

Not everyone had good intentions. In its extreme form, Outer Child is a sociopath. The limbic brains of most sociopaths are found to have a glitch that interferes with their ability to feel anxiety—especially the anxiety of getting caught. Fear of punishment, of suffering painful consequences, is the primal root of guilt, and part of what holds the rest of us back from committing crimes. We non-sociopaths are too aware of the consequences of getting caught. We simply have too many fears to *knowingly* pursue illegal or dishonest schemes. (Notice the emphasis on the word *knowingly.*)

But even non-sociopaths can get into financial difficulty, because Outer Child tends to follow the herd. If everyone else is doing something questionable, Outer Child tends to join in—an unfortunate example of mirror neurons at play. Monkey see, monkey do. Leading up to the recession, for example, buyers saw everybody else overborrowing, lenders saw everybody else overlending, so Outer Children said, *"It'll be okay. Let's do it."*

CREEPING CORRUPTION

When corruption becomes more blatant, some Outer Children look the other way: hear no evil, speak no evil, see no evil. An organization might have a few rotten apples—dishonest investors who can spoil the bunch— and Outer Child can remain oblivious to it all. Many would rather "switch than fight," especially if blowing the whistle would mean losing their jobs. So they deny what they're seeing. Denial is exactly how corruption sneaks up and becomes pervasive.

Indeed, corruption can creep up on you insidiously. Maybe you work for a company that is slowly becoming corrupt, but its image remains good and the corruption is so gradual and well disguised that it doesn't set off the trip wire of your anxiety. You don't hear the usual warning bells—those internal fear signals about getting caught—so you fail to notice you're doing something "wrong," and unknowingly cross over into corrupt behavior.

Outer Child culture is about pushing the envelope. When it comes to money and power, Outer can become spoiled, reckless, and downright underhanded. Since some Outer Children can't be trusted to keep their hands out of the cookie jar and others don't know when they're doing something wrong, the financial markets need clear boundaries to guide everyone's behavior. The parent needs to tell the child, *"That's naughty. You can't do this."* But the parent system—our official overseers—have, as we've seen, had their own Outer Child problems.

YOUR FINANCIAL FUTURE

Outer Child culture, in responding to encroaching world threats, has affected all of us on a personal level. We can't make the underlying fear go away by willing it away, but we can change our behavioral response to it— both personally and collectively. The Outer Child tools empower us to work through our shared fears and personal worries and build a new personal economy, laying a new brick in the foundation of the world economy, one action at a time.

In transforming fear into constructive action, creating vision is crucial. Consider your financial goals—both short- and long-term—and use your imagination to form a clear and definite vision of them, as if already accomplished. Keep this Future Vision firmly fixed on the screen of your mind. Your imagination is larger than your fear. In your imagination, you can soar above and beneath and through fear. In your imagination, fear is no longer a wall, but a springboard. Your Future Vision lifts you to the level of solution—the space beyond the fear—allowing you to "focus through" your cinder block of fear. Imagination is limitless. It is not bound by the crippling rules of your internal gatekeepers—those unconscious mental barriers erected by your Outer Child to overprotect you from all of your fears (fear of disappointment, fear of making a fool of yourself, fear of change, fear of success, fear of failure, etc.). In your imagination, you never lose; you just try, try again until you succeed.

Using your imagination in a goal-directed way produces a surge of brain activity, strengthening the nerve centers of your brain's higher command. So to get your mirror neurons and other brain processes working on your behalf, create a clear picture of yourself in the future engaged in the act of fulfilling your financial goals. By imagining yourself taking real behavioral steps you are exercising these significant neural connections and rehearsing the skill set to take these steps. Next, imagine the future lifestyle and physical surroundings you enjoy as a result, having incrementally achieved your goals. Creating this Future Vision and referring to it frequently increases your likelihood and capability to make this happen.

To boost the power of your imagination, you can enclose your financial Future Vision within your Dream House. Your Dream House is a crucible in which to transform fear into achievement. Imagine sitting before your beautiful view with your fear tucked safely and warmly in your breast pocket, feeling good about yourself for what you've accomplished. Your Dream House embodies your goals, obstacles overcome, and fulfillment— a pleasurable image to conjure up as you go about your day.

Then take another leap and imagine feeling *gratitude* to the powers of existence for being able to enjoy this fulfillment. You don't have to actually feel gratitude—you just have to imagine what gratitude *would feel like*. To imagine a feeling is almost the same as feeling it—and to certain regions in your brain, they are indistinguishable. When you conjure up gratitude, you intensify your *sense of reality* about your financial Future Vision, giving the as-if function in your brain an extra workout. Remember, belief isn't the essential ingredient here, it's the act of creating the mental image that performs the work of physical therapy for the brain. So don't waste energy trying to believe that you can actually accomplish these goals. Just conjure up the frequent image of yourself in the act of achieving them and of later enjoying their benefits. Stamp these images on the screen of your mind, and skeptical or not, they will make you more conscious and alert to new financial possibilities and keep you working toward your goals. Frequent contemplation of your Future Vision increases your mental and even physical capacity to move forward.

I encourage you to write down financial goals and post them around your home and workplace—on the mirror, the refrigerator, the desk. Post them in your checkbook, wallet, and other places you look at when you're engaged in your financial life. Rewrite them and repost them frequently to keep them fresh in your mind. Make new signs and doodle your favorite designs on them while daydreaming about yourself in the act of working toward financial success. When you see one of these signs, let it enhance your emotional motivation to follow through. Move these reminders around to allow their messages to catch you off guard. When you notice one, think of your Dream House or some pleasurable image associated with your financial goals to keep your mental muscles toned and action-ready.

TALK IT OUT

Beyond daydreaming about your Future Vision, where do you get the motivation to follow through? By looking to others? Competing against others? External validation? Heaven forbid! By now you know where the most potent motivation comes from—within. You know how to get it: by tuning in to yourself—listening to Little's fears and needs. You get motivation by feeling compassion for your own internal needs. In developing self-compassion, this heightened level of self-love empowers you to take constructive actions. When Little You tells you what it needs, you won't want to leave this helpless, blameless part of yourself behind:

> I'm the ambitious type. My Outer Child always went for the best because I was afraid of not being the best. If I didn't have the best, I was no good, as if I was disappointing somebody. When I connected with my Inner Child, I got in touch with my fears about "being no good." It started me down a whole new path—to help the Little

Guy. I turned self-negation into self-love. Now I do something every day—actions for me that aren't to impress anyone else. I still want the best, but I bought a VW Beetle the other day and I feel proud driving around in it because it's small (like my Little Guy) and it's okay that it's not a Ferrari.

Little You wants what all little children want: security, to enjoy life, to feel entitled. Little is afraid of being neglected, unworthy, "less than," left out, not having what other people have:

> Little Me was mad because she wanted beautiful clothes and things. I reminded her that I couldn't afford them and that this was because she was so afraid all the time and that it held me back in my career. My Little retorted with, "Don't blame me. I can't help being afraid. You hate me and you don't do anything to make it better for us." Her anger was so forceful, I realized that I had to get Little Me out of this bind and make bolder moves in my work. Learning how to handle Little's fear about taking initiatives helped me stop pandering and become responsible for my life.

Little's greatest need is to be taken care of. Your current financial problems are forsaking that need. In writing your Outer Child dialogues, use the power of your imagination to make Big You as caring, wise, sincere, competent, reliable, and mature as you can. Imagine an Adult Self who is fully capable of taking care of an Inner Child's needs and taming an obstreperous Outer Child. Use the dialogue to practice becoming that Adult for Little You. As writer, you step into the role of the ideal parent toward yourself, and in the process you inculcate self-love along with greater Adult capability:

> My Inner Child was afraid that I'd never get what I want unless I got it now, so my Outer Child maxed out my credit cards. Little Me was filled with emotional hunger, but spending more than I made caused her to feel even emptier and more afraid. This gave me reason to sober up from shopoholism. I planned activities to substitute for spending, like walking the two miles home from work. Not only does it help me stay trim, but in leaving my car home, it's impossible to swing by the mall.

Empathically coax Little You to express itself about your financial problems. You can also ask Outer to turn around and listen to what Little You needs Big You to do. As your Inner Child expresses its deepest needs and fears, your unconscious becomes conscious. As your Adult Self listens, your motivation to take action increases. As you respond to Little's needs with concrete actions, you become that loving, competent adult who incrementally works toward your goals.

LISTENING IS NOT ENOUGH

Soothing Little's feelings is not enough. Your Inner Child remains in jeopardy until you take action to improve your financial life. Make solemn promises to Little You to do things every day to move things forward. Keep your promises. It is not words, but deeds that cement your internal love-connection and make the difference in your bank account, as these testimonials from workshop members illustrate:

> My Outer Child had to have everything. I asked Little about this and found out how afraid she was of being nobody and nobody caring. After a few dialogues about this, Little convinced me I was making her miserable. I promised I'd do something about Outer and that very same day I returned some things to the mall—things Outer bought (Ha!). In my next dialogue, I told Outer to answer to me from now on. Who was listening, I don't know, it was just me writing at my desk. But it was an emotional moment because I felt change coming. I started taking action steps every day, the first being a phone call to find out about consolidating my debt. And so it went, action step by action step, day by day, until the shopping bags disappeared and I became solvent.

> I was feeling like a loser. My Outer Child was way too strong. When I asked him to turn around and listen, he just laughed. I talked to Little every day and found out that being broke made him afraid—not just of poverty, but of success, of getting a competitive backlash from peers if I started making real money. But I told Little that he had an Adult on his financial team now: me. It meant getting a better job—and another job on top of that. I had a lot of fear but I took the steps anyway. My first was to get outside help. Then I followed

up with more action steps: I went to Debtors Anonymous, got a sponsor, followed the program, got help from Job Corp, signed up with headhunters, got a financial advisor to create capitol out of the real money I started to make. It took a lot of work to climb out of the hole I'd dug, but it got Outer to stop laughing at me.

FIFTEEN

Outer Child and Depression

Depression is ubiquitous. The term is used colloquially (*"That movie was depressing."*), and clinically to denote a condition whose parameters are still debated by experts (*"I've been depressed for two and a half years."*).

You can be depressed about something such as the death of a loved one, the state of your finances, or the fact that it's going to rain again today. Or you can be depressed about nothing in particular, at least nothing you're aware of. You just feel blah, melancholic (*"I feel lifeless and drained but don't know why."*) Or you can be depressed about *everything*—the way a friend just spoke to you, your lost keys, your employer's wage freeze, the nice guy who didn't call. Doesn't anything ever go right? You say you're depressed, but often, you could just as well substitute the word *unhappy* or *sad, frustrated, miserable, worried, inadequate, frantic, bothered,* or *upset.*

CLINICAL DEPRESSION

There's a big difference between the relatively short mood dip that follows a bit of bad luck (you're facing possible layoffs at work just as you're trying to buy a house) and clinical depression, where you feel low so routinely that you need professional help. Does the term *chronic depression* describe you? Do you feel low and have negative feelings about your life and yourself most of the time?

Sometimes chronic depression hides behind other life issues. You might *think* your malaise reflects a relationship that's lost its passion or a frustrating job, but when you change lovers or jobs it follows you to the new venue. This suggests that your Outer Child has commandeered your depression and projected it onto an external situation *inappropriately.* In other words, Outer *externalized* your depression. Your job didn't cause your depression, although your performance was affected by it. The real problem was something more internal—a neurochemical process gone awry, perhaps, or an emotional issue (such as loneliness, unresolved grief, or chronic feelings of unworthiness) that had been affecting you more than you realized.

Your Outer Child can do the same thing with anxiety. You might have an undercurrent of anxiety and Outer externalizes it—projects it onto people or events. For instance, you might attribute an anxious moment to a comment someone made that got you riled up, when actually the problem was already there. Someone may have inadvertently triggered an agitated response in you, but that person was an innocent bystander to your hyper-reactive nervous system.

Often, anxiety and depression go together. You can be anxious about being depressed and depressed about being anxious. In many instances, depression is squelched anxiety—a way of turning inward and shutting down during a full-blown state of panic to protect yourself and preserve your strength for healing; think of a wounded animal crawling off to lick its wounds.

Depression can also be acute. It can descend upon you—an otherwise contented person—like a ton of bricks when you experience a profound loss—loss of a job, loss of a dream, loss of a bodily function, or loss of a loved one. Like with Brenda:

When my fiancé broke up with me, I went from being happy to profoundly depressed. I panicked, having suddenly lost my future, terrified I'd be alone forever. I was so depressed I could hardly get out of bed, and went about with a tight ball of anxiety in my stomach. Antidepressants helped somewhat, but I still wasn't me for a long time.

There are many stories like Brenda's. Abandonment and loss create conditions that resemble major depression. The grief and separation anxiety can linger indefinitely.

Depression can become so infused into your daily life that you develop a depressive personality:

I was too isolated and anxious to meet anybody. I freaked out too easily when I tried to get to know someone, which was pretty depressing. Always alone, I sat at the computer, watched TV, and slept a lot to escape. I felt like a freak or a depressive or whatever, like it was just who I turned out to be. I'd been that way for so long, I didn't know what "normal" felt like. I used to think back to when I was a kid full of hope and feel sad that things didn't turn out right—and it was all my fault, at least that's how it felt.

SELF-OBSESSION

Sometimes obsessive compulsive disorder (OCD) gets combined into depression in the form of obsessive thoughts that tick tick tick away in your head and prevent you from being in the moment. You observe yourself experiencing life from a distance rather than being a part of the experience.

When you obsess, it seems voluntary because it involves conscious thinking. As your mind works away, you believe you're directing the show. You're trying to *think* your way out of your depression. But when you go to shut off the constant ruminating—*enough already!*—you find you can't turn off that feed. The tape keeps rolling on its own. Obsession turned out to have its own mind. In fact, Outer Child has been hijacking the problem-solving corner of your brain to perpetuate this exhausting pattern, appropriating your cognitive resources for its own defensive purposes.

Obsessive thinking is one of Outer Child's most tenacious defenses. The amygdala contributes to this process, prompting the brain to figure out what's wrong so it can mount the proper defense. The mind's questioning goes on and on: *"What happened here? Where did my peace of mind go? What is making me sick? How come I'm not acting like other people? What am I doing wrong? Who can I blame? What am I up against?"* On and on, your runaway brain constantly chases after explanations to find its lost happiness. Your brain is "searching for the lost object."

Searching for the lost object is a term coined by attachment theorist John

Bowlby. It refers to a primary mental process involved in the first stages of grief and loss, similar to the phantom pain of searching for a lost limb. When the loss is caused by abandonment—someone leaves you—this obsessive "searching" causes you to obsess about your ex. You study old photographs, review details of your last encounter, and drive by his house or call over and over again. When the thing you've lost isn't a person but your peace of mind, then rather than study, review, and stalk a lover, you study, review, and stalk yourself. It's the brain's attempt to track its missing mental state.

Obsession is a form of protest—a willful rebuttal against the loss (*"I refuse to accept this!"*). Protest is an exhausting emotional process involved in bereavement and loss. With depression, Outer Child is waging a relentless protest against an internal psychic injury.

Recognizing that your obsession is involuntary—an automatic Outer Child defense—can help you break through your depression. You can turn the volume down on your obsessive thoughts, not take them seriously, not listen to them, not fuel the protest, not acquiesce to Outer's futile attempt to think its way out of the depression. You can't think your way out; you must act your way out. Your mind won't stop searching, spooling, and protesting until a stronger Adult Self takes charge of your recovery.

THE SCIENTIFIC STUDY OF DEPRESSION

Your Adult Self needs to direct your brain search away from self-obsession and toward exploring helpful information about overcoming depression. So much has been discovered about depression's emotional, psychological, and neurobiological dimensions that it's enough to fill whole libraries. You don't need to become an expert on the latest research to deal with the problem, but I think it's helpful to know some of the inroads scientists have been making. Then we'll leave a final analysis about the physical causes to the researchers and get down to the business of what we can do about it.

A DEPRESSION SWITCH

Recent studies using brain scans (fMRI studies) have identified an area called "Area 25" that lights up in depressed people. Area 25 also lights up in nondepressed people instructed to think depressing thoughts! Quieting Area 25 immediately reduces depression. By implanting electrodes in the brain, Area 25 can be turned off (through a procedure called deep brain stimulation), causing depressed feelings and thoughts to immediately go away.

Deep brain stimulation (DBS) involves surgery. Other medical treatments involve something less drastic—medication.

THE CHEMICAL THEORY

One of the older theories of depression sees the brain as a bowl of biochemical soup. Serotonin is considered one of the key ingredients in well-being and pleasure, so to treat depression you just add serotonin and stir. I call this the "chemical theory."

That's more or less what some patients believe when they take antidepressants like Prozac, Paxil, or Zoloft. Many think antidepressants contain serotonin, but that's not quite right. Instead these medications block the reabsorption of your own supply of serotonin, which accounts for the name of this class of drugs: selective serotonin reuptake inhibiters, or SSRIs. In other words, these antidepressants cause your own internal supply of serotonin to dwell longer in the synapses (spaces) between your neurons, where it reportedly continues to bombard the neurons' receptor sites. Proponents of the chemical theory believe (though this idea is disputed by others) that this prolonged bombardment is what accounts for antidepressants' ability to lift depression.

THE NEUROPLASTIC THEORY

In a departure from the chemical theory, other researchers believe that depression and anxiety are reversible neurodegenerative disorders, which involve not a chemical imbalance, but atrophy of certain brain areas. According to this school of thought, antidepressant therapies (including electroshock therapy) work by repairing atrophied dendrites (connective branches at the ends of neurons) and sprouting new neurons in key brain regions. In promoting neuronal growth (neurogenesis), antidepressants are taking advantage of the brain's plasticity. Antidepressant therapies, for example, are known to increase receptor sites for serotonin.

THE PLACEBO EFFECT

Research has shown that half of the people who benefited from anti-depressant drug trials were not taking a chemical substance; instead they were taking a dummy pill. Their condition improved due to something called the "placebo effect"—a manifestation of the brain's own pharmacy of powerful internal mood-stabilizers, pleasure enhancers, painkillers, "uppers," "downers," healers, and cell-progenitors. This effect is mediated by *autonomic* brain processes, since it is produced when the cognitive mind is "tricked" rather than by conscious will.

The Outer Child program is designed to enhance benefits of your own internal pharmacopeia through many means. One way is by personifying the three functional parts of the psyche, stimulating areas of the brain that coordinate the emotional (Inner), cognitive (Adult), and behavioral (Outer). Another is by rewarding your brain with visualizations and action steps that are pleasurable to keep your chemistry flowing (i.e., dopamine, endorphins) and reinforce positive new behaviors.

DEPRESSION AS A PHYSICAL DISORDER

Another interpretation of the scientific findings is that depression results from a reduction in overall brain functioning—not just with regard to mood, but with deficits in learning, memory, sleeping, sex drive, weight control, the ability to experience pleasure, and the senses of smell and taste. In other words, depression is more than a single condition; it is a syndrome characterized by a cluster of disabilities. Sadness just happens to be its most notable symptom.

This interpretation views depression as a physical disorder misinterpreted by the brain. Feelings are the brain's representation of what's going on in the body. The brain reads the sickness as sadness; low mood is a secondary response. "Withdrawing from activity," a commonly expressed symptom of depression, is seen as the body's way of conserving energy and minimizing risk—an evolved pattern of behavior mediated by the immune system.

This way of viewing depression would resolve some old quandaries. For instance, the neuroplastic theory's claim that antidepressants work by promoting neurogenesis (rather than by enhancing serotonin) would rectify a number of seeming contradictions. The lag time for an antidepressant to take effect, for one thing. It usually takes weeks for someone's depression to lift, even though serotonin levels increase within hours. The researchers in this camp say that's because it takes about that long for neural growth and repair to make an impact on mood. It would also explain why *reducing* serotonin is known to neither worsen nor create depression and why tianeptine, a chemical that dampens serotonin, actually *helps* with depression.

YES, WE CAN (CHANGE OUR BRAINS)

Whatever the final analysis, it's always worth repeating: Depression is reversible. The brain is plastic, moldable, and regenerative. The brain adapts by sprouting new branches (dendrites) from neurons, repairing receptor sites, and generating new neurons. The brain's capacity for repair and growth allows you to learn, remember, and change your behavior. It's what the Outer Child exercises are designed to accomplish—create new neural topiaries in the brain.

START YOUR ENGINES

The Outer Child program is in its glory when it comes to depression, anxiety, and obsession. It doesn't matter what caused the condition—persistent stress, profound loss, genetic predisposition, frontal-lobe malfunction, or trauma-induced brain damage—the three prongs of the program can help you alleviate it. You'll need to fire up all three engines—visualization, emotional attunement, and taking action—and keep them running. Half measures don't get the job done. Depression calls for a special application of the exercises. Please note that these tools are not designed to replace other recovery efforts, such as psychotherapy, support groups, nutrients, and/or medication, but to complement and enhance their benefits.

In applying the Outer Child program, the Adult Self knows not to expect immediate results, that recovery takes concerted effort. Just as a musical performance requires a written composition, players, and their execution of the piece, so does your recovery concert consist of composing a vision, orchestrating your emotional and behavioral parts, and performing action steps.

DREAM HOUSE REVISITED

We'll begin with a special application of the visualization exercise. Creating a Future Vision involves resurrecting your dreams and setting your mind on a trajectory toward the far-reaching goals of peace, contentment, and happiness.

I know that the unquiet state of the depressed mind, along with its self-obsession and pervasive sense of hopelessness, makes it difficult to focus and concentrate, let alone visualize yourself achieving this goal. That's why this exercise is so ideally suited for the depressed. Its effectiveness doesn't rely on overriding your self-doubt and despair. You don't have to believe the content of your vision or have faith in a positive future; you just have to imagine it. Play pretend. I'm not talking about magical thinking here. You're an adult who is learning that when you use your imagination in a goal-directed way, you get parts of your brain working that have been shut down for a long time. You're making furrows, planting seeds, and fertilizing soil in the landscape of your brain.

The more depressed and anxious you feel, the more effort it takes to create a vision of a future time in which you experience contentment. That's one of the reasons I developed the Dream House exercise. Conjuring a Dream House in your mind doesn't ask you to create a new mental image of your future achievements each time. The first time you create it, your unconscious mind projects your goals, obstacles, and personal resources onto its imaginary structure, design, and setting, without you consciously having to think about how you accomplish it. Once created, the Dream House *symbolizes* your brighter future in a goal-directed region of your mind and it stimulates those areas every time you conjure it up.

Yet even this—constructing a Dream House for the first time—can be a challenge for the depressed who are low on energy and short on patience. But the more difficult it is, the more benefit you gain from doing it. Remember, it is physical therapy for the brain. The more severe your depression, the more important it is to massage and exercise this part of the mind.

If you've already created a Dream House, you're ready to move on (if not, go back to Chapter Six for detailed instructions). Your job right now is to create new elements in your Dream House that make it so spectacular that when you are there (two years from now), you feel far less depressed or anxious than you do today. Imagine what new elements you would need to add to this house to give it the ability to elevate your mood. Maybe you need to bring more light into your favorite room, or create more open space, or make it cozier by filling it with books, blankets, photographs, or pets. Do you need higher ceilings? New views to gaze upon through your windows, or the sounds of a nearby waterfall, ocean, or brook? Whatever you need, imagine it there.

Imagine having created a wonderful space for social gatherings. If you wish, imagine weekend guests (who enjoy your home and you as much as you do) or frequent visits from friends, neighbors, clients, community. Add whatever elements (including relationships) your Dream House would need to make it a depression-free environment. Just make sure they are in keeping with the laws of reality. Remember, your house can't fly and you can't bring someone back from the dead. The more physically concrete and detailed you make this setting for your Future Vision, the greater its impact on your mind.

Imagine that you're sitting in your favorite spot in your house (two years from now), looking out at your beautiful view, feeling good about yourself because you have resolved all of your current problems, including your depression and anxiety. You feel deep satisfaction for that accomplishment. Even if you're only able to picture this positive image for a few seconds at a time, it leaves an imprint on the brain.

> As I conjured up my Dream House, I added a piano. For some reason it needed to be in the next room, out of sight, in order to make me feel happy about its being there. That silent piano represented victory over the depression, I suppose, and my whole Dream House vibrated with new life even though, in reality, I was still depressed. So it was quite a dichotomy—happy vision, sad life—but it helped.

You can alternate time frames for your Future Visions. For instance, you can imagine yourself three months from now, sitting in your own home (in keeping with reality, your Dream House would only be in the planning stages), feeling lighter, more in control, and *good* about creating the improvements you'd made. Conjure up this positive image for a few seconds and imagine feeling gratitude for it, *as if you were already enjoying this elevated mood.* To make the image more detailed, you can imagine changing an element in your own home to symbolically represent the possibility of real change. You can even force yourself to smile as you imagine it.

Psychologist Paul Ekman's extensive research in emotion and facial training has proven that even a forced smile leads to involuntary positive bodily reactions: "The face is a means of activating emotions."

> I imagined three months from now that I removed the curtains in my apartment and had sunlight streaming in from the eastern sky. A few weeks later I actually tore my living room curtains down, but the sun was glaring and suddenly the room looked dingy. A few weeks after coping with that, I picked up some chiffon curtains at a garage sale. It was a long time before I got around to taking them to the dry cleaners. But I finally hung them on the old bare curtain rods. Those billowing curtains letting light in were a new beginning for me.

You might prefer to imagine a very small symbol of improvement— something small enough to hold in your hand, maybe a rock you found or a favorite book you pulled from the shelf—something that represents the changes you're making. You may even want to go out and buy this item— this token of future improvement.

> I imagined a little stuffed teddy bear. I bought a blue velvet one with little movable arms. I held it when I practiced my visualization.

HAVING THAT HEART-TO-HEART

Keep your imagination fired up because you're going to need it to perform the next exercise: separation therapy. To prepare, consider this: Outer Child has been interfering in your relationship with yourself, thriving on your depression, and sabotaging your recovery at every turn. As a result, your Inner Child feels sad, alone, abandoned, frustrated, and anxious—waiting for Big You to take control.

Writing dialogues between the three parts of your psyche will help you reverse your depression, but writing them takes effort—something you might feel too emotionally depleted to take up without someone there to support you. So get help from a friend, coach, sponsor, therapist, or someone from your support group, someone to sit with you and transcribe or help you write your dialogue, or just to provide encouragement.

Let's get started on a practice run. The first step is to imagine yourself writing a dialogue. Imagining the process first is good preparation for over-coming the inertia of depression. Picture having a heart-to-heart with your Outer Child, and getting it to turn around and listen. Then imagine your-self actively engaged in writing a dialogue with your Inner Child and soothing and calming its feelings. Create a vivid image of these activities lifting your mood.

The next task is to put pen to paper. Write today's date and make a list of all of the things you do (or fail to do) that interfere in getting better, and immediately attribute these self-defeating behaviors to your Outer Child. You're sparing your innocent Inner Self from bearing the brunt of all of the self-rage, self-hatred, and self-blame you feel toward yourself about being depressed. Then coax Little You to open up about what it is feeling inside about your depressed state. Make sure Big You is reassuring, kind, and gentle. Writing these words is an act of self-love.

As Little You opens up, you may uncover some surprising emotional issues, issues that may not have *caused* the depression, but which *come to the fore* during this time of recovery. Whether they caused your depression or not, the issues provide healing moments. They offer access to your restora-tive center. You may not have started out with the following emotional needs, but once depression hit, you sure did acquire them: the need to be emotionally taken care of; the need to fill a void; the need to believe in your-self; and the need to believe in the future. Your depression has created urgency around these four needs. Outer Child dialogues address them.

URGENT SELF-CARE

The need to be taken care of requires extra focus. We can all identify with it—it's human and natural to want to be taken care of, especially when we feel sick inside and out. This need comes in handy, because learning how to take care of your Inner Child helps lift your depression.

Where does this need come from? Maybe you came from a loving fam-ily but your current life stands in stark contrast to it; you yearn for the nur-turance you had. Maybe the need to be cared for has been intensified by the absence of someone—perhaps you've been through a painful loss or aban-donment. Or maybe as a child your parents had needs of their own and your need to be taken care of was never entirely satisfied. Maybe they were sick, narcissistic, or alcoholic, and you took care of their emotional needs instead of the other way around. You and your parents' roles were reversed, and as a child, you had to do all sorts of work to get your parents to parent you.

A lot of people who suffer depression have experienced role reversals of this sort. I see them in workshops all the time. When Patricia—who you might remember from earlier chapters—had initially read her dialogue aloud, her role reversal was glaring.

> LITTLE PATRICIA: You need to stop obsessing, Big. Barry isn't worth it. You need to focus on yourself instead of him. Don't you realize he is never going to change? You need to get stronger, Big, and stop lying around all day. You can do it, I know you can—you just have to believe in yourself."
>
> BIG PATRICIA: You're right, Little, I'll try to do better.

You can hear Little Patricia acting more like the adult than Big Patricia. Her Inner Child was making all of the suggestions, giving pep talks to Big Patricia, and doing all of the problem solving, while her Adult Self is passively taking emotional support *from* her child self!

I asked Patricia if she'd had to work hard as a child to get her parents to parent her and her answer (no surprise) was an emphatic yes. As you read in Chapter Eight, her mother had been incapacitated with multiple sclerosis when Patricia was still a child.

When I help a workshop participant see a role reversal, lightbulbs start appearing over other people's heads, one after another, around the circle —it's synergy, no doubt, owing to the mirror neuron effect. These are breakthrough moments. People realize what's been wrong inside their psyches all along: Inner Child and Adult Self have changed places. In resolving their internal reversals, people's relationships with themselves take a sharp turn for the better. Big You takes charge, positioned to take care of Little You. Little You finally becomes the *recipient* of your own intensive self-care.

When I see someone's Inner Child doing too much work during a dialogue, I imagine the brain activities involved. I picture an engorged amygdala. Inside is a small heart pulsating with emotion (wearing a halo to signify our blameless inner self), struggling to get its needs met. Outside is the cracked, crusty shell (wearing a backward baseball cap), and it's grabbing the cerebral cortex (carrying a briefcase to signify the Adult brain) and pulling it along. If you don't take this imagery too literally, it offers a concrete way to conceptualize what goes on in depression (Inner Child being mishandled by Outer Child, and Adult Self being overpowered), suggesting what kind of physical therapy you need to do, beginning with exercising the atrophied muscles of your cognitive adult mind.

Patricia was careful to correct her role reversal in her next dialogue. She got Big to make the effort instead of expecting Little to be the "parent." Big Patricia had found a new purpose—to find ways to administer to her Inner Child's needs.

> Little Me had a hard time accepting all this help from Big Me. She didn't feel entitled to be taken care of. This was the first time she was ever *invited* to be dependent. Little thought her job was to fix Big Me. Big had to keep reminding her, "Don't worry, Little, it's my job, not yours. You can relax and let me take charge of your needs. It might take time, but I'm going to help you feel better."

Writing dialogues encourages you to feel enough compassion for yourself to motivate you to take action. By addressing your *need to be taken care of,* you overcome self-abandonment. In assigning blame for your self-defeating patterns to your Outer Child, you leave your Inner Child blameless and unconditionally loved. In radically accepting your feelings, you address your *need to believe in yourself.* As you build a new self-loving relationship, you *fill a long-empty void.*

In reviewing Paul's dialogue, his role reversal was also impossible to miss. He explained that his mother had been critical and angry all of the time. He'd always tried to anticipate her needs to make her happy, in hopes of getting her to care about him. He saw that as an adult, his Inner Child was doing the same thing. It was time to change all that.

> I told Little Me he didn't have to keep trying so hard anymore, that he was special to me, that I enjoyed loving and caring for him. And it was an extremely emotional moment for me. Life-changing.

As you're writing a dialogue, to get the most benefit, use the *universal need to be taken care of* as a spur. Imagine that this human need has been frustrated. It doesn't matter for the moment whether this is true for you. Just suspend your judgment for now and follow in this thought groove: Imagine that your Inner Child's greatest need is to be emotionally cared for and that you have been forsaking that need. Your Adult Self has dropped the ball, abdicated responsibility for your emotional self-care. In writing the dialogue, all of this changes: Little You finally gets to sit back and take it all in.

DO YOUR WAY OUT

Paving the road to recovery involves taking action steps—and diligently, one step at a time. If you need motivation, where do you look for it? From listening to Little You, of course. Remember the child on the street you promised to care for? When you attend to that child's needs, you automatically circumvent your internal role reversal. To get ideas for action steps, you can ask Little You, *"What would you like me to do for you to take better care of you?"*

Remember that reading and conceptualizing will not reverse depression. What reverses it is *doing*. You know you can't think your way out of depression. Self-obsession is not a solution. It's just your brain spooling, searching for its lost peace of mind. You're going to work your way out of the depression. Act your way out. Walk or jog your way out. Interact your way out. *Do* your way out. You must diligently practice your visualization exercise, write Outer Child dialogues, and follow through with action steps—for a minimum of three months—to get real results.

> My depression became a monster living in my brain. I really didn't think daily actions would help. But I did them anyway—at first only a few times a week—and finally they opened doors. One of the best activities I accomplished was to join a chanting group. This was a real stretch for me, but it was fun and I felt better afterward. It got me to laugh and be with people.

Don't let your Outer Child continue displacing your energy on self-defeating indulgences, like isolating, ruminating, sleeping, spending, eating, drinking, procrastinating, cluttering. Likewise, don't let it manifest your depression through underachieving, overachieving, underinitiating, underearning, overextending yourself, and a host of other Outer Child compensations for not taking care of yourself. Outer Child is certainly adept at squandering your energy and spinning your wheels. Now it's time to commit your energy to taking action. Here are some pointers about action steps to think about. It's time to start doing!

- Make an entry in your Outer Child notebook, however brief, to record each daily action. Start today!
- If you have trouble initiating an action, first visualize yourself taking the action, to prepare and motivate you to physically *take* the action.
- Make any problems with inertia the subject of your next dialogue. Let Little You weigh in and tell you how badly it needs you to *do* something for it and how much better it feels when you accomplish something, even if small.
- Look for incremental improvements over time. The need for immediate gratification belongs to your Outer Child. Remind yourself that you are taking baby steps whose impact will be cumulative. The actions don't reach critical mass until about three months have passed.
- Make sure you do something every day that brings you into the moment, even if it's only for five minutes.
- Dedicate each action to reaching your goals. Your conscious intention to reach those goals will aid your progress, even if today's action does not seem directly related.
- Make sure each action moves some muscles. You've been moving the muscles of your mind (through personifying parts, Future Visions, and increasing consciousness and intention) and your hands (writing the dialogues). Now move your body.
- Structure is your friend. Many depressed people do better with structure. Structure can be a job or a commitment that gets you up and out and task-focused. Build as much structure into your life as you can.

The more you physically move the better. Movement not only provides a good release, but stimulates neurohormones (like endorphins) that promote well-being.

The daily actions are the antidote to the virus that was invading my body, mind, and soul. Who would have thought that taking a fifteen-minute walk around the block would help with the torment? It made just the smallest difference, but it was the difference that made the difference.

Remember that you have your own personal medicine chest of antidepressants, stimulants, tranquilizers, and painkillers within your body/brain. The three prongs of the program help you produce them through positive visualizing, emoting and releasing, and getting active and physical.

Once you have completed your five-minute baby step, you have accomplished your action task for the day. If those five minutes create momentum and you want to extend your time on this action, so much the better. Let it carry you as far as you like. If you miss a day, just pick up where you left off the next day.

My depression sent tentacles into my brain, strangling my every thought, hope, and dream, until I forced myself to get out. I got a part-time job. This was a good start, but I didn't stop there. I got a personal trainer; I started going to a woman's group. Getting moving helped me get moving.

To inspire ideas for your own baby steps, here are some ideas for getting into the moment:

- Eat an apple slowly and consciously. With each bite, savor its flavor and crunchy texture.
- Open the blinds. Carefully observe the change of light, the way it plays off reflective surfaces and fills the room. Now close them. Notice the difference. Mentally dedicate this moment of focus to your goals and dreams.
- When you go to your mailbox or retrieve your newspaper from your front stoop, walk a little farther down the block. Be conscious of the length of your stride, the temperature of the air, its currents, its smells, the outdoor sounds.
- Play a song or playlist you enjoy. Hum along if you can. Listen consciously and intentionally. If your mind drifts, no matter, just return your focus to the music again. The idea is to "favor" the music, the way you would favor a mantra during meditation.
- Call a friend or acquaintance—someone who would appreciate the outreach. Call with the intention of giving them something, maybe just to let them know you were thinking about them. Your own emotional needs are not pertinent for this particular baby step: It's all about reaching out to give.

- Have a conversation in which you consciously and intentionally focus on the positive for a few minutes. Don't have any expectations that this will lift your mood. Just compare your mood before and after.
- Find something that needs doing, then take a good long look at the task. Imagine yourself tackling it. If you feel overwhelmed by a task, break it down into tiny steps and do one or two as your action step for the day.
- Research an organization you might want to join. Make a phone call just to get information.
- Visit outerchild.net and check if there might be others out there struggling with challenges similar to yours. Consider making contact.
- Even if you hate your job, take five minutes and practice your conscious intention to expand your presence or performance at work. This is what Wallace B. Wattles called "more than filling your present place" in his 1910 book, *The Science of Getting Rich*. Recognize that for depression, work is occupational therapy, and its benefits are likewise incremental and cumulative.
- Smile and laugh. Even if forced, fMRI brain scans show that moving your face into a smile activates significant areas of the brain—good mental therapy. So at least once in a while, force yourself to laugh or smile, even if it means you'll occasionally be laughing in the dark, whistling while you work, smiling through your tears, or singing in the rain—anything to get your facial muscles moving.
- Walk inside the house. Walk outside the house. Get fresh air. Move a little farther every day. Get aerobic. Move your muscles with the conscious intention of reaching your goals.

For more information about neurobiological factors related to depression and potential treatments, go to page 256 at the end of this book. Also visit my website, outerchild.net, for some additional visualization exercises and bulleted scientific information presented as fact-tidbits; click on "topics" and download information on this subject.

SIXTEEN

Living a Conscious Life

We've been through a journey together and we're in the home stretch. You have your life ahead of you; and I, mine. So many choices face us. We can go back to the familiar and let our energy dissipate into old patterns, or we can choose to do things differently and move our lives in the direction of our goals.

By now you understand that transforming your life is not a matter of simply waiting for newly gained insight to create spontaneous change, or holding out for a final breakthrough that will free you from the tethers of the past. No, you must take the necessary behavioral steps to change your life. You have a right to feel good about yourself for having arrived at this understanding. Your daily actions will be more conscious and deliberate. While you notice other people still leading their lives on automatic pilot, caught up in their usual cycles, you have found a way out.

An enlightened adult remains fully conscious and goal-directed, always striving to be more than he or she is now, reaching to a higher self to expand the mind, fulfill dreams, achieve goals, and nurture love. As a stronger Adult Self, you seek a balance that reconciles forward-looking vision with a sublime acceptance of the now. You accept reality on its own terms and invest your energy in what you can do in the present.

Embarking on this new path means preparing yourself for ongoing commitment. A single effort will not suffice. You have acquired tools that work most effectively when applied consistently over an extended period of time. For most people this means performing the exercises daily for about three months to see new initiatives take hold and yield rewards you didn't know were possible.

As you continue to expand your life, it's important to remain acutely aware of what your Outer Child is up to. Keep daily tabs on that part of your psyche. Outer is waiting for you to let down your guard so that it can revert to its old habit of seeking immediate gratification. Outer belongs to the realm of quick fixes and substitute fulfillments and will use almost any ploy—denial, avoidance, self-indulgence—to satisfy its need for instant relief. But these Outer Child defenses need no longer derail your Adult mission. You have the tools to live your life with conscious intention to reach your potential, one action at a time.

Using the separation framework to connect with your primal emotions has been critical to the process of change because it motivates your Adult Self to take behavioral steps to fulfill your long-standing needs in substantial, life-building ways.

BUILDING MENTAL MUSCLE

To drive home this final point—that change involves activating mental muscle enforced with behavioral muscle—I'd like to tell you about a former client of mine, Mary.

Early in my career, I worked with a beautiful young woman who was severely addicted to dangerous drugs. Mary's mother wanted to understand what could cause her intelligent daughter to risk her life like that. What dark secret was she guarding, what terrible pain was she suffering, what past trauma gripped her that could make her want to do this to herself? She hoped that if I could help Mary uncover her hidden emotional conflicts, it would set her free.

Indeed, Mary shared her secrets with me, worked through long-buried pain from past traumas, and shed many tears in the process. When she left therapy to go away to college, she possessed deep emotional understanding about why she'd been involved in serious drugs and a firm resolve to change her life.

Her resolve lasted about a year. One day in her sophomore year, she got a shot of Novocain during a visit to the dentist's office. She disliked the fact that it made her tongue feel numb and that she couldn't smile for a few hours. This was the extent of her conscious awareness of the physical impact of the Novocain. But her body secretly recognized the numbing as compellingly familiar and associated it with the pleasurable feelings of her former heroin highs, sending it into automatic drug-seeking mode. Mary began getting insistent drug cravings that did not reach full consciousness, but affected her nonetheless.

The impact was gradual. Mary didn't know why, but one night she decided to break her sobriety and join her friends for a few beers; her body recognized the relaxed feeling and automatically stepped up its drug-seeking efforts, still undetected by Mary's consciousness. A week later Mary, still unaware, binged on vodka, and a few weeks after that, feeling buzzed again, she found herself thinking, *"Why not, just for a kick, just for tonight, go off campus and buy some heroin."* And so it went until this beloved, beautiful, intelligent young woman was back out on the street.

Although therapy had helped Mary acquire astute psychological insight, she had not acquired a strong enough mental muscle to overrule repetitive subliminal messages emanating from her body. I would certainly have handled her case differently if I had had my fully developed bag of Outer Child tricks, but this was years before that work began. The tools would have helped Mary make an even deeper emotional connection to her core needs and I would have prescribed a regimen of mentally integrative tasks, ones that would have strengthened the neural pathways in her brain that mediated the drug-seeking urges.

Thanks to new information from scientific research, I have since learned that no matter how many repressed emotions Mary released and resolved in the course of therapy, it would not have stopped those signals from reaching her brain. The cables leading from the trigger-points in the limbic brain to the higher thinking centers are much more powerful—thicker and faster—than the ones leading from the thinking centers back down to the limbic brain. In other words, we get strong, fast, urgent messages from the nonthinking brain, but we don't have equally powerful, speedy brain circuits for preempting those mammalian urges. Our cerebral output is weaker and slower than our mammalian input, so we can have automatic reactions to triggers before we can plan a reasoned counterchallenge.

But biology is not destiny. The Outer Child program is designed to strengthen the thinking mind's capacity to respond to our urgent mammalian drives. The exercises promote neural growth in the relay stations that moderate trigger-points for your automatic behaviors. In Mary's case, until she strengthened these significant brain functions, she would remain unprepared to cope with drug-seeking impulses whose origins her conscious mind was not able to recognize. That's why her Outer Child was able to fly in under the radar and act out—at first with a few beers and many rationalizations, but eventually with the same drug that brought her to me in the first place. Fortunately that's not the end of Mary's story. She reconnected with me many years later and reported:

> I didn't find the groove for staying alive until I learned about my Outer Child and started doing separation therapy. I had an Outer Child who was extremely well camouflaged, who wore my tailored clothes, used my speech patterns, and said all the right things to countless drug counselors. Since my Outer Child pretended to speak for me, the true me stayed asleep at the wheel. I was so badly submerged with my Outer Child, I couldn't recognize my own rationalizations. This meant that my Outer Child would act them out when I least expected and get me to flirt with my drug addiction once again.
>
> My Outer Child would take me to the edge of the slippery slope, and then would make it seem safe to take a step. So I'd suddenly decide to have a beer after work with a friend without seeing the danger. I was two months out of my last rehab and I was already hanging around with friends who routinely drank wine with dinner. Who was I kidding? It was just a matter of time before I let them pour me a glass. But just then I got lucky and found out that my old therapist was giving workshops in overcoming "Outer Child" patterns. I signed up for one to surprise her, but I was the one who was surprised. As soon as I started practicing the exercises, I realized that a part of me, Big Me, was too weak to protect me. This part spoke well and impressed everyone with its insight, but my addicted Outer Child was much stronger.

I learned the Outer Child maxim: *The Weaker Your Adult Self, the Needier Your Inner Child and the More Intrusive Your Outer Child.* Well, an addict like me needs a much stronger Adult Self than an average person would need. I had to rise up to the level of CEO of my own life.

I'd spent twenty years in psychotherapy and rehab programs, having searched my soul many times over, but doing this work was the first time I encountered my real Inner Child. Once I found that true voice, I realized I'd been walking around with a complete internal disconnect. I don't know how I'd managed to remain this unconscious for so long. Maybe it's because I'm such an addict, that my psyche only cared about having access to drugs and nothing more.

As soon as I tuned in to my Inner Child's sad little feelings and saw how abandoned she felt, I wanted to do something to help her. I felt so much compassion for her. She was always scared, waiting for the other shoe to drop. During a break in the workshop, I took her for a walk through the beautiful landscape at Esalen, over the brook, past the waterfall, and down the steps to the sea crashing against the rocks. I felt close to myself and responsible for myself in a way that I'd never felt before. Was this another false breakthrough? Well, maybe so, because I was hoping that just having these feelings would be "it"—I certainly didn't want to have to start doing exercises every day. But I also knew that to continue doing the right thing for Little, it meant staying conscious, and THAT would take work. If I slacked off, I'd lose touch with her, and one day down the road, I'd pick up a glass of wine and start the cycle all over again...

I knew that my Outer Child would always try to deaden my consciousness so that the little she-devil could get me to the edge of the slippery slope again. The addiction in my body wasn't going away, so I couldn't afford to zone out again. This was several years ago and I'm still on track, more conscious every day. I maintain strength by keeping the tools in my pocket.

At its core, Outer doesn't want you to stay conscious because it doesn't want to *feel*. But feeling is how you know you're alive. Feeling is how you know when there's need for change. Outer is always working to form a layer of encrustation around Little's uncomfortable feelings. Outer's crust prevents you from feeling, from being fully conscious. In fact, Outer's arsenal is aimed at deadening consciousness to fend off uncomfortable feelings. This is how most people remain stuck in their patterns; they are out of touch with their core needs and instead focus on the Outer crust—the superficial layer of Outer Child's incessant desire for substitute fulfillments. To break free, you must get underneath Outer's crust to connect with your real Inner Child. Little You beholds your pure emotional essence, your basic human, mammalian need for security, closeness, bonding, and love. Outer is accustomed to pursuing illusions of connection, quick fixes, and counterfeit achievement. The Adult gains strength as it takes hold of Outer Child's energy to guide your life toward greater meaning, purpose, and connection.

A NEW ROLE FOR YOUR OUTER CHILD

As you employ the dialogues, visualizations, and action steps in this book, you strengthen your brain's ability to coordinate among the regions that control emotion (Inner Child), behavior (Outer Child), and cognition (Adult Self). Your cognitive mind grows powerful enough to divert urges into new goal-seeking behaviors. After several repetitions of new behaviors, you'll see your patterns changing. Yes, even your most deeply entrenched patterns! With enough repetition, these healthy new behaviors become habits (new learned behaviors!) and doing the right thing isn't the struggle it was at the beginning. The process is akin to the way you learned to drive. It required intense focus at first, but eventually you made a habit of obeying traffic laws and keeping your eyes on the road without giving it much thought. In a nutshell, it gets easier.

Research shows that when an animal or human is rewarded for learning new behavior, changes occur in the neurons of the basal ganglia. Patterns of neural activity change permanently after learning takes place. In teaching your Outer Child new tricks, your stronger Adult Self can now welcome your habit-prone, knee-jerk Outer Child as your new best friend and ally.

Yes, this moment comes—when Outer Child becomes your friend! Over the years I have brought the Outer Child framework to groups and individuals and gotten a wealth of feedback in return. From time to time, workshop members have expressed key concerns that sent me back to the drawing board.

One such concern has been that in blaming Outer Child for bad behavior, we've left it out in the cold. "Shouldn't we love every part of ourselves?" people ask. The answer is a resounding *"Yes!"* and I am grateful to my workshop members for helping me appreciate the ultimate role of the Outer Child—that of friend. Since then, I have been sure to emphasize the need to extend our capacity for unconditional love to Outer Child.

The second concern goes something like this: *"I thought the goal was to become integrated, but you keep telling us to separate the parts of the personality."* Clarifying the first concern automatically resolves the second. In order to achieve integration, first the functional parts of the personality must be separated. This is because they had been merged and misaligned. Little You was submerged within the other parts, and sent out distress signals that Outer Child automatically picked up on and acted out. As your Adult Self transforms Outer's energy into constructive new habits, Adult and Outer stand side by side, allies acting together on behalf of your Inner Child's needs and your Adult goals. This concerted effort reintegrates the three parts of your personality.

The reintegration process is facilitated first through your imagination and then through taking consciously intended action steps. Your Adult mind does the work here and, whether you realize it or not, has been helping your Outer Child mature. Outer will always be Outer and embody the impulsive, automatic, defensive, behavioral part of yourself. But as your Adult Self grows stronger, Outer no longer has to react in its old, patterned ways to every subliminal signal sent from the amygdala. Outer learns to carry out new "learned behaviors" initiated by the Adult, behaviors that move you toward your goals.

AN ONGOING STORY

The program has brought us through a lot of firsts: It is the first time in applied theoretical psychology that the acting-out part of the psyche has been given its own identity and voice. It is the first time your pure emotional essence has been securely isolated from its reactive counterpart, creating the proper contrast for Inner Child's descant voice to be clearly heard above Outer Child's constant racket. It is the first time your Inner Child is freed from blame; heretofore, Inner's identity had been enmeshed with Outer's behavioral antics and we were unconsciously angry with it. It is the first time your Inner Child can ask for what it wants from an Adult who can tell the difference between a true need and a grab for substitutes—an Adult who is increasingly conscious, compassionate, and responsible. It is the first time your Inner Child can confront its overprotector—the first time Inner can say *"No"* and wrest itself from Outer's interference. It is the first time your Adult Self can dialogue with your argumentative, oppositional self-saboteur and give it guidance and direction; unless we are otherwise reconstituted, the Adult remains too weak and too easily overruled, and Outer Child rules the roost, misappropriating Inner Child's needs. It is the first time you have behavioral tools for reversing self-abandonment, exercising self-control, administering self-love, strengthening your Adult mind, overcoming your patterns, and incrementally becoming your higher self.

The application of this new conceptual framework is an ongoing story—for you and for others. In creating the story line for your new life, never underestimate the power of your imagination. All three prongs of the program give your imagination a healthy workout and increase your forward range of motion. As you continue using the Outer Child framework, use the power of your imagination to make Outer Child, Inner Child, and the Adult Self as different from one another as you can possibly make them. The more you tease out their differences, the more emotionally powerful their exchange. Make Outer as behavioral, habit-prone, oppositional, and underhanded as is true for you, filling in with your growing awareness about all of the sabotaging traits that apply to your Outer Child. Make Little as needy, vulnerable, blameless, and helpless as is true for you, filling in with your growing awareness about your innermost needs and strongest urges. Make your Adult Self as compassionate, caring, consistent, competent, and responsible as you can imagine yourself *becoming*. The person performing the dialogues is your emerging higher self. Through writing, you step into the character of this higher self and practice your finest attributes in the act of nurturing your emotional self and retraining your energetic, rambunctious Outer Child to perform on your behalf.

When you practice the tools enough times, they become second nature. When you get stuck, go back and make use of the special hands-on applications we've been over. For instance, you can use the Turn Around Exercise (see Chapter Seven) when you hit a tight spot. This puts your Outer Child in the observer seat and teaches it to delay its response time. Outer's habit has been to go from point A (urge) to point C (knee-jerk reaction) without stopping at point B (thinking and planning). Being in the observer role trains Outer to pause at Point B. You're forcing your automatic behavior (Outer Child) to observe the impact of its own destructive impulses! This imagery brings clarity and resolution to internal conflict areas. It reminds you that your behavior needs to come from the executive in charge of the personality, rather than from the urgent yearnings of the child self.

OTHER RESOURCES

Please visit my website, www.outerchild.net, to get ongoing support for your recovery.

On the website, you will find out how to join or even create an Outer Child support group. Positive peer pressure from supportive groupmates can really rev up your progress. After a group has been meeting regularly for a while, you'll start reaching your goals. If your group runs out of steam, rather than disband, I suggest scheduling regular reunions, perhaps three, six, or twelve months down the line, to coincide with people's longer-range goals. This adds accountability to the process and increases incentive as you anticipate reporting your progress back to the group. You gain inspiration by witnessing how far people have come, what issues they still struggle with, and which of the exercises seem to promote the most forward motion.

Find an eBuddy through outerchild.net so you can help each other hone your Future Visions and chart your progress. The idea here is that others who are taming their Outer Children can motivate you to stay on task, write dialogues, commit to and actually *take* action steps. And, of course, as you do the same for them, you gain an extra benefit.

Take your Outer Child inventory—a checklist posted on outerchild.net of myriad Outer Child characteristics—to keep your self-awareness fresh and your motivation charged. You have an option to send me a sample of your Outer Child traits and contribute to my data collection.

Continue exploring important issues related to Outer Child by downloading information under the topics section:

Take your Outer Child inventory
Outer Child love survey
Outer Child clutterers and hoarders: resources, tools, and tidbits
Biological factors in depression; new horizons for treatment
Reasons for weight gain (besides overeating)
How childhood abandonment leads to patterns of self-sabotage

How stress hormones affect cognitive learning and memory, create
   depression, and even shrink the brain! The good news is . . .
Outer Child is a notorious abandoholic. Let's start an Abandoholics
   Anonymous
Instructions for setting up peer-run Outer Child groups; 25 group
   recipes for professionals
Outer Child goes global and brings down the economy
Outer Child takes the celebrity spotlight
Outer Child points fingers—favorite pastime of the general public
   and more

MAINTAINING RECOVERY

Keep at it and avoid complacency. Science has shown that learned behaviors are extremely resistant to extinction and can rebound when your system is under stress. The program helps you build a repertoire of new
"learned behaviors" so that you have a wide range of healthy responses to
fall back on when you encounter unexpected triggers. The message is,
Don't stop when you achieve just one or two goals. The collected wisdom
from recovery programs has taught us that addiction doesn't go away; one
doesn't recover from an "ism," one is *in recovery*—recover*ing*. Recover*ing*
involves ongoing vigilance and daily reinforcement.

Remember Sarah who struggled with her diet?

The exercises got me where I wanted to go. They took me deep
enough to find the spur that got me to change. When I saw how powerful the tools were I decided to keep up the daily regimen for a year.
I lost all the weight and then started noticing everything else change
as well. At the beginning I wrote a dialogue almost every day, but
eventually I wrote one only when I felt out of sorts, or when I lapsed
into an old pattern. It always put me back on track. This tool helped
me tune in to myself on the deepest level and motivated me to resolve
the problem no matter what. I still visualize my Dream House every
day. The image is posted in my mind as a kind of symbolic reference
point for where I'm taking my life, always onward and upward.

I've polled workshop members, clients, friends, and colleagues who've
worked with the program to get their suggestions for maintenance strategies.

Many of them recommended keeping an ongoing journal. Journaling helps establish a way of regularly checking in with yourself. You can incorporate dialogues and future letters in this journal, keep track of your goals, chart your progress, plan new action steps, expand your awareness, and expand your Future Vision.

Remember Brad who'd lost passion for his wife? He presents this testimonial:

> Writing in my journal means I have to slow down and take time to reflect. I've found it doesn't work to just think things through; it's too easy to get distracted and go off on mental tangents. The journal helps me get clear, listen to my own thoughts—the thoughts of my higher self. I've learned how to order my life, how to avoid pitfalls, what I'm all about inside, what's important to me, what my goals are—it's all there in my journal. I've made a commitment to go no more than a week without checking in with myself in my journal. Any longer than that and my wisdom begins to dissolve into everyday matters. I could easily get sidetracked by something or someone that has nothing to do with my chosen path. The problem of passion I had in my marriage turned out to be good for me, because learning how to resolve it helped me grow into a person I can accept. I can honestly say I love my wife, my family, and even myself.

Keep all of the tools handy. Continue giving voice to the functional parts of your psyche. Keep your imagination trained on your Future Vision. Sustain a mental image of your goals, target your behavior with conscious intention, and continue building a deep internal connection of self-love. I encourage you to continue using the tools of the program until you reach your dreams. Your human potential is waiting for you.

Acknowledgments

Yay, Team! I am indebted to so many contributors to this book, beginning with Peter Yelton, ACSW, co-parent of the Outer Child concept. Peter provided a virtual wealth of conceptual material for developing Outer Child's personality profile and theoretical base. I'm also deeply grateful to Lisa Considine who bailed me out with her excellent skills in writing, editing, and administering author's first aid when I short-circuited in the midst of writing this book.

Woven into this book are Outer Child descriptions sent to me from people all over the world. Heartfelt thanks to visitors of my website who've been contributing to my anecdotal research project for over a decade; to members of my workshops for openly sharing their Outer Child struggles and helping me design new applications for the program; to beautiful Esalen Institute, Breitenbush Hot Springs, New York Open Center, and Kripalu Institute for welcoming this project into their folds; to my clients, fellow therapists, family, and friends for confiding their Outer Child tendencies and trusting I would never expose their secrets. What doozies you've all contributed!

Heartfelt gratitude to those who helped get this book into print: Susan

Golomb and Terra Chalberg for believing in my work and placing it in good hands; Marnie Cochran who pored over the manuscript with loving care and the rest of the Random House team, Sophie Epstein and Shona McCarthy. Special thanks to Spencer Petticrew-Shawcross for his meticulous editing of the endnotes and bibliography, and to Clive Clayton, Ph.D., for his input on the financial chapter and other key points. I am grateful to have known psychoanalyst Richard Robertiello MD, coauthor of *Big You Little You: Separation Therapy,* who mentored and nurtured my development as a psychotherapist and theoretician. Thank you to Robert Gossette, Ph.D., my research mentor, for helping me find cutting edge materials and challenging my unsupported assumptions, and Barbara Allis MD and Angela Hegarty MD for helping me improve the neurobiological portions of the manuscript.

Thank you to Patrick Lupinski for outerchild.net's creative web design and Vernon McAuley for donating his "Sticks & Stones" drawings, which use a simple line and dot to convey the subtlest nuance of emotion, gesture, and behavior. Thank you to Tyler Jordan for his wizardry as webmaster, Bridget Hieronymus for site production, Amy Michelin for social networking and writing, and Jessica Gerardi for writing backup. Thank you to my photo doctor, Monica Mohan, a miracle worker!

Thank you to my son, Adam, and my daughter, Erika, for their steadfast love; my father, Dexter Griffith, for striking the balance between creativity and self-discipline; my sister, Marcia Gerardi, and my brothers Dexter and Robert Griffith for their constant love and support; for Mark Gerardi, Karen Griffith, Randy Davis Griffith, Alex, Laura, Jesse Cohen, Jessica Gerardi, Kristi, Dylan, and Bryan Griffith for always being there. Thank you to my friends for putting up with unreturned phone calls, cancelled plans, and total absences while I was writing this book, also to Jill Mackey, Amy Wapner, Carole Anne Price, Pat Malone, Celeste Carlin, Donna Carsen, Edith Drucker, Dilys Purdy, Diedre Olsen, Pat Dennis, Fran Friedman, Linda Whol, Gina Hoffman, Edith Winkler, Debra Greenwood, Doug Khazzam, Nancy Bautzmann—as well as to T.K., Sheila, and Rigo at T.K.'s Galley—for creating the morning's perfect writing environment.

Endnotes

CHAPTER 1

3   You may already be familiar Writers developing the Inner Child concept have included: W. Hugh Missildine, *Your Inner Child of the Past* (New York: Simon & Schuster, 1963); Grace Elish Kirsten and Richard Robertiello, *Big You, Little You: Separation Therapy* (New York: Dial Press, 1977); Alice Miller, *Drama of the Gifted Child* (New York: Basic Books, 1979); Charles Whitfield, *Healing the Child Within: Discovery and Recovery for Adult Children of Dysfunctional Families* (Deerfield Beach, Fl.: Health Communications, 1987); John Bradshaw, *Homecoming: Reclaiming and Championing Your Inner Child* (New York: Bantam Books, 1990); Pia Mellody, *Facing Love Addiction: Giving Yourself the Power to Change the Way You Love* (New York: Harper Collins, 2003).

CHAPTER 2

12   The reason I believe Habit formation is centered in the basal ganglia (located between the cortex and brainstem) and involves "chunking" a series of steps into patterns. Chunking is mediated by dopamine, a powerful brain chemical involved in reward and addiction, whose involvement makes the newly learned steps extremely difficult to "unchunk" (unlearn). See Ann M. Graybiel, "The Basal Ganglia and Chunking of Action Repertoires," *Neurobiology of Learning and Memory* 70 (1998): 119–136. Interestingly, cocaine and amphetamines heighten dopamine activity in the basal ganglia, turning new behavioral steps into an addiction instantly—rather than through a gradual accrual of repetitions. See M. K. McGovern, "Habits," *Serendip* (Spring 2005), http://serendip.brynmawr.edu. (Also see endnote for page 77, "When your brain receives rewards".)

14 **Following Freud's example** Internal Family Systems (IFS) is a more elaborate framework that divides the psyche into over 10 parts, each of which, like Freud's Id, encompasses both emotional and reactive behavioral elements rather than keeping the two separate (not in error, just conceptualized differently from the Outer Child framework). See Richard C. Schwartz, *Internal Family Systems Therapy* (New York: The Guilford Press, 1995).

CHAPTER 3

33 **Anger is Outer's favorite emotion** Although I focus on the amygdala as an emotional center, the hypothalamus is implicated in anger. Lab research shows that stimulating the hypothalamus elicits anger; lesions in the hypothalamus create placidity. See C. George Boeree, "The Emotional Nervous System," *Webspace* (2009), http://webspace.ship.edu.

33 **In the extreme, abandonment rage** Abandonment homicide (wife murder is called "uxoricide") is associated with high levels of norepinephrine (NE) and low levels of serotonin in a part of the brain that controls aggressive impulses (the orbitofrontal cortex), which is similarly found in long-range effects of trauma. See Donald G. Dutton, "The Neurobiology of Abandonment Homicide," *Aggression and Violent Behavior* 7, no. 4 (2002): 407–21.

33 **So when you become angry** Higher alcohol use is also associated with low serotonin. See Daniel Schiele, "The Neuropsychobiology of Addiction, Trauma, and Dissociation," a paper presented at the Western Clinical Conference in Multiple Personality and Dissociation, Costa Mesa, Calif., 1992.

CHAPTER 4

44 **Outer Child's repetitious behaviors** Although I focus on the dopamine-rich basal ganglia as a key site for automatic behaviors, it is not possible to map a set of behaviors to any one brain region due to the complex web of interactions involved. For example, the cingulate cordate is involved in "priming" (where previous learning has primed you to fall into a particular pattern). The primary motor cortex (M1) coordinates with premotor areas engaged in planning and executing movements, sending long branches (axons) of its Betz cells down to the spinal cord to initiate movement in the muscle. Brodmann area 6 is involved in planning complex coordinated movements. One neuroscientist, Rodolfo Llinas at NYU, points to the thalamus as being the conductor of the brain's orchestra; cells oscillate between the thalamus and primary motor cortex at the same frequency to facilitate movement (and awakeness), activating the hypothalamus, cerebellum, basal ganglia, brain stem, orbitofrontal cortex (OFC), and other areas in the frontal lobes. Llinas was featured in Sandra Blakeslee's article "In a Host of Ailments, Seeing a Brain Out of Rhythm," *New York Times,* December 2, 2008, New York edition, D2.

45 **Fear tends to incubate** Joseph E. LeDoux in *The Emotional Brain: The Mysterious Underpinnings of Emotional Life* (New York: Simon and Schuster, 1996), 203.

49 **Neuroscientist Richard Davidson, using fMRI brainscans** Whereas the left frontal lobe is associated with positive states, the *right* is associated with sadness, worry, and anxiety. Davidson's research shows that compassion visualizations when practiced regularly promote a leftward tilt in the ratio from right to left prefrontal activity, thus facilitating improved ongoing well-being and increased functioning. Reported in Daniel Goleman, *Destructive Emotions, How Can We Overcome Them? A Scientific Dialogue with the Dalai Lama* (New York: Bantam Dell, 2003), 3–19. Also see *Visions of Compassion: Western Scientists and Tibetan Buddhists Examine Human Nature*, eds. Richard J. Davidson and Anne Harrington (New York: Oxford University Press, 2002).

49 **Researchers can induce positive emotions** See M. A. Neitsche, J. Koschack, H. Pohlers, S. Hullermann, W. Paulus, S. Happe, "Effects of frontal transcranial direct current stimulation on emotional state and processing in healthy humans," *Frontiers in Psychiatry* 3 (June 2012): 58.

CHAPTER 5

54 **In fact, strengthening the brain's integrative functions** The anterior cingulate cortex (ACC) and orbitofrontal cortex (OFC) coordinate among higher, middle, and lower brain regions, so when the Outer Child exercises are able to strengthen their neural connections, the benefits have a widespread neural impact. We know how important those connections are because from 1935 to 1961 well-intended surgeons cut them in performing lobotomies, inadvertently rendering tens of thousands of people in the United States (including Rosemary Kennedy) deficient in judgment, problem solving, impulse control, spontaneity, planning, or their ability to read social clues or relate to emotional experience. See Elliot S. Valenstein, *Great and Desperate Cures: The Rise and Decline of Psychosurgery and Other Radical Treatments for Mental Illness* (New York: Basic Books, 1986).

56 **It helps you picture yourself** Mirror neurons, discovered in 1992 by Giacomo Rizzolatti, map pictorial images from the visual cortex onto their motor counterpart in the premotor cortex, allowing your brain to rehearse motor steps just by observing them. By envisioning a goal-directed activity (pulling a fish from the sea), motor neurons mentally simulate the action, thereby practicing the new skill set. Mirror neurons are involved in other functions, such as language, sensing the intention of another's movements, and empathy. See Marco Iacoboni, *Mirroring People: The New Science of How We Connect with Others* (New York: Farrar, Straus and Giroux, 2008), 126–79.

CHAPTER 6

67 **In focusing your cognitive mind** Visualization improves performance via mirror neurons. Iacoboni, *Mirroring People*, 3–34. Visualizing something in the mind's eye takes place in the parietal lobe, stimulating corresponding neurons in the premotor cortex. Daniel Goleman, *Social Intelligence: The New Science of Human Relations* (New York: Bantam Dell, 2006), 41–42.

69 **Rather than focus his psychological energy** This exercise transports your mental energy from the problem to the level of solution—the meta level—the domain of change. See Paul Watzlawick, John Weakland, and Richard Fisch, *Change: Principles of Problem Formation and Problem Resolution* (New York: W. W. Norton, 1974).

74 **Einstein formed pictorial images** Marian C. Diamond, "Why Einstein's Brain?" *New Horizons for Learning* 4, no. 5 (July, August, September 1999), http://www.newhorizons.org. Also see Goleman, *Destructive Emotions*, 190.

77 **When your brain receives rewards** Behavioral memory (learning new behaviors) is not dependent on limbic structures but on dopamine-reward in the basal ganglia. The dopamine-rich basal ganglia (specifically in the striatum) lights up when you develop sequential motor acts, reacting to reward signals. When behaviors are reinforced by dopamine-reward in the basal ganglia, patterns of neural activity change permanently. Also, once exposed to an addictive agent, it recognizes it forever. See Graybiel, "The Basal Ganglia and Chunking of Action Repertoires."

CHAPTER 7

81 **Whereas your emotional memories** When context memory is retrieved, it takes "molten form" and becomes malleable to revision. Your current context, bias, personal agenda, or emotional state can greatly distort a retrieved memory. When reset into long-term memory banks, the newly altered memory resumes a "solid form." So reports Richard Gray, who features Karim Nader's research, which raised the question: "Can drugs help to alter memory beneficially?" Nader found that when lab rats were given a drug (propranolol) to turn down the emotional part of a memory, they remembered details without showing an emotional response (they are less traumatized by it). See Richard Gray, "Scientists Find Drug to Banish Bad Memories," *Daily Telegraph*, June 1, 2007.

81 **Stressful events trigger the production** In causing neuronal connections to corrode, stress hormones shrink the hippocampus, as shown in autopsies on adult brains of people who grew up in orphanages (where separation distress is common). Research shows that early childhood stress can reduce neurogenesis in adulthood, impairing the brain's ability to repair hippocampal damage. Yashmin J.G. Karten, Ana Olariu, and Heather A. Cameron, "Stress in Early Life Inhibits Neurogenesis in Adulthood," *Trends in Neuroscience* 28, no. 4 (April 2005): 171–72.

82 **Thanks to an underdeveloped hippocampus** CREB, a brain protein in the amygdala, is involved in storing fear memories. By targeting CREB (in mice), research found that fear memories can be eliminated. See Joseph Hall, "Erasing Traumatic Memory Possible, Researchers Say," *Toronto Star*, March 12, 2009.

82 **Some stress hormones can also cause the exact opposite** See Joseph E. LeDoux, "Emotional Memory," *Scholarpedia* (2007), http://www.scholarpedia.org.

87 **Outer has been walking the perimeter** "Outer walking perimeter" imagery was bequeathed by colleague and co-architect of the Outer Child concept, Peter Yelton, LCSW, during consultation in 2008.

87 **The dialogues are helping you** Mirror neurons are associated with empathy (along with spindle cells). when you see emotion in someone's face, your mirror neurons activate identical areas within your brain, enabling you to sense the feel-

ing within yourself. People who score high on empathy scales are found to have active mirror neuron systems. Conversely, autistic children are found to have a deficit in their mirror neuron systems. Reconstructive play therapies using "mimicking and mirroring" to stimulate mirror neuron development show some promise. See Iacoboni, *Mirroring People*, 106–29, 172–77. (Also see endnote for page 67, "In focusing your cognitive mind".)

CHAPTER 8

96   **I'm not suggesting** Not everyone is traumatized by the same stressor; it has to do with your personal history and context, as well as your neurological makeup. For instance, fifty soldiers were studied: Those with high neuropeptide Y were clearer thinkers and more resilient; those with lower levels tended to be more easily traumatized. See Charles Morgan et al., "Relationship Among Plasma Cortisol, Catecholamines, Neuropeptide Y, and Human Performance During Exposure to Uncontrollable Stress," *Psychosomatic Medicine* 63, no. 3 (May/June 2001): 412–22.

97   **memory of your birth** Without a developed hippocampus, the natal brain can't record the birth context—the sudden drop in temperature, perhaps glaring lights and noise, or jolt into its first breath of air—nonetheless, a disembodied emotional response to the trauma can intrude into later experiences. See A. J. DeCasper and W. P. Fifer, "Of Human Bonding: Newborns Prefer Their Mothers' Voices." *Science* 208, no. 4448 (June 6, 1980): 1174–76. Also see William P. Smotherman and Scott R. Robinson, "The Development of Behavior Before Birth," *Developmental Psychology* 32, no. 3 (May 2, 1996): 425–34.

98   **Gilbert Kliman, MD, trauma specialist** All of the information in this paragraph as well as the terms *behavioral pantomime* and *post-traumatic behavioral narrative* were taken from Gilbert Kliman's "Toward a Unifying Theory of Post-Traumatic Stress Disorder: Integrating Data from Studies of Post-Traumatic Behavior, Memory, Symptom Formation, Physiology, Cerebral Imaging, Psychoanalytic Findings and Evolutionary Theory," a paper presented to the first joint scientific meeting of the American College of Psychoanalysts and the American Academy of Psychoanalysis and Psychodynamic Psychiatry, Washington, D.C., May 3, 2008.

102   **Daniel Schiele, a trauma expert** The insights in this paragraph were taken from Schiele's paper "The Neuropsychobiology of Addiction, Trauma and Dissociation," in which he also states that since a terrifying scene can't be integrated within your established cognitive knowledge base, it remains isolated and autonomous; it develops an emotional life of its own and can be easily triggered to repeat itself.

103   **Robert Sapolsky, a neurobiologist** "Lever of Control" and the ensuing discussion detailing five categories of stressful situations were taken from Robert Sapolsky's groundbreaking *Why Zebras Don't Get Ulcers* (New York: W.H. Freeman, 1994), 214–24, 252–54.

104   **Psychologist Martin Seligman, an expert** See Martin Seligman, *Helplessness: On Depression, Development, and Death* (San Francisco: W.H. Freeman, 1975) and "Can Happiness Be Taught?" *Dædalus* 133, no. 2 (Spring 2004): 80–87.

104   **Research into stress response** Stewart D. Winser, "Incidence of Perforated Peptic Ulcer: Effect of Heavy Air-raids," *Lancet* 28 (February1942): 259–61.

104   **When a baboon is stressed** Sapolsky, *Why Zebras Don't Get Ulcers,* 318–20.

106   **In depersonalization, you are blunted** In his paper "The Neuropsychobiology of Addiction," Daniel Schiele states that depersonalization and derealization serve to blunt reality and enable us to mitigate stress helplessness with "magical thinking."

107   *Stress hormone expert Robert Sapolsky* See Robert M. Sapolsky, "Social Subordinance as a Marker of Hypercortisolism," *Annals of the New York Academy of Sciences* 771, *Stress Basic Mechanisms and Clinical Implications* (December 1995): 626–39.

107   *Amygdala expert Joseph LeDoux* See LeDoux, "Emotional Memory."

107   *Ann Graybiel's study of habit formation* See Ann Graybiel and Yasuo Kubota, "Understanding Corticobasal Ganglia Networks as Part of a Habit Formation System, *Mental and Behavioral Dysfunction in Movement Disorders,* ed. Marc-André Bédard et al. (Totowa, N.J.: Humana, 2003).

107   *Howard Hoffman and others who study endogenous opiates* See Howard S. Hoffman, *Amorous Turkeys and Addicted Ducklings: A Search for the Causes of Social Attachment* (Fullerton, Calif.: Authors Publishing Cooperative, 1994); Jaak Panksepp, Stephen M. Siviy, and Lawrence A. Normansell, "Brain Opioids and Social Emotions," *The Psychobiology of Attachment and Separation,* Martin Reite and ed. Tiffany Field (San Diego: Academic Press, 1985); Myron Hofer, "Hidden Regulators: Implications for a New Understanding of Attachment, Separation, and Loss," *Attachment Theory: Social, Developmental and Clinical Perspectives,* eds. Susan Goldberg, Roy Muir, and John Kerr (Hillsdale, N.J.: Analytic Press, 1995).

107   *Bessel van der Kolk says a withdrawal phase* See Bessel A. van der Kolk, "Clinical Implications of Neuroscience Research in PTSD," *Annals of the New York Academy of Sciences* 1071, *Psychobiology of Posttraumatic Stress Disorder* ed. Rachel Yehuda (July 2006): 277–94.

107   *Daniel Schiele says we rechoreograph* See Schiele, "The Neuropsychobiology of Addiction." (Schiele refers to the Karpman Drama of victim, persecutor, rescuer.)

107   *Gilbert Kliman suggests that by producing* See Kliman, "Toward a Unifying Theory of PTSD."

107   **through repeated effort, helps strengthen neural connections** The program is designed to stimulate areas in the brain that serve integrative functions, including the orbitofrontal cortex (OFC) and the anterior cingulate cortex (ACC) (see endnote for page 54, "In fact, strengthening the brain's integrative functions"). There are thick bundles of spindle cells between these areas. Spindle cells are high-velocity, jumbo-sized neurons rich in receptors for serotonin, dopamine (neurochemicals that facilitate pleasure, reward, punishment), and vasopressin (associated with social bonding and fidelity). Among their many functions, spindle cells within the ACC recognize facial expressions involved in empathy (along with mirror neurons: see endnote for page 67, "In focusing your cognitive mind"). Goleman, *Social Intelligence*, 66. Also see Rebecca Roth, "Gambling and the Brain," student paper posted on Serendip's Exchange, a website hosted by Bryn Mawr College (April 23, 2002), http://serendip.brynmawr.edu.

CHAPTER 9

122 **Out of compassion for those** Biological factors can increase your appetite, promote excessive fat storage, and/or slow metabolism, yet they remain unknown to most dieters who suffer the struggle for weight control in isolation, shame, and frustration. I present the following tidbits of information to give them validation and hope: Science is closing in on the problem.

- **White versus brown fat cells** Your weight can be affected by the proportion of your white to brown fat cells. *White cells* are known to lower your metabolic rate, whereas *brown* burn more calories. Associated Press, "Focus on 'Good' Body Fat in Battle against Weight Gain," *Newsday,* April 9, 2009.

- **Infectious Ad-36 and fat storage** A high percentage of a fat-associated infectious virus, Ad-36 (also in pink-eye), is found in obese populations as compared with nonobese populations. In the laboratory, stem cells exposed to Ad-36 turn into fat cells. In identical twins, the one who'd had the Ad-36 virus (as shown by antibodies) weighs significantly more than the other twin. Epidemiological studies show obesity distribution across geographic regions to be similar to the way viral infections distribute, independent of variations in regional dietary habits. Robin Marantz Henig, "Fat Factors," *New York Times Magazine,* August 13, 2006; Associated Press, "More Evidence of Virus Link to Obesity," *New York Times,* August 20, 2006.

- **Microbes and fat storage** *Microbes:* Trillions of microbes colonize the gut— i.e., bacteria, fungi—and depending on their composition, can promote fat stockpiling. Mice raised in a sterile lab, to prevent microbe colonization, do not lay down fat unless they are transplanted with microbes from "normally exposed" mice. Microbes can be harmful or helpful; depending on proportions of certain bacteria (i.e., *B. theta* and *M. smithii* bacteria) in the gut, your body either lays down fat or sloughs it off. Ibid.

- **Biochemistry and fat storage** Some elements in the biochemistry of appetite/ fat storage/metabolism have been identified—i.e., leptin, ghrelin, NPY, insulin, etc. Chemistry involved in *countering the urge to eat* includes MPH, PYY, and obestatin. See Ruben Noguerias and Matthias Tschop, "Separation of Conjoined Hormones Yields Appetite Rivals," *Science* 310, no. 5750 (November 2005): 985–86.

- **Leptin (appetite shut-off switch) and fat storage** Leptin, made by fat cells, is an appetite shut-off switch—it signals the brain to know when you're full. Research shows that adding leptin after weight loss helps people keep weight off, because it tricks the brain into believing your fat cells are full. See Gina Kolata, "Will a New Drug Melt Pounds?" *New York Times*, Health, December 5, 2004.

- **Ghrelin and fat storage** Ghrelin is made in the gut and intestines and slows metabolism, promotes fat storage, and increases your urge to eat. Ibid.

- **History of dieting and fat storage** Fat cells are particularly resistant in people who have dieted. Fat cells shrink but fight back by storing lipids or by stimulating appetite through hormones like leptin or ghrelin. There are different types of fat cells; one is the precursor fat cell, which creates new fat cells that are highly resistant to giving up their fat stores. Extensive research shows that two nonobese people of the same weight require different amounts of calories to stay thin; a *formerly fat* person has to eat fewer calories. Furthermore, people with a history of obesity have more fat cells, so even when they're thin (which means their fat cells are deflated versus engorged) they look heavier than naturally thin people (who have fewer fat cells). Mi-Jeong Lee et al., "Acute and chronic regulation of leptin synthesis, storage, and secretion by insulin and dexamethasone in human adipose tissue," *American Journal of Physiology—Endocrinology and Metabolism* 292 (2007): 858–64.

- **Set point and fat storage** Set point refers to the self-regulating range of an individual's weight, above which and below which an individual's metabolism works automatically to return to this average weight. Each person's set point is well established and varies greatly from person to person. Some people's range gets established at a high set point and their metabolism adjusts downward to keep them within that higher range (fatter). Henig, "Fat Factors."

- **Genes and fat storage** Some people are genetically predisposed to stockpile fat, particularly if their genes originated from famine-prone geographic areas that would have selected for "thrifty genes" (capable of lowering metabolism and resisting fat burning during famine—i.e., Pima Indians). Conversely, populations from the food-abundant "Fertile Crescent" selected for genes for sloughing off excess fat, since obesity would make people slower, easier prey. There are up to 1,000 genes implicated in metabolism and weight. Kolata, "Will a New Drug Melt the Pounds?"

- **Hypothalamus and fat storage** An important site for weight control is the hypothalamus, as evidenced by a nine-year-old boy with an injury to his hypothalamus who rapidly grew to 400 pounds. If the hypothalamus is destroyed in rats, they grow massively obese. Ibid.

- **Prenatal and fat storage** Obesity can develop in utero. For instance, in a pregnant woman with high blood sugar, glucose levels build and can cross over to the fetus, causing the fetus' pancreas to secrete high levels of insulin, which promotes fat storage. Roni Rabin, "Obesity Begins in Utero," *Newsday,* November 7, 2005.

- **Estrogen and progesterone and fat storage** These hormones, which spike to overcompensate at onset of menopause, can cause women (and men on hormone therapy for prostate cancer) to lay down significant fat in the lower body, where it resists weight loss.

- **Stress and fat storage** Having discussed the chronic release of cortisol's potential to interfere in hippocampal memory, here it is again interfering in our diets. Although extreme stress initially reduces your appetite, the longer-acting stress hormones, like cortisol, increase our appetites to get us to regain our fat stores. Sapolsky, *Why Zebras,* 74–78. Also see "Stress Linked to Obesity: Hormone Triggers Growth of Fat Cells," Bloomberg News, *Newsday,* July 3, 2007.

- **Neuropeptide Y and fat storage** Another stress hormone, neuropeptide Y (NPY) causes fat cells to double in size and multiply. In rats, if receptors for NPY are blocked, they stop laying down fat, no matter how much they eat. En-Ju Deborah Lin, "Combined Deletion of Y1, Y2, and Y4 Receptors

Despite Persistence of Hyperphagia and Obesity," *Endocrinology* 147, no. 11 (2006): 5094–101.

- **Sleep and fat storage** The "clock gene" is implicated in disturbances in circadian rhythm—a sleep/appetite self-adjusting system that varies according to position of sun to earth based on shifting light-darkness patterns. Another factor involves stress hormones (i.e., cortisol) that interrupt sleep, slow metabolism, and increase the urge to eat. Joseph Takahashi, et al., published online in Science Express (May 2005).

- **Gastric bypass and fat storage** Dieter's bodies produce more ghrelin to restore their fat stores. Gastric bypass reduces ghrelin by reducing its production site—the gut. It is believed that weight loss from bypass surgery is due *not* to people's reduced food intake, but to reduced ghrelin production; less ghrelin means increased metabolism and reduced eating urge. D. Cummings et al. "Plasma Ghrelin Levels After Diet-Induced Weight Loss or Gastric Bypass Surgery," *New England Journal of Medicine,* 23: 346, 21 (May 2002): 1623–30.

- **Liposuction and fat storage** Liposuction removes belly-type fat, but it can leave precursor fat cells (which recruit other cells into fat) or visceral fat (known to resist weight loss). Ibid.

- **Insulin and fat storage** Insulin is a fat-mobilizing hormone. If you're insulin-resistant, it means that the more you gain weight, the more insulin you pump out of your pancreas. As mega-doses of insulin bombard your cells, they become insensitive to insulin, so you pump out more insulin to compensate, with the result that you store more fat.

- **Magic weight loss remedies** Science hasn't yet found magic pills to eliminate the need for dieting and exercising; yet research continues exploring these remedies. Under study: Rimonabant and Acomplia, two drugs that block cannabis (marijuana) receptors in the brain to block appetite (reducing the "munchies") and increase metabolism. Obese people have more receptors for these endocannabinoids. See Jamie Talan, "New Weight-Loss Drug Works in Trial," *Newsday,* February 14, 2006; and Gina Kolata, "Will a New Drug Melt the Pounds?" *New York Times,* Health, December 5, 2004. Mesotherapy injections containing various agents reportedly make "fat and cellulite melt away" in specific areas of the body, according to Dr. Marion Shapiro, as reported in "European Method Can Slim You with Injections" (2002), WNBC.com/health.

- **The "exercise pill"** increases mitochondria in muscles that burn fat (transforming sugar burning switches into fat burning switches), as if you'd strenuously exercised. Alan Zarembo, "Now, Exercise in a Pill Form?" *Newsday,* August 1, 2008.

125 **For those of us who** I believe there is a built-in evolutionary mechanism that makes us (perhaps women more than men) hypervigilant toward something that potentially causes us to be deemed visually unattractive. On an evolutionary level, in parts of the world where food supply is scarce and people die of starvation, being heavier is deemed attractive for a woman. But in parts of the world where food is abundant, eating too much food could be seen from an evolutionary perspective as a potential threat to survival in that weight gain could limit our desir ability as a mate and therefore threaten the survival of our genes. The female body shape considered unattractive varies from society to society, but with over-abundant food in America, being overweight is considered *un*attractive. Our idealization of "skinny" has heightened our collective amygdaloid response to food.

134   **You gain radical acceptance** See Tara Brach, *Radical Acceptance: Embracing Your Life with the Heart of a Buddha* (New York: Bantam Dell, 2003).

CHAPTER 10

147   **Procrastination—whether occasional, chronic** See "Brain's Reward Circuitry Revealed in Procrastinating Primates," *National Institute on Mental Health* online (August 10, 2004), http://www.nimh.nih.gov. Also see Zheng Liu et al., "DNA Targeting of Rhinal Cortex D2 Receptor Protein Reversibly Blocks Learning of Cues that Predict Reward," *Proceedings of the National Academy of Sciences* 101, no. 33 (August 17, 2004): 12336–41.

149   **Like most chronic procrastinators** Depression and anxiety are also symptoms of chronic procrastination, according to Jenny Maryasis, "Procrastination: Habit or Disorder?" a student paper posted on Serendip's Exchange (2002), http://serendip.brynmawr.edu.

CHAPTER 11

157   **Traumatic Bonds** Howard Hoffman spent decades studying social bonds mediated by pain-induced opioids and explains, for instance, that when you send mild electric shocks (pain) to a duckling it bonds more closely to a moving object; when its opioid receptors are blocked, the duck no longer bonds to the object. See Hoffman, *Amorous Turkeys and Addicted Ducklings*.

159   **The Stockholm syndrome** Nils Bijerot, "The Six-Day War in Stockholm," *New Scientist* 61, no. 886 (1974): 486–87.

160   **Repeated teasing strengthens latah's** Ronald Simons, *Boo! Culture, Experience, and the Startle Reflex* (New York: Oxford University Press, 1996): 161–62.

CHAPTER 12

181   **Make yourself sexually available** Some of my couples have benefited from participating in weeklong Tantric workshops (held in beautiful tropical resort settings) to commence a new sensual relationship.

CHAPTER 14

199   **plastic fundamentally changes the way we spend** Jonah Lehrer, *How We Decide* (Boston: Houghton Mifflin Harcourt, 2009).

200   **A research study** Psychologist Daniel Kahneman, economist Alan B. Krueger, et al., "Would You Be Happier If You Were Richer? A Focusing Illusion," *Science* 312, no. 5782 (June 30, 2006): 1908–10.

      When researchers enhance dopamine Susana Peciña et al., "Hyperdopaminergic

Mutant Mice Have Higher 'Wanting' but not 'Liking' for Sweet Rewards," *J Neuroscience* 23, no. 28 (October 15, 2003): 9395–02.

201 **Deregulated dopamine can shorten attention span** See Terje Sagvolden et al., "A Dynamic Developmental Theory of Attention Deficit/Hyperactivity Disorder," *Behavioral and Brain Sciences* 28, vol. 3 (June 2005): 397–419.

201 **Cocaine and amphetamines increase** Cocaine and amphetamines affect dopamine in different ways: Cocaine inhibits dopamine uptake to increase its lifetime in the synapse; amphetamines increase dopamine in synapse by forcing dopamine molecules back into the synapse. See "Disorders of Dopaminergic Systems," a table on the website of researcher Shamim Khaliq, http://shamimkhaliq.50megs.com.

202 **Research shows that financial windfalls** This paragraph was paraphrased from Jonah Lehrer in an online article, August 19, 2007.

202 **Surging dopamine can heighten your awareness** See K. C. Berridge and T. E. Robinson, "What Is the Role of Dopamine in Reward: Hedonic Impact, Reward Learning, or Incentive?" *Brain Research Reviews* 28, no. 3 (December, 1998): 309–69.

204 **We can look at the impact** See Scott Burns, "The Subprime Mortgage Crisis Began on 9/11," *Dallas Morning News*, February 10, 2008. Also see *Intervention and Resilience After Mass Trauma*, eds. Michael Blumenfield and Robert J. Ursano, (New York: Cambridge University Press, 2008): 69–70.

209 **To imagine a feeling** fMRI studies of people's brains engaged in meditating on a positive emotion like gratitude show significant long range, positive changes in specific areas known to modulate emotion. Goleman, *Destructive Emotions*, 12. Also see note for page 67, "In focusing your cognitive mind."

CHAPTER 15

215 **Often, anxiety and depression go together** Depression is often associated with elevated stress hormones—i.e., cortisol, chronic renal failure, which can cause shrinkage in the hippocampus, and is considered a risk factor for Alzheimer's, a progressive hippocampal illness. Yvette I. Sheline, Mokhtar H. Gado, and Helena C. Kraemer, "Untreated Depression and Hippocampal Volume Loss," *American Journal of Psychiatry* 160 (August 2003): 1515–18. Cortisol (heightened by depression) is also known to rob the skeleton of calcium, leading to osteoporosis. Depressed women have lower bone density. David Michelson et al., "Bone Mineral Density in Women with Depression," *New England Journal of Medicine* 335, no. 16 (October 17, 1996): 1176–81. Depression causes blood platelets (that help blood clot) to be stickier, to aggregate when they should be flowing, thereby making heart attacks more deadly. See Dominique L. Musselman et al., "Exaggerated Platelet Reactivity in Major Depression," *American Journal of Psychiatry* 153, no. 10 (October 1996): 1313–17. *Please note: Owing to the brain's capacity for neurogenesis, these damages can be mitigated.* See Norman Doidge, *The Brain That Changes Itself: Stories of Personal Triumph from the World of Brain Science* (New York: Penguin, 2007).

216 **Depression can become so infused** Depressive episodes can affect the brain similarly to seizures by creating a neurological vicious cycle, feeding on itself thro

a process called "kindling"—a progressive neurobiological process. At first, stress can affect the brain without causing depression, but each event acts like kindling wood for a fire; eventually the impact of stress leads to "an open blaze of depression." Once the brain becomes kindled for depression, the more episodes of depression you have, the worse they get, the less stress it takes to trigger them, and the harder they are to treat—similar to epilepsy, where seizures tend to be more easily triggered and more powerful with each occurrence. Both major depressive episodes and seizures can damage areas in the brain, suggesting the importance of intervening quickly to prevent further damage. See Peter D. Kramer, *Against Depression* (New York: Viking, 2005), 144–45. *Reminder: Owing to the brain's capacity for neurogenesis, these damages can be mitigated.* (Doidge, *The Brain That Changes Itself*).

216   ***Searching for the lost object*** See John Bowlby, "Loss, Sadness and Depression," *Attachment and Loss,* vol. III (New York: Basic Books, 1983).

217   **"Area 25" that lights up** Area 25 is in the ACC, localized to the subgenual—which has connections to amygdala, hypothalamus, and orbitofrontal cortex (OFC)—and instigates the stress response. See H. Johansen-Berg et al., "Anatomical Connectivity of the Subgenual Cingulate Region Targeted with Deep Brain Stimulation for Treatment-Resistant Depression," *Cerebral Cortex* 18, no. 6 (October 2007): 1374–83.

217   **Quieting Area 25 immediately reduces depression** Different types of depression (bipolar, unipolar, and major depression) light up different sites in Area 25, a fact that has implications for developing specifically targeted treatments. Ibid.

218   **Deep brain stimulation (DBS) involves** Sending electrodes into Area 25 breaks abnormal oscillation patterns. Helen S. Mayberg et al., "Deep Brain Stimulation for Treatment-Resistant Depression," *Neuron* 45, no. 5 (March 3, 2005): 651–60. For more about oscillating patterns, see Thomas Boraud et al., "Oscillations in the Basal Ganglia: the Good, the Bad and the Unexpected," *The Basal Ganglia VIII*, vol. 56 of *Advances in Behavioral Biology*, eds. J. P. Bolam, C. A. Ingham, and P. J. Magill (New York: Springer Science and Business Media, 2005), 1–24.

218   **The Chemical Theory** Besides serotonin, other neurochemicals include norepinephrine (NE), dopamine, and others. Some people think blood tests measure your brain's "serotonin level" but as yet, blood tests cannot give reliable results because 95% of serotonin is in the gut, serving other bodily functions; the total amount of serotonin in the blood does not reflect how serotonin is being utilized in the brain; also there is a blood-brain barrier.

218   **Serotonin is considered** "Just add serotonin and stir" is from David Dobbs, "A Depression Switch?" *New York Times Magazine,* April 2, 2006.

218   **The Neuroplastic Theory** Kramer, in *Against Depression* (p. 70), says this theory awakens the echoes of William James, who called depression "psychical neuralgia." The systems view would explain why antidepressants are good for lazy eye in that they repair weakened brain cells in other areas such as those in the visual cortex. Ronald S. Duman et al., "Neuronal Plasticity and Survival of Mood Disorders," *Biological Psychiatry* 48, no. 8 (October 15, 2000): 1181–91.

18   **In promoting neuronal growth** Grigori Enikolopov, a neuroscientist at Cold Spring Harbor Laboratories, near my home, discovered in 2006 that Prozac

increases the number of neurons in the dentate gyrus. Neurogenesis converts unspecialized stem cells into specialized neurons. Prozac promotes the second step in this process by stimulating "amplifying neural progenitors" to divide and generate more neural cells. *Cold Spring Harbor Lab Newsletter,* Spring 2006. (Also see endnote for page 215, "Often, anxiety and depression go together.")

219   **The Placebo Effect** See Irving Kirsch and Guy Sapirstein, "Listening to Prozac but Hearing Placebo: A Meta-Analysis of Antidepressant Medication," *Prevention & Treatment* 1 (June 26, 1998).

219   **Another interpretation** Research shows that early-life stress can prime people for later depression. People with early trauma have elevated stress hormones, which in turn contribute to the scaffolding of later depression. Sheline, Gado, and Kraemer, "Untreated Depression and Hippocampal Volume Loss." For example, sex abuse in girls before puberty has been shown to create hyperactivity of the stress hormone system, priming them for depression as adults. See Hara Estroff Marano, "Depression: Beyond Serotonin," *Psychology Today*, March 1, 1999. Stress hormones "permanently" sensitize neurons and receptors so they perpetually overrespond to stress. M. Liotti et al., Department of Psychiatry, U. of Texas, *Biological Psychiatry:* 48 (July 1, 2000): 30–42. Children diagnosed with anxiety disorders are found to have larger amygdala volumes than non–anxiety prone children, causing even a small degree of stress to provoke an outpouring of stress hormones, producing depression's vegetative state, sleep disturbances, cognitive dullness, and loss of pleasure. Stress causes the amygdala to go into overdrive, hurling out negative emotions that promote anxiety states and depression. *Reminder: Owing to the brain's capacity for neurogenesis, stress damages are reversible.* (Doidge, *The Brain That Changes Itself*).

219   **Feelings are the brain's representation** See Antonio R. Damasio, *Descartes' Error: Emotion, Reason, and the Human Brain,* (New York: Putnam, 1994).

219   **"Withdrawing from activity"** Benjamin Hart, "Biological Basis of the Behaviour of Sick Animals," *Neuroscience & Biobehavioural Reviews,* 12 (1988): 123–137.

220   **tianeptine, a chemical that dampens serotonin** Tianeptine is believed to promote neurogenesis, including sprouting new neurons and new connections between cells. Kramer 100–01.

220   **Depression is reversible** The exercises are designed to help repair stress' impact on the brain and ease depression. See Maggie Fox, "The Brain Can Produce Antidepressants with the Right Signal, a Finding That Suggests That Meditation or Going to Your 'Happy Place' Truly Works," Science News, posted online through *NewsDaily*, Oct 8, 2008. See Daniela D. Pollak et al., *Neuron* 60, no. 1 (October 9, 2008): 149–61.

220   **The brain is plastic, moldable** Doidge, *The Brain That Changes Itself.*

223   **Psychologist Paul Ekman's** Paul Ekman, "Facial Expressions of Emotion: New Findings, New Questions," *Psychological Science* 3 (1992): 34–38.

230   **Smile and laugh.** Here's an article that illustrates Ekman's findings about smiling: "Putting on a Happy Face: A Small Pilot Trial Indicates That Injecting Botox into Frown Lines of Women Can Reduce or Eliminate Depression," *Newsday (from Los Angeles Times)*, June 12, 2006.

230 **Walk** Research shows that walking or running for a minimum of 20 minutes three times a day is an effective therapy for depression. Gregg A. Tkachuk and Garry L. Martin, "Exercise Therapy for Patients with Psychiatric Disorders: Research and Clinical Implications," *Professional Psychology: Research and Practice* 30, no. 3 (June 1999): 275–282.

CHAPTER 16

240 **Science has shown that learned behaviors** Stress enhances habit formation (and addiction), causing people (and laboratory rats) to fall into "automatic pilot," the survival benefit being that it frees up the "thinking" mind to focus on the *source* of the stressor. Stress-induced habit formation involves complementary changes in the brain, including shrinkage of the prefrontal cortex (decision making) and oversprouting of neuronal dendrites in the basal ganglia's sensory-motor striatum (habit formation, chunking of behaviors—see endnote on page 246). When rats were stressed, they were able to learn new tasks (i.e., pressing a bar to get food), but had trouble deciding when to stop pressing the bar (Natalie Angier, "Brain Is a Co-Conspirator in a Vicious Stress Loop," *New York Times,* August 18, 2009, New York edition, D2). This would partially account for the perseveration of compulsive hoarding and other types of OCD. The Outer Child program helps increase your repertoire of healthy patterns by providing activities that are easy and pleasurable enough to stimulate brain reward systems that reinforce new behaviors, turning them into habits with repeated practice. When reinforced by dopamine, new behavioral steps develop (chunk) into new automatic patterns. As an added incentive, animal and human studies show that learning new behaviors actually makes the brain grow larger, as first observed by Donald Hebb. See D. O. Hebb, *The Organization of Behavior: A Neuropsychological Theory* (New York: Taylor & Francis, 2006), first edition published in London by John Wiley & Sons, 1949.

Bibliography

Acevedo, B., A. Aron, H. Fisher, and L. L. Brown. "Neural Correlates of Long-Term Pair Bonding in a Sample of Intensely In-Love Humans." Presented as a poster to the Society for Neuroscience's annual meeting, Washington, D.C., November 15–19, 2008.

Alonso, P., et al. "Genetic Susceptibility to Obsessive-Compulsive Hoarding: The Contribution of Neurotrophic Tyrosine Kinase Receptor Type 3 Gene." Presented as a poster at the XVth World Congress on Psychiatric Genetics, New York, October 7–11, 2007.

Anderson, Susan. "Peer-Facilitated Adult Education." *New Directions* for Adult and Continuing Education, 1999: 15–23.

———. *Black Swan: The Twelve Lessons of Abandonment Recovery.* Huntington, N.Y.: Rock Foundations Press, 1999.

———. *The Journey from Abandonment to Healing: Turn the End of a Relationship into the Beginning of a New Life.* New York: Berkley, 2000.

———. *The Journey from Heartbreak to Connection.* New York: Berkley, 2003.

Angier, Natalie. "Brain Is a Co-Conspirator in a Vicious Stress Loop." *New York Times,* August 18, 2009, New York edition, p. D2.

Ariely, Dan. *Predictably Irrational: The Hidden Forces That Shape Our Decisions.* New York: HarperCollins, 2008.

Associated Press. "Focus on 'Good' Body Fat in Battle Against Weight Gain." *Newsday,* April 9, 2009.

————. "More Evidence of Virus Link to Obesity." *New York Times,* August 20, 2007.

Atkins, Robert C. *Dr. Atkins' New Diet Revolution.* New York: M. Evans and Co., 1992.

Balint, Michael. *The Basic Fault: Therapeutic Aspects of Regression.* Evanston, Ill.: Northwestern University Press, 1992.

Barohn, Ellen. "Journaling: When the Pen Really Can Be Mightier." *Newsday,* March 19, 2002.

Beckman, Mary. "The Mice That Don't Miss Mom: Love and the μ-Opioid Receptor." *Science* 304, no. 5679 (June 25, 2004), 1888–89.

Beer, Hollace M., and Richard C. Robertiello. "Bulimia as a Failure in Separation." *Journal of Contemporary Psychotherapy* 23, no. 1 (March 1993): 41–45.

Begely, Sharon. "Religion and the Brain." *Newsweek,* Science and Technology, May 7, 2001.

Berridge, K. C., and T. E. Robinson. "What Is the Role of Dopamine in Reward: Hedonic Impact, Reward Learning, or Incentive?" *Brain Research Reviews* 28, no. 3 (December 1998): 309–69.

Bejerot, Nils. "The Six-Day War in Stockholm." *New Scientist* 61, no. 886 (1974): 486–87.

Blakeslee, Sandra. "Brain-Updating Machinery May Explain False Memories." *New York Times,* September 19, 2000, New York edition, F7.

————. "Cells That Read Minds." *New York Times,* January 10, 2006.

————. "In a Host of Ailments, Seeing a Brain out of Rhythm." *New York Times,* December 2, 2008, New York edition, D2.

————. "Placebos Prove So Powerful Even Experts Are Surprised." *New York Times,* October 13, 1998, New York Edition, F1.

Bloomberg News. "Stress Linked to Obesity: Hormone Triggers Growth of Fat Cells." *Newsday,* July 3, 2007.

Blumenfield, Michael, and Robert J. Ursano, eds. *Intervention and Resilience After Mass Trauma.* New York: Cambridge University Press, 2008.

Boeree, George C. "The Emotional Nervous System." George Boeree's Homepage, Shippensburg University (2009), http://webspace.ship.edu/cgboer/limbicsystem.html.

Boggs, Will. "Mystery of Permanent Memory Revealed." *Reuters* Health, May 16, 2001.

Boraud, Thomas, et al. "Oscillations in the Basal Ganglia: The Good, the Bad, and the Unexpected." *The Basal Ganglia VIII,* vol. 56 of *Advances in Behavioral Biology,* 1–24. Ed. J. P. Bolam, C. A. Ingham, and P. J. Magill. New York: Springer Science and Business Media, 2005.

Bowlby, John. *Loss: Sadness and Depression. Attachment and Loss* trilogy vol. III. New York: Basic Books, 1980.

Brach, Tara. *Radical Acceptance: Embracing Your Life with the Heart of a Buddha.* New York: Bantam Books, 2003.

Bradshaw, John. *Homecoming: Reclaiming and Championing Your Inner Child.* New York: Bantam Books, 1990.

Brand, Sarah, et al. "The Effect of Maternal PTSD Following in Utero Trauma Exposure on Behavior and Temperament in the 9-Month-Old Infant." In Yehuda, *Psychobiology of Posttraumatic Stress Disorder.*

Bratiotis, Christiana. "Cognitive Behavioral Treatment Interventions for Compulsive Hoarding." Poster presented at Mass Housing's Community Service Conference,

Thinking Outside Our Box(es): A Housing, Service, Clinical and Enforcement Team Approach to Hoarding, Marlborough, Mass., December 12, 2007.

Bremmer, J. Douglas, et al. "Noradrenergic Mechanisms in Stress and Anxiety." *Synapse* 23, no. 1 (December 7, 1996), 28–38.

Brown, Walter A., and Zsuzsa Meszaros. "Hoarding." *Psychiatric Times* 24, no. 13 (November 1, 2007).

Bryan, Jenny. "Could Fat Be Catching?" Televised segment of the Wellness and Wellbeing series produced by Channel 4, Belfast, 2006.

Burns, Scott. "The Subprime Mortgage Crisis Began on 9/11." *Dallas Morning News,* February 10, 2008.

Cahill, Larry. "MRIs Reveal Possible Source of Woman's Super-Memory." *Online for University of California–Irvine.* January 28, 2009.

Cahill, Larry, and Michael T. Alkire. "Epinephrine Enhancement of Human Memory Consolidation: Interaction with Arousal at Encoding." *Neurobiology of Learning and Memory* 79 (2003), 194–98.

Carey, Benedict. "For the Brain, Remembering Is Like Reliving." *New York Times,* September 5, 2008.

———. "Lotus Therapy." *New York Times,* May 27, 2008.

———. "Some Protect the Ego by Working on Their Excuses Early." *New York Times,* January 6, 2009.

———. "Standing in Someone Else's Shoes, Almost for Real." *New York Times,* December 2, 2008, New York edition, D5.

———. "Surgery for Mental Ills Offers Both Hope and Risk." *New York Times,* November 27, 2009, New York edition, A1.

———. "Watching New Love as It Sears the Brain." *New York Times,* May 31, 2005.

Cheever, Susan. "Mystery of Love: What's Oxytocin Got to Do with It?" *Newsday,* March 12, 2003.

Cloninger, Robert. "Genetic and Environmental Factors in the Development of Alcoholism." *Journal of Psychiatric Treatment Evaluation* 10 (1982): 78–83.

Cooke, Robert. "Hatching a New Theory: Chick Experiment Sheds Light on Newborn Perception." *Newsday,* 2002.

———. "Mice Over Matter: New Studies Counter Long-Held Beliefs About Brain Cell Growth." *Newsday,* February 26, 2002.

Coopersmith, Stanley. *The Antecedents of Self-Esteem.* San Francisco: W. H. Freeman, 1967.

Coren, Stanley. "Building a Better Brain for Your Dog." Posted to Canine Corner, Coren's blog on the website of *Psychology Today* magazine, November 5, 2008, http://www.psychologytoday.com/blog/canine-corner/200811/building-better-brain-your-dog.

Cummings, D., et al. "Plasma Ghrelin Levels After Diet-Induced Weight Loss or Gastric Bypass Surgery." *New England Journal of Medicine,* 346, 21 (May 23, 2002): 1623–30.

Damasio, Antonio R. *Descartes' Error: Emotion, Reason, and the Human Brain.* New York: Putnam, 1994.

Davidson, Richard J., and Anne Harrington, eds. *Visions of Compassion: Western Scientists and Tibetan Buddhists Examine Nature.* New York: Oxford University Press, 2002.

Dębiec Jacek, and Joseph LeDoux. "Noradrenergic Signaling in the Amygdala Contributes to the Reconsolidation of Fear Memory: Treatment Implications for PTSD." In Yehuda, *Psychobiology of Posttraumatic Stress Disorder: A Decade of Progress.*

DeCasper, A. J., and W. P. Fifer. "Of Human Bonding: Newborns Prefer Their Mothers' Voices." *Science* 208, no. 4448 (June 6, 1980), 1174–76.

Delahanty, Douglas, and Nicole Nugent. "Predicting PTSD Prospectively Based on Prior Trauma History and Immediate Biological Responses." In Yehuda, *Psychobiology of Posttraumatic Stress Disorder.*

Diamond, Marian C. "Why Einstein's Brain?" *New Horizons for Learning* 4, no. 5 (July, August, September 1999). http://www.newhorizons.org/journal/journal23.htm.

Dobbs, David. "A Depression Switch?" *New York Times Magazine,* April 2, 2006.

Doidge, Norman. *The Brain That Changes Itself: Stories of Personal Triumph from the Frontiers of Brain Science.* New York: Penguin, 2007.

Doka, Kenneth, ed. *Living with Grief After Sudden Loss: Suicide, Homicide, Accident, Heart Attack, Stroke.* Washington, D.C.: Hospice Foundation of America, 1996.

Drevets, Wayne C., Jonathan Savitz, and Michael Trimble. "The Subgenual Anterior Cingulate Cortex in Mood Disorders." *CNS Spectrums* 13, no. 8 (August 2008): 663–81.

Dugatkin, Lee Alan. *The Imitation Factor: Evolution Beyond the Gene.* New York: Free Press, 2000.

Duman, Ronald S., et al. "Neuronal Plasticity and Survival in Mood Disorders." *Biological Psychiatry* 48, no. 8 (October 15, 2000): 732–39.

Dutton, Donald G. "The Neurobiology of Abandonment Homicide." *Aggression and Violent Behavior* 7, no. 4 (2002): 407–21.

Ekman, Paul. "Facial Expressions of Emotion: New Findings, New Questions." *Psychological Science* 3, no. 1 (April 7, 1992): 34–38.

Elias, Marilyn. "MRIs Reveal Possible Source of Woman's Super-Memory." *USA Today,* Health and Behavior, January 27, 2009.

Encinas, Juan M., Anne Vaahtokari, and Grigory Enikolopov. "Fluoxetine Targets Early Progenitor Cells in the Adult Brain." Study communicated by James D. Watson in the *Cold Spring Harbor Laboratory Newsletter,* March 15, 2006.

Etcoff, Nancy. *Survival of the Prettiest: The Science of Beauty.* New York: Anchor Books, 1999.

Eysenck, H. J. "Anxiety, Learned Helplessness, and Cancer." *Journal of Anxiety Disorders* 1, no. 1 (1987): 87–104.

Field, Tiffany. "Attachment as Psychobiological Attunement: Being on the Same Wavelength." In Reite, *The Psychobiology of Attachment and Separation.*

Fox, Maggie. "Mice Overcome Fear, Depression with Natural Prozac." Reuters, October 8, 2008.

Francis, Darlene D. and Michael J. Meaney. "Maternal Care and the Development of Stress Responses." *Current Opinion in Neurobiology* 9, no. 1 (1999): 128–34.

Freud, Sigmund. "Beyond the Pleasure Principle." 1920.

Freud, Sigmund. "The Ego and the Id." 1923.

Frewen, Paul, and Ruth A. Lanius. "Toward a Psychobiology of Posttraumatic Self-Dysregulation: Reexperiencing, Hyperarousal, Dissociation, and Emotional Numbing." *Annals of the New York Academy of Sciences* 1071, no. 1 (July 2006):110–124.

Friedman, Jeffrey. "Research Identifies Enzyme Involved in Fat Storage." Online article about Friedman's research: Howard Hughes Medical Institute, July 11, 2002.

Fromm, Eric. *The Art of Loving*. Perennial Library Edition. New York: HarperCollins, 1989.

Gautam, Sandeep. "The Faculty of Imagination: Neural Substrates and Mechanisms." *Science* 2.0, June 5, 2007.

Gekakis, Nicholas D., et al. "Role of the CLOCK Protein in the Mammalian Circadian Mechanism." *Science* 280, no. 5369 (June 5, 1998): 1564–69.

Gershon, Michael D. *The Second Brain: A Groundbreaking New Understanding of Nervous Disorders of the Stomach and Intestine*. New York: HarperCollins, 1999.

Gilbert, Daniel. *Stumbling on Happiness*. New York: Alfred A. Knopf, 2006.

Glover, Dorie. "Allostatic Load in Women with and without PTSD Symptoms." In Yehuda, *Psychobiology of Posttraumatic Stress Disorder*.

Goleman, Daniel. *Social Intelligence: The New Science of Human Relations*. New York: Bantam Dell, 2006.

———. *Destructive Emotions, How Can We Overcome Them? A Scientific Dialogue with the Dalai Lama*. New York: Bantam Dell, 2003.

———. *Emotional Intelligence*. New York: Bantam Books, 1995.

Gossette, Robert L., and Richard M. O'Brien. "The Efficacy of Rational Emotive Therapy in Adults: Clinical Fact or Psychometric Artifact?" *Journal of Behavior Therapy and Experimental Psychiatry* 23, no. 1 (1992): 9–24.

———. "Irrational Beliefs and Maladjustment: When are Psychometric Effects Clinically Meaningful?" Paper presented in 1990.

Gray, Richard. "Scientists Find Drug to Banish Bad Memories." *Daily Telegraph*, July 1, 2007.

Graybiel, Ann M. "The Basal Ganglia." *Current Biology* 10, no. 14 (July 17, 2000): R509–11.

———. "The Basal Ganglia and Chunking of Action Repertoires." *Neurobiology of Learning and Memory* 70 (1998): 119–36.

——— and Yasuo Kubota. "Understanding Corticobasal Ganglia Networks as Part of a Habit Formation System." In *Mental and Behavioral Dysfunction in Movement Disorders*. Marc-André Bédard et al., eds. Totowa, N.J.: Humana, 2003.

Grella, Maria. "Compulsive Hoarding Syndrome." Posted to the website The Sop (October 13, 2009), http://thesop.org.

Hall, Joseph. "Erasing Traumatic Memory Possible, Researchers Say." *Toronto Star*, March 12, 2009.

Hanh, Thich Nhat. *The Miracle of Mindfulness: A Manual on Meditation*. Boston: Beacon Press, 1987.

Harris, Judith. *The Nurture Assumption: Why Children Turn Out the Way They Do*. New York: Free Press, 1998.

Hassabis, Demis, Dharshan Kumaran, and Eleanor A. Maguire. "Using Imagination to Understand the Neural Basis of Episodic Memory." *Journal of Neuroscience* 27, no. 52 (December 26, 2007): 14365–74.

Hebb, D. O *The Organization of Behavior: A Neuropsychological Theory* (New York: Taylor & Francis, 2006), first edition published in London by John Wiley & Sons, 1949.

Henig, Robin Marantz. "Fat Factors." *New York Times*, August 13, 2006.

Herman, Judith Lewis *Trauma and Recovery: The Aftermath of Violence—from Domestic Abuse to Political Terror* New York: Basic Books, 1992.

Hitti, Miranda. "Gambling Addiction Resembles Brain Problem: Poorer Choices, More Errors Seen in Chronic Gamblers' Mental Tests." *WebMD Health News,* April 13, 2005.

Hobson, J. Allan. *The Dreaming Brain.* New York: Basic Books, 1988.

Hofer, Myron. "Hidden Regulators: Implications for a New Understanding of Attachment, Separation, and Loss." In *Attachment Theory: Social, Developmental, and Clinical Perspectives.* Susan Goldberg, Roy Muir, and John Kerr, eds. Hillsdale, N.J.: Analytic Press, 1995.

Hoffman, Howard S. *Amorous Turkeys and Addicted Ducklings: A Search for the Causes of Social Attachment.* Boston, Mass.: Authors Publishing Cooperative, 1994.

Horney, Karen. *Our Inner Conflicts: A Constructive Theory of Neurosis.* New York: W. W. Norton, 1993.

Hunsberger, J., et al. "Novel Role of Exercise-Regulated Gene VGF in Models of Depression." *Nature Medicine* 13 (2007): 1476–82.

Hurvich, Leo M., and Dorothea Jameson. "An Opponent Process Theory of Color Vision." *Psychological Review* 6, no. 51 (November 1957): 384–404.

Iacoboni, Marco. *Mirroring People: The New Science of How We Connect with Others.* New York: Farrar, Straus and Giroux, 2008.

Johansen-Berg, H., et al. "Anatomical Connectivity of the Subgenual Cingulate Region Targeted with Deep Brain Stimulation for Treatment-Resistant Depression." *Cerebral Cortex* 18, no. 6 (October 10, 2007): 1374–83.

Kabat-Zinn, Jon. *Full Catastrophe Living: Using the Wisdom of Your Body and Mind to Face Stress, Pain, and Illness.* New York: Delacorte Press, 1990.

Kagan, Jerome. *Galen's Prophecy: Temperament in Human Nature.* New York: Basic Books, 1994.

Kahneman, Daniel, et al. "Would You Be Happier If You Were Richer? A Focusing Illusion." *Science* 312, no. 5782 (June 30, 2006): 1908–10.

Kandel, Eric R., and James H. Schwartz, eds. *Principles of Neural Science and Behavior.* East Norwalk, Conn.: Appleton and Lange, 1991.

Kapur, S., R. Mizrahi, and M. Li. "From Dopamine to Salience to Psychosis—Linking Biology, Pharmacology and Phenomenology of Psychosis." *Schizophrenia Research* 79, no. 1 (2005): 59–68.

Karten, Yashmin J.G., Anna Olariu, and Heather A. Cameron. "Stress in Early Life Inhibits Neurogenesis in Adulthood." *Trends in Neuroscience* 28, no. 4 (April 1, 2005): 171–72.

Kelley, A. E., and L. Stinus. "Disappearance of Hoarding Behavior After 6-Hydroxydopamine Lesions of the Mesolimbic Dopamine Neurons and its Reinstatement with L-Dopa." *Behavioral Neuroscience* 99, no. 3 (June 1985): 531–45.

Kelly, Dennis D., ed. "Stress-induced Analgesia." *Annals of the New York Academy of Sciences* 467 (June 1986).

Kernberg, Otto F. *Borderline Conditions and Pathological Narcissism.* Northvale, N.J.: Aronson, 1975.

Khaliq, Shamim. "Disorders of Dopaminergic Systems." A table on Khaliq's website, http://shamimkhaliq.50megs.com/Psychology/Neurotransmitters/diseases_of_dop amine.htm.

Kirsch, Irving, et al. "The Emperor's New Drugs: An Analysis of Antidepressant Medication Data Submitted to the U.S. Food and Drug Administration." *Prevention & Treatment* 5 (2002).

——, and Guy Sapirstein. "Listening to Prozac but Hearing Placebo: A Meta-Analysis of Antidepressant Medication," *Prevention & Treatment* 1 (June 26, 1998).

Kirsten, Grace Elish, and Richard Robertiello. *Big You, Little You: Separation Therapy*. New York: Dial Press, 1977.

Klein, D. F. "Listening to Meta-Analysis but Hearing Bias." *Prevention and Treatment* 1 (1998).

Klein, Donald, "Anxiety Reconceptualized." In *Anxiety: New Research and Changing Concepts*. Donald Klein and Judith Rabkin, eds. New York: Raven Press, 1981.

Klein, Melanie. *Love, Guilt, and Reparation and Other Works, 1921–1945*. New York: Free Press, 1984.

——. "On the Theory of Anxiety and Guilt." In *Envy and Gratitude and Other Works, 1946–1963*. New York: Delacorte Press, 1975.

Kliman, Gilbert. "Toward a Unifying Theory of Post-Traumatic Stress Disorder: Integrating Data from Studies of Post-Traumatic Behavior, Memory, Symptom Formation, Physiology, Cerebral Imaging, Psychoanalytic Findings and Evolutionary Theory." Paper presented to the first joint scientific meeting of the American College of Psychoanalysts and the American Academy of Psychoanalysis and Psychodynamic Psychiatry, Washington, D.C., May 3, 2008.

Kohut, Heinz. *The Restoration of the Self*. New York: International Universities Press, 1977.

Kolata, Gina. "How the Body Knows When to Gain or Lose." *New York Times*, October 17, 2000.

——. "Will a New Drug Melt Pounds?" *New York Times*, Health, December 5, 2004.

Kramer, Peter D. *Against Depression*. New York: Viking, 2005.

Kringelbach, Morton L. "The Orbitofrontal Cortex: Linking Reward to Hedonic Experience." *Nature Reviews: Neuroscience* 6 (2005): 691–702.

Lebrun, Yvan. "Cluttering After Brain Damage." *Journal of Fluency Disorders* 21, nos. 3–4 (1996): 289–95.

LeDoux, Joseph E. "Emotional Memory." *Scholarpedia* (2007), http://www.scholarpedia .org/article/Emotional_memory.

——. *The Emotional Brain: The Mysterious Underpinnings of Emotional Life*. New York: Simon and Schuster, 1996.

——. "Emotion, Memory, and the Brain." *Scientific American,* June 1994.

——. *Synaptic Self: How Our Brains Become Who We Are*. New York: Viking, 2002.

Lee, Mi-Jeong, et al. "Acute and Chronic Regulation of Leptin Synthesis, Storage, and Secretion by Insulin and Dexamethasone in Human Adipose Tissue." *American Journal of Physiology—Endocrinology and Metabolism* 292 (2007): E858–64.

Lehrer, Jonah. "Head Fake: How Prozac Sent the Science of Depression in the Wrong Direction." *Boston Globe,* Ideas, July 6, 2008.

——. *How We Decide*. Boston: Houghton Mifflin Harcourt, 2009.

——. Online article for *Seed* magazine, August 19, 2007.

Lewis, Helen Block. *Shame and Guilt in Neurosis*. New York: International Universities Press, 1971.

Lewis, Michael. *Altering Fate: Why the Past Does Not Predict the Future.* New York: Guilford Press, 1998.

———. *Shame: The Exposed Self.* New York: Free Press, 1992.

Lidz, Franz. *Ghost Men: The Strange but True Story of the Collyer Brothers, New York's Greatest Hoarders.* New York: Bloomsbury, 2003.

Lin, En-Ju Deborah, et al. "Combined Deletion of Y1, Y2, and Y4 Receptors Prevents Hypothalamic Neuropeptide Y Overexpression-Induced Hyperinsuline-mia Despite Persistence of Hyperphagia and Obesity." *Endocrinology* 147, no. 11 (2006): 5094–101.

Liotti, M., et al. "Differential Limbic-Cortical Correlates of Sadness and Anxiety in Healthy Subjects: Implications for Affective Disorders." *Biological Psychiatry* 48, no. 1 (July 2000): 30–42.

Liu, Zheng, et al. "DNA Targeting of Rhinal Cortex D2 Receptor Protein Reversibly Blocks Learning of Cues That Predict Reward." *Proceedings of the National Academy of Sciences* 101, no. 33 (August 17, 2004): 12336–41.

Lucentini, Jack. "A Game of Cash and Carry a Grudge." *Newsday,* July 9, 2002.

Lynch, William. *The Willie Lynch Letter and the Making of a Slave.* Chicago: Lushena Books, 1999.

MacMillan, Duncan, and Patricia Shaw. "Senile Breakdown in Standards of Personal and Environmental Cleanliness," *British Medical Journal* 2 (October 29, 1966): 1032–37.

Madden, John, ed. *Neurobiology of Learning, Emotion and Affect.* New York: Raven Press, 1991.

Mahler, Margaret S. *On Human Symbiosis and the Vicissitudes of Individuation: Infantile Psychosis.* New York: International Universities Press, 1968.

Maier, Steven F., Linda R. Watkins, and Monika R. Fleshner. "Psychoneuroimmunol-ogy: The Interface Between Behavior, Brain and Immunity." *American Psychologist* 49, no. 12 (December 1994): 1004–17.

Marano, Hara Estroff. "Depression: Beyond Serotonin." *Psychology Today*, March 1, 1999.

Maryasis, Jenny. "Procrastination: Habit or Disorder?" Student paper posted on *Serendip*'s Exchange (2002), http://serendip.brynmawr.edu.

Masterson, James F. *New Perspectives of Psychotherapy of the Borderline Adult.* New York: Brunner Mazel, 1978.

Mathews, C. A., et al. "Heritability and Clinical Features of Multigenerational Families with Obsessive-Compulsive Disorder and Hoarding." *American Journal of Medical Genetics Part B* 144B, no. 2 (March 5, 2007): 174–82.

Mayberg, Helen S., et al. "Deep Brain Stimulation for Treatment-Resistant Depression." *Neuron* 45, no. 5 (March 3, 2005): 651–60.

McEwen, Bruce S. "Allostasis and Allostatic Load: Implications for Neuropsychophar-macology." *Neuropsychopharmacology* 22, no. 2 (2000): 108–24.

McGovern, M. K. "Habits." *Serendip*, Spring 2005. http://serendip.brynmawr.edu/bb/neuro/neuro05/web1/mmcgovern.html.

McKinney, William T. "Separation and Depression: Biological Markers." In Reite, *The Psychobiology of Attachment and Separation*.

McLean, Paul. *The Triune Brain in Evolution.* New York: Plenum Press, 1990.

Meaney, M. J., et al. "The Effects of Postnatal Handling on the Development of the Glucocorticoid Receptor Systems and Stress Recovery in the Rat." *Progress in Neuro-Psychopharmacology and Biological Psychiatry* 9 (1985): 731–34.

Mellody, Pia. *Facing Love Addiction: Giving Yourself the Power to Change the Way You Love.* New York: HarperSanFrancisco, 2003.

Mestel, Rosie. "Fat Luck: The Life and Hard Times of Our Lard Cells." *Newsday,* May 7, 2002.

Michelson, David, et al. "Bone Mineral Density in Women with Depression." *New England Journal of Medicine* 335, no. 16 (October 17, 1996): 1176–81.

Miller, Alice. *The Drama of the Gifted Child.* New York: Basic Books, 1997.

Missildine, W. Hugh. *Your Inner Child of the Past.* New York: Simon & Schuster, 1963.

Moles, Anna, Brigitte Kieffer, and Francesca D'Amato. "Deficit in Attachment Behavior in Mice Lacking the μ-Opioid Receptor Gene." *Science* 305, no. 5679 (June 25, 2004): 1983–86.

Monti-Bloch, L. and B. I. Grosser. "Effect of Putative Pheromones on the Electrical Activity of the Human Vomeronasal Organ and Olfactory Epithelium." *Journal of Steroid Biochemistry and Molecular Biology* 39. no 4B (1991): 573–82.

Morgan, Charles, et al. "Relationship Among Plasma Cortisol, Catecholamines, Neuropeptide Y, and Human Performance During Exposure to Uncontrollable Stress." *Psychosomatic Medicine* 63, no. 3 (May/June 2001): 412–22.

Morgenstern, Julie. *Organizing from the Inside Out.* New York: Henry Holt and Company, 2004.

Musselman, Dominique L. "Exaggerated Platelet Reactivity in Major Depression." *American Journal of Psychiatry* 153, no. 10 (October 1996): 1313–17.

Nader, Karim, Glenn E. Schafe, and Joseph E. LeDoux. "Fear Memories Require Protein Synthesis in the Amygdala for Reconsolidation after Retrieval." *Nature* 406 (August 17, 2000): 722–26.

National Institute on Mental Health. "Brain's Reward Circuitry Revealed in Procrastinating Primates," NIMH website (press release, August 10, 2004), http://www.nimh.nih.gov.

Noguerias, Ruben, and Matthias Tschöp. "Separation of Conjoined Hormones Yields Appetite Rivals." *Science* 310, no. 5750 (November 2005): 985–86.

Online post, unspecified author. "My Subgenual Cingulate Is Sad." Online, The Neurocritic: Deconstructing the Most Sensationalist Recent Findings in Human Brain Imaging, October 30, 2007.

Online post. "European Method Can Slim You with Injections," *Health,* November 27, 2002.

Panksepp, Jaak, *Advances in Biological Psychiatry* 1, Greenwich: JAI Press Inc, 1995.

Panksepp, Jaak, Eric Nelson, and Marni Bekkedal. "Brain Systems for the Mediation of Social Separation-Distress and Social-Reward Evolutionary Antecedents and Neuropeptide Intermediaries." *Annals of The New York Academy of Sciences* 807, *The Integrative Neurobiology of Affiliation* (January 1997): 78–100.

Panksepp, Jaak, Stephen M. Siviy, and Lawrence A. Normansell. "Brain Opioids and Social Emotions." In Reite, *The Psychobiology of Attachment and Separation.*

Pavlov, I. V. *Conditioned Reflexes.* Mineola: Dover Publications, 1922.

Peciña, Susana, et al. "Hyperdopaminergic Mutant Mice Have Higher 'Wanting' but Not 'Liking' for Sweet Rewards." *J Neuroscience* 23, no. 28 (October 15, 2003): 9395–402.

Pert, Candace B. *Molecules of Emotion: Why You Feel the Way You Feel.* Foreword by Deepak Chopra. New York: Scribner, 1997.

Pollak, Daniela D., et al. "An Animal Model of a Behavioral Intervention for Depression." *Neuron* 60, no. 1 (October 9, 2008): 149–61.

Preuschoff, Kerstin, Peter Bossaerts, and Steven R. Quartz. "Neural Differentiation of Expected Reward and Risk in Human Subcortical Structures." *Neuron* 51, no. 3 (August 3, 2006): 381–90.

Quiñones, Eric. "Link Between Income and Happiness Is Mainly an Illusion." Online, June 29, 2006 (referring to Princeton study, researchers David Schkade and Arthur Stone).

Rabin, Roni. "Hormone May Be Key to Weight Loss." *Newsday,* October 15, 2003.

———. "Obesity Begins in Utero." *Newsday,* November 7, 2005.

Ramin, Cathryn Jakobson. *Carved in Sand: When Attention Fails and Memory Fades in Midlife.* New York: HarperCollins, 2007.

Real, Terrance. *I Don't Want to Talk About It.* New York: Scribner, 1997.

Reite, Martin. *The Psychobiology of Attachment and Separation.* Ed. Tiffany Field. Orlando, Fla.: Academic Press, 1985.

Riesberg, Barry. *Guide to Alzheimer's Disease.* New York: Free Press, 1983.

Rinpoche, Sogyal. *The Tibetan Book of Living and Dying.* San Francisco: Harper, 1992.

Robertiello, Richard, and Terril T. Gagnier, PhD. "Sado-masochism as a Defense Against Merging: Six Case Studies." *Journal of Contemporary Psychotherapy* 23 (1993).

Robertiello, Richard. *Hold Them Very Close, Then Let Them Go.* New York: Dial, 1975.

Roth, Rebecca. "Gambling and the Brain." *Serendip* (April 23, 2002), http://serendip .brynmawr.edu/bb/neuro/neuro02/web2/rroth.html.

Ruden, Ronald A. *The Craving Brain: The Biobalance Approach to Controlling Addiction.* With Marcia Byalick. New York: HarperCollins, 1997.

Sagvolden, Terje, et al. "A Dynamic Developmental Theory of Attention-Deficit/ Hyperactivity Disorder (ADHD) Predominantly Hyperactive/Impulsive and Combined Subtypes." *Behavioral and Brain Sciences* 28, vol. 3 (June 2005): 397–419.

Salamone, John D. "Antidepressants and Placebos: Conceptual Problems and Research Strategies." *Prevention and Treatment* 5, no. 1 (July 2002).

Sandford, John J., Spillos V. Argyropoulos, and David J. Nutt. "The Psychobiology of Anxiolytic Drugs: Part 1: Basic Neurobiology." *Pharmacology and Therapeutics* 88, no. 3 (December 3, 2000): 197–212.

Sapolsky, Robert M. *A Primate's Memoir: A Neuroscientist's Unconventional Life Among Baboons.* New York: Scribner, 2001.

———. "Social Subordinance as a Marker of Hypercortisolism." *Annals of the New York Academy of Sciences* 771, *Stress Basic Mechanisms and Clinical Implications* (December 1995): 626–39.

———. *Why Zebras Don't Get Ulcers.* New York: W. H. Freeman, 1994.

Saxena, Sanjaya, et al. "Cerebral Glucose Metabolism in Obsessive-Compulsive Hoarding." *American Journal of Psychology* 161 (June 2004): 1038–48.

———. "The Neurobiology and Medication Treatment of Compulsive Hoarding." *International OCD Foundation Newsletter* 18, no. 1 (Winter 2004).

Schiele, Daniel R. "The Neuropsychobiology of Addiction, Trauma, and Dissociation." Paper presented at the Western Clinical Conference in Multiple Personality and Dissociation, Costa Mesa, Calif., 1992.

Schleifer, Steven J., et al. "Suppression of Lymphocyte Stimulation Following Bereavement." *Journal of the American Medical Association* 250, no. 3 (1983): 374–77.

Schwartz, Richard C. *Internal Family Systems Therapy*. New York: Guilford Press, 1995.

Scripps Howard News Service. "Hormone Is Hunger's 'On' Switch." *Newsday*, May 23, 2002.

Seligman, Martin E. P. "Can Happiness Be Taught?" *Dædalus* 133, no. 2 (Spring 2004): 80–87.

———. *Helplessness: On Depression, Development, and Death*. San Francisco: W. H. Freeman, 1975.

Selye, Hans. *Advances in Psychoneuroimmunology*. Istvan Berczi and Judith Szélenyi, eds. New York: Plenum Press, 1994.

Serra, G., M. Collu, and G. L. Gessa. "Endorphins and Sexual Behavior." In *Endorphins, Opiates and Behavioral Processes*. R. J. Rodgers and S. J. Cooper, eds. New York: John Wiley & Sons, 1988.

Shaw, Therese, and Ajit Shah. "Senile Squalour Syndrome: What to Expect and How to Treat It." *International Psychogeriatrics* 8, no. 4 (1996): 669–74.

Sheline, Yvette I., Mokhtar H. Gado, and Helena C. Kraemer. "Untreated Depression and Hippocampal Volume Loss." *American Journal of Psychiatry* 160 (August 2003): 1516–18.

Simons, Ronald. *Boo! Culture, Experience, and the Startle Reflex*. New York: Oxford University Press, 1996.

Smale, Steve. "The Prisoner's Dilemma and Dynamical Systems Associated to Noncooperative Games." *Econometrica* 48, no. 7 (November 1980): 1617–34.

Small, Gary, and Gigi Vorgan. *iBrain: Surviving the Technological Alteration of the Modern Mind*. New York: Harper, 2009.

Smotherman, William P., and Scott R. Robinson. "The Development of Behavior Before Birth." *Developmental Psychology* 32, no. 3 (May 2, 1996): 425–34.

Steketee, Gail, and Randy O. Frost. *Compulsive Hoarding and Acquiring: Therapist Guide*. New York: Oxford University Press, 2007.

Sternberg, Esther. *The Balance Within: The Science Connecting Health and Emotions*. New York: W. H. Freeman, 2001.

Stewart, D. N., and D. M. DeR. Winser. "Incidence of Perforated Peptic Ulcer: Effect of Heavy Air-raids," *Lancet* 239 (February 28, 1942): 259–61.

Suomi, Stephen. "Early Stress and Adult Emotional Reactivity in Rhesus Monkeys." In *The Childhood Environment and Adult Disease*. Ciba Foundation Symposium 156, pp. 171–206. New York: John Wiley and Sons, 1991.

Talan, Jamie. "Art of Bouncing Back: By Studying Soldiers in Action, Researchers Hope to Understand Why People React Differently to Pressure." *Newsday*, March 1, 2004.

———. "Don't Call It Love, Call It Chemistry." *Newsday*, February 11, 2003.

———. "Doubts on Debriefing." *Newsday,* October 2, 2001.

———. "'Fear' Gene Found in Mice." *Newsday,* November 21, 2005.

———. "Gene Directs Eating Habits." *Newsday,* September 14, 2005.

———. "Genetic Variants Linked to Mania and Depression Are Under Study; May Lead to Treatments." *Newsday,* November 1, 2006.

———. "Hope for Depression." *Newsday,* May 2, 2006.

——. "Ketamine in Low Doses Alleviated Some Depression…Symptoms." *Newsday,* August 7, 2006.

——. "New Drug Treats Heroin Addiction." *Newsday,* May 22, 2002.

——. "New Weight-Loss Drug Works in Trial." *Newsday,* February 14, 2006.

——. "Possible Clue to Obesity: How the Brain Listens." *Newsday,* August 21, 2001.

——. "Scientists Studying Depression Identify Abnormalities in Some Brain Regions…" *Newsday,* October 26, 2006.

——. "Special Protein Linked to Less Forgetful Fruit Flies." *Newsday*, April 2, 2002.

——. "Targeting the Structure of Horrific Memories." *Newsday*, January 29, 2002.

——. "Technique Offers Hope to Addicts." *Newsday,* September 5, 2001.

——. "Where in the Brain Is Our Identity?" *Newsday*, January 29, 2002.

Tallis, Frank. *Love Sick: Love as a Mental Illness.* New York: Thunder's Mouth, 2005.

Tavris, Carol. *Anger: The Misunderstood Emotion.* New York: Touchstone, 1989.

Taylor, Beverly. "Clutter and Hoarding—The 6 Secrets of Success for De-Cluttering." EzineArticles.com. August 19, 2009.

Tice, Dianne, and Roy Baumeister. "Controlling Anger Self-Induced Emotion Change." In Wegner and Pennebaker, *Handbook of Mental Control.* Englewood Cliffs, eds. Upper Saddle River, N.J.: Prentice Hall, 1992.

Tkachuk, Gregg A., and Garry A. Martin. "Exercise Therapy for Patients with Psychiatric Disorders: Research and Clinical Implications." *Professional Psychology* 30, no. 3 (1999): 275–82.

Tolin, David F., Randy O. Frost, and Gail Steketee. *Buried in Treasures: Help for Compulsive Acquiring, Saving, and Hoarding.* New York: Oxford University Press, 2007.

——. "An Open Trial of Cognitive-Behavioral Therapy for Excessive Hoarding." *Behaviour Research and Therapy* 45, no. 7 (July 2007): 1461–70.

Trudeau, Michelle. "Study Sheds Light on Compulsive Hoarding: Brain Signatures Different for Those with 'Saving' Disorder." Radio segment about a study of hoarding that appeared in the June 2009 issue of the *American Journal of Psychiatry.* Broadcast on NPR, June 7, 2004.

Tully, Tim. "Fruit Flies, Mind, Memory." Lectures at Cold Spring Harbor Labs, C. W. Post 2001–4.

Valenstein, Elliot S. *Great and Desperate Cures: The Rise and Decline of Psycho surgery and Other Radical Treatments for Mental Illness.* New York: Basic Books, 1986.

Van der Kolk, Bessel A. "Clinical Implications of Neuroscience Research in PTSD." In Yehuda, *Psychobiology of Posttraumatic Stress Disorder.*

Van der Kolk, Bessel A., et al. *Traumatic Stress: The Effects of Overwhelming Experience on Mind, Body, and Society.* New York: Guilford Press, 1996.

Vaughan, Susan. *The Talking Cure: The Science Behind Psychotherapy.* New York: Putnam, 1997.

Vedantam, Shankar. "Against Depression, a Sugar Pill Is Hard to Beat: Placebos Improve Mood, Change Brain Chemistry in Majority of Trials of Antidepressants." *Washington Post*, May 7, 2002.

Wapner, Seymour, et al. "An Examination of Studies of Critical Transitions Throughout the Life Cycle." In *Toward a Holistic Developmental Psychology.* Seymour Wapner and Bernard Hillsdale, N.J.: Erlbaum, 1983.

Wattles, Wallace B. *The Science of Getting Rich.* 7th edition. Largo, Fla.: Top of the Mountain Publications, 1996 (originally 1910).

Wátzlawick, Paul, John Weakland, and Richard Fisch. *Change: Principles of Problem Formation and Problem Resolution.* New York: W. W. Norton, 1974.

Weiss, Jay M. "Stress-Induced Depression: Critical Neurochemical and Electrophysiological Changes." In *Neurobiology of Learning, Emotion and Affect.* John Madden, ed. New York: Raven Press, 1991.

Weiss, R. S. *Loneliness: The Experience of Emotional and Social Isolation.* Cambridge, Mass.: MIT Press, 1973.

West, Jean. "Children's Drug Is More Potent than Cocaine." *The Observer,* September 9, 2001.

Whitfield, Charles L. *Healing the Child Within: Discovery and Recovery for Adult Children of Dysfunctional Families.* Deerfield Beach, Fla.: Health Communications, 1987.

Winnecott, Donald W. "The Capacity to Be Alone." In *The Maturational Processes and the Facilitating Environment: Studies in the Theory of Emotional Development.* Madison, Wisc.: International Universities Press, 1965.

Wise, Roy A. "The Neurobiology of Craving: Implications for the Understanding and Treatment of Addiction." *Journal of Abnormal Psychology* 97, no. 2 (May 1988): 118–32.

Wolff, P. H. "The Serial Organization of Sucking in the Young Infant." *Pediatrics* 42, no. 6 (December 1968): 943–56.

Worthington, Everett. *Five Steps to Forgiveness: The Art and Science of Forgiving.* New York: Crown, 2002.

Yehuda, Rachel, ed. *Psychobiology of Posttraumatic Stress Disorder: A Decade of Progress.* Boston: Blackwell Publishing, 2006. First edition published in *Annals of the New York Academy of Sciences* 1071 (July 1997). Rachel Yehuda and Alexander C. McFarlane, eds.

Zarembo, Alan. "Now, Exercise in a Pill Form?" *Newsday,* August 1, 2008.

Zillmann, Dolf. "Mental Control of Angry Aggression." In *Handbook of Mental Control.* D. M. Wegner and J. W. Pennebaker, eds. Upper Saddle River: N.J.: Prentice Hall, 1992.

Index

© Marci Gerardi

ABOUT THE AUTHOR

Susan Anderson is a psychotherapist who has devoted more than thirty years of clinical experience and research to working with the victims of trauma, abandonment, grief, and loss. The creator of the Outer Child concept and the founder of the abandonment recovery movement, she is the author of *The Journey from Abandonment to Healing, Black Swan: The Twelve Lessons of Abandonment Recovery,* and *The Journey from Heartbreak to Connection.* In addition to her lectures and workshops, she continues private practice in Manhattan and on Long Island.

ABOUT THE TYPE

This book was set in Granjon, a modern recutting of a typeface produced under the direction of George W. Jones, who based Granjon's design upon the letterforms of Claude Garamond (1480–1561). The name was given to the typeface as a tribute to the typographic designer Robert Granjon.

NEW WORLD LIBRARY is dedicated to publishing books and other media that inspire and challenge us to improve the quality of our lives and the world.

We are a socially and environmentally aware company. We recognize that we have an ethical responsibility to our customers, our staff members, and our planet.

We serve our customers by creating the finest publications possible on personal growth, creativity, spirituality, wellness, and other areas of emerging importance. We serve New World Library employees with generous benefits, significant profit sharing, and constant encouragement to pursue their most expansive dreams.

As a member of the Green Press Initiative, we print an increasing number of books with soy-based ink on 100 percent postconsumer-waste recycled paper. Also, we power our offices with solar energy and contribute to non-profit organizations working to make the world a better place for us all.

Our products are available in bookstores everywhere.

www.newworldlibrary.com

At NewWorldLibrary.com you can download our catalog,
subscribe to our e-newsletter, read our blog,
and link to authors' websites, videos, and podcasts.

Find us on Facebook, follow us on Twitter, and watch us on YouTube.

Send your questions and comments our way!
You make it possible for us to do what we love to do.

Phone: 415-884-2100 or 800-972-6657
Catalog requests: Ext. 10 | Orders: Ext. 52 | Fax: 415-884-2199
escort@newworldlibrary.com

NEW WORLD LIBRARY
publishing books that change lives   14 Pamaron Way, Novato, CA 94949